THE ARAB WORLD TODAY

For Mark and John;
and for Min, who proved there is life after life

THE ARAB
WORLD TODAY

EDITED BY
DAN TSCHIRGI

LYNNE RIENNER PUBLISHERS ▪ BOULDER & LONDON

Published in the United States of America in 1994 by
Lynne Rienner Publishers, Inc.
1800 30th Street, Boulder, Colorado 80301

and in the United Kingdom by
Lynne Rienner Publishers, Inc.
3 Henrietta Street, Covent Garden, London WC2E 8LU

Library of Congress Cataloging-in-Publication Data
The Arab world today / edited by Dan Tschirgi.
    p. cm.
    Includes bibliographical references and index.
    ISBN 1-55587-459-2 (alk. paper)
    ISBN 1-55587-479-7 (alk. paper: pbk.)
    1. Arab countries—Politics and government—1945– I. Tschirgi,
Dan.
DS63.1.A697 1994
909'.09749270829—dc20   93-29379
                                                CIP

British Cataloguing in Publication Data
A Cataloguing in Publication record for this book
is available from the British Library.

Contents

Acknowledgments

No book of this nature can be produced without the help of many people. Although space does not permit me to list all who contributed, some were truly indispensable.

In the grim days of early 1991, Donald McDonald, president of the American University in Cairo (AUC), planted the seed of the idea that led to this work by encouraging efforts to fathom the significance of the crisis then gripping the Middle East and pledging institutional support toward that end. AUC Assistant Provost John Swanson's organizational abilities and unflappable sense of balance soon proved essential.

The United States Institute of Peace provided most of the funds that permitted authors from various corners of the Arab and non-Arab worlds to meet in Cairo to discuss first drafts of the chapters this book comprises. Naturally, neither AUC nor the United States Institute of Peace bears responsibility for views expressed in the following pages.

I also thank my colleagues in the Department of Political Science at AUC for permitting me time to undertake this project. Particular mention must be made of three young assistants—Brad Johnson, Gordon Knox, and Heba-Tallah Salah Shaaban—upon whose unfailing efficiency I rather shamelessly relied.

The University of the Americas–Puebla (UDLA-P), in Puebla, Mexico, was a congenial host during the portion of a sabbatical I devoted to editing this volume. I am grateful to Román López Villicaña, chairman of the Department of International Relations at UDLA-P, and Concepción Añorve for having helped make my stay productive, interesting, and delightful.

Finally, I extend very special thanks to Dr. David Kuebrich, of George Mason University, for his many, thorough, and exceedingly valuable comments on various stages of the manuscript that eventually metamorphosed into the present work.

D. T.

Abbreviations and Acronyms

ACC	Arab Cooperation Council
AUC	American University in Cairo
CENTO	Central Treaty Organization
CIS	Commonwealth of Independent States
EC	European Community
ECO	Economic Cooperation Organization
EEC	European Economic Community
FIS	Front Islamique du Salut (Islamic Salvation Front [Algeria])
FLN	National Liberation Front (Algeria)
GCC	Gulf Cooperation Council
GNP	gross national product
HDI	Human Development Index
IMF	International Monetary Fund
ISI	import-substituting industrialization
LAS	League of Arab States
mbd	million barrels per day
MEBRD	Middle East Bank for Reconstruction and Development
MWC	Modern Working Class
NATO	North Atlantic Treaty Organization
NCC	National Consultative Council (Jordan)
NMC	New Middle Class
NSCP	National Society for Consumer Protection
ODA	official development assistance
OECD	Organization for Economic Cooperation and Development
OPEC	Organization of the Petroleum Exporting Countries
PLO	Palestine Liberation Organization
RDF	Rapid Deployment Force
TLHR	Tunisian League for Human Rights
UAE	United Arab Emirates
UAR	United Arab Republic

UDLA-P   University of the Americas—Puebla
ULP   Urban Lumpen Proletariat
UNDP   United Nations Development Program
UNESCWA   United Nations Economic and Social Commission for West
            Africa
YAR   Yemen Arab Republic

Introduction

DAN TSCHIRGI

Though the Middle East has seen its fate linked to Western influence for centuries, never before has the West—and particularly its current principal actor, the United States—been so directly involved in shaping the course of events in the Arab world. Throughout the region, virtually all aspects of communal life—from macropolicies involving long-term strategies for national security, regime maintenance, and economic development to tactical decisions taken by Arab governments struggling with immediate problems—now respond to a chain of calculations that quickly link Arab decisions to Arab expectations, fears, hopes, and analytical judgments regarding Western, primarily U.S., reactions. In this way, through the mediating filter of existing regimes, the vast populace of the Arab world finds its own daily life now influenced by the external world as never before.

Thoughtful Westerners who understand this—again, particularly those in the United States—must find something awesome, indeed frightening, in the situation. To be a determining factor in the lives of others is not a comfortable position, especially when one knows little of those lives. Yet, this is precisely the situation that faces the populations and governments of the West.

A Welcome Casualty

Both Western and non-Western students of the Arab world have long ruefully recognized that their area of concern stubbornly remained a terra incognita to most beyond its borders. Myths, biases, and—perhaps above all—simple indifference were hallmarks of the Western perspective on the Arab world. The crucial and probably inevitable point, given the preva-

1

lence of democratic systems in the West, is that the outlooks of governing decisionmakers as well as those of the man on the street could be characterized in this way.

The rapid, downward slide to war launched by Iraqi President Saddam Hussein's initiation of the 1990–1991 Gulf Crisis suddenly stirred enormous curiosity in the West about the Arab world. "What are we doing there, and why?" was the question of the day. It was a compelling question. Politicians had to decide whether to fight; citizens had to decide how to respond to the decisions of politicians. All had to explain their reactions, if only to themselves.

Ironically, the groundwork for the dimensions reached by the Gulf Crisis had largely been laid by the West itself, for the contemporary Arab world—with its full complement of complex political tensions and potentially explosive problems—is to a great extent (though obviously not exclusively) a product of historical and ongoing Western influence. It is sad that the catalyst for the widespread intensification of curiosity in the West was something as tragic as the Gulf Crisis.

Sad though it may be, it was also probably inevitable. Most people become deeply interested in topics only when they themselves are actually or potentially directly affected. As the Gulf Crisis and the possibility of Western intervention developed, potential personal vulnerability to Middle Eastern events touched many in the West—from the decisionmaker, to the soldier and the soldier's family, to the proverbial taxpayer. In the first instance, the range of pressing questions focused on issues of immediate relevance to Westerners: Should we intervene? What will it cost us? What will we gain? Will the cost be commensurate with the gain?

But the very effort to deal with such questions automatically raised a series of equally pressing but far more specific questions arising from the concrete political context created by Iraq's move into Kuwait on August 2, 1990: Is it worthwhile to act against Iraq on behalf of Kuwait? Is there any difference between the regime in Baghdad and that in Kuwait City that affects us? How, and why, should we act in concert with Arab allies as diverse as our long-standing pro-Western friend, Egypt, and our even more long-standing antagonist, Syria, against Iraq, with which we have had a long, ambivalent relationship?

In turn, such questions inevitably pushed those attempting to proffer answers into the realm of far more regionally specific questions: What is the difference between the regimes in Iraq and Kuwait, and why does it exist? What are the real differences between these regimes and those of Syria and Egypt; why do such differences exist; and what do they signify regarding the political context of the Arab world? What, indeed, is the Arab world's *political context*—that is, what are the area's dominant political dynamics, and how do they operate? Why do these dynamics exist; where and what are their societal roots?

In short, starting from the immediate self-centered realm of questions that required only a cost-benefit analysis, Western efforts to cope with the developing Gulf Crisis were necessarily driven to two further levels of analysis. The first, an intermediate level of questioning, made more specific the issue of Western interests and their connection with political realities in the Arab world. The second, even deeper level focused on questions regarding the nature of the Arab world itself.

The progression outlined here can be seen in the mountains of printed pages generated by the Gulf Crisis: from early debates between Henry Kissinger and Zbigniew Brzezinski that looked at the issue from purely realpolitik perspectives, to a range of literature that sought to justify or castigate Western support of the Arab allies acquired in the crisis, to more extended and reflective efforts to understand the significance of the Gulf Crisis in terms of its Arab setting.

Although the primary focus of most works falling into this last category has remained fixed on the West—that is, on the significance of the Gulf Crisis *for the non-Arab world*—the analytical approaches employed have tended to look closely at the Arab world itself. Issues attracting scholarly attention in this regard have been wide-ranging, as is evident from the burgeoning postcrisis literature. Thus, for example, the authors in Victoria Brittain's *The Gulf Between Us* are largely preoccupied by the meaning of the Gulf Crisis for the United States and Great Britain.[1] On the other hand, the implications of the Gulf Crisis for the emerging post–Cold War international system are the central concern of the volume edited by Haim Bresheeth and Niri Yuval-Davis, *The Gulf War and the New World Order.*[2] Much attention has also been paid to philosophical, ethical, and religious questions raised by the Gulf Crisis. Charles A. Kimball's *Religion, Politics and Oil,* Kenneth L. Vaux's *Ethics and the Gulf War,* and Jean Elshtain and colleagues' *Reflections on the Morality of the Persian Gulf War* form part of this intellectual direction.[3]

Despite the multiplicity of topics with which these representative works deal, they share a basic common feature: Although they retain a primary focus on questions raised for the West by the Gulf Crisis, they seek answers largely by trying to understand and explain the Middle East, particularly the Arab world. Although this may seem an obvious methodological step, I contend that its generalized appearance in post–Gulf Crisis considerations of non-Arab relations with the Arab world is something of a novel departure.

An incident comes to mind that graphically illustrates the point. Some years ago, on the eve of Ronald Reagan's first inauguration, I attended a seminar at which a prominent U.S. strategic thinker addressed a group of both scholars and executives of U.S. defense industries. It was rumored that this individual would receive a major appointment in the incoming administration, and indeed he was later named to an important ambassadorship. He spoke to the group on plans to upgrade the Rapid Deployment Force (RDF) (later renamed the Central Command) with a view to enhancing the security of the Gulf. His presentation left at least one participant, a young Middle Eastern scholar, puzzled. Would the speaker, she asked, please clarify the precise nature of the threat to be met by a revitalized RDF: Was it an external power, or was it rooted in the internal nature of Arab politics? The presiding eminence glanced at her and then solemnly intoned, "The question is academic."

We would hope, and it seems likely, that today hoots of well-deserved ridicule would greet such a facile dismissal of the need to distinguish between essential regional factors and more global, and hence more abstract, factors at play in the formulation of Western policies toward the Arab world. Only recently, they did not.

The Gulf Crisis and its aftermath may, then, have occasioned at least one welcome casualty: the demise of the complacent and long-predominant Western assumption that little of importance is to be learned by heeding and trying to understand Middle East realities on their own terms. In this book we try to help secure this outcome, to hammer another nail into the coffin of complacency, by focusing tightly on political, economic, and social implications of the Gulf Crisis for the Arab world. To be sure, historical, actual, and potential roles of non-Arab actors in the fortunes of the Arab world figure prominently in many of the following chapters. Yet, the starting point and thrust of analysis remain unswervingly tied to that world itself.

Obviously, the full range of possible topics to be treated in such an endeavor is beyond reach. Selectivity has been required. Yet, the issues we deal with are key, and we hope the treatment they receive will give the reader extensive insight into today's Arab world.

Considering the Gulf Crisis and the Arab World

The culminating event of the Gulf Crisis was the Gulf War. The U.S. Pentagon labeled the war a "Desert Storm," whereas Oxford's Roger Owen likens the crisis and ensuing war to an "earthquake." If we adhere to these metaphorical visions, we must admit that now, nearly three years later, the dust of Desert Storm still clouds efforts to perceive its real significance; the fault lines and long-term regional changes in the Arab world that may have been wrought by this politically seismic upheaval have not been clearly manifested.

The real questions for anyone interested in going beyond the 1991 headlines that proclaimed the International Coalition's massive victory over Iraq are profound. Has the whole affair really altered the dynamics that led to the confrontation in the first place? If so, how? If not, why not, and what does this imply?

At a superficial level, it seems almost impossible to think that a confrontation of the magnitude of the 1990–1991 Gulf Crisis would not produce a lasting and radical impact. Yet, looking at today's Arab world, this assumption is called into question. Where is the impact? Where is the fundamental and permanent change?

Perhaps it is there, someplace; however, perhaps "someplace" exists only in the determined, logical constructs of analysts. Perhaps the reality is that the Arab world has become so inured to defeat and catastrophe that this latest example, despite superficial indications to the contrary, has no implications beyond being yet another in a series.

All this essentially circumscribes the central issues explored by the various contributors to this book: What—if any—are the implications of the Gulf Crisis for the Arab world, and, therefore, what can Arabs as well as non-Arabs expect in the future? Given the Arab world's importance in the international system, these issues are compelling.

It is still too early to expect pristine, conclusive answers from the events of 1990–1991. Yet, the lapse of three years provides sufficient validity for an effort to suggest preliminary answers to some of the multiple aspects of the questions raised. In this volume we present the considered judgments of a variety of Arab and non-Arab professional students of the Middle East. In a sense, then, the following pages constitute a snapshot, a freezing in time of the appraisals of a broad and interdisciplinary segment of these students. Again, time will eventually provide a firm basis upon which these appraisals themselves must ultimately be judged.

Three considerations give the snapshot both intellectual and practical value. First is the immediate value: the extent to which analyses and arguments advanced in these chapters may come to bear upon discourses that will produce decisions affecting the Arab world. Second is the extent to which this 1994 snapshot may lead students of the Middle East and the Arab world to review, alter, or modify their approaches to understanding the region. Finally, the freezing in time of this analytic moment will inevitably be of some historical interest: Regardless of what eventually happens in the Middle East, these pages stand as a record of a wide spectrum of current analytical outlooks on the significance of the Gulf Crisis.

The book is divided into four sections. In Part 1 we consider the fundamental academic problem of the implications of the Gulf Crisis for analytical approaches to understanding the Arab world. The question is obviously and painfully valid: Few, if any, professional students of the Middle East anticipated the Gulf Crisis or foresaw the dimensions it would reach. Does this imply that the study of the region has suffered from a degree of analytical blindness? Roger Owen's chapter provides both a contextual framework for the ensuing chapters and a thought-provoking and encouraging challenge to those who hope to know something about the area.

L. Carl Brown, Nicholas Hopkins, and Cynthia Nelson address the problems of assessing standard approaches to the study of the Arab world and considering possible new orientations. Turning a practiced historian's eye on events in the Middle East and on the efforts of contemporary scholarship to come to grips with those events, Brown offers a balanced and persuasive judgment. Nicholas Hopkins's stimulating chapter reviews a variety of explanations of the Gulf Crisis and, making creative use of political sociology and political anthropology, suggests specific areas of research that may help deepen our understanding of that event and, by extension, of the Arab world. Cynthia Nelson's contribution calls bluntly for an alternative construction of knowledge as a necessary step toward gaining a true understanding of the Arab world. Proceeding from a woman's perspective, she provides a cogent argument supporting the need for a feminist critique of current wisdom regarding that world.

In Part 2 we emphasize more substantive questions, examining the implications of the Gulf Crisis for economic and social developments in the Arab world. Exploring the impact of the crisis on the Arab region's socioeconomic matrix is vital if serious efforts are to be made to cope with very serious problems: the disparity of wealth afflicting today's Arab world; the prospects for movement toward more participatory political systems; the immediate and long-term consequences of population displacement during and after the Gulf Crisis; and the possibilities for overall economic growth and political stability in non–oil-producing Arab states.

Alan Richards examines the nature of Arab oil wealth and its impact on the Arab world as a whole in the years before the Gulf Crisis. He then suggests economic and political implications of the crisis for the region's future. Sociologist Saad Eddin Ibrahim provides a wide-ranging and timely analysis of the impact of the Gulf Crisis on current Arab regimes. Focusing on the significance of nontraditional social classes that emerged in the Arab world during the past three or four decades, and linking this to events since the Gulf Crisis, he offers a thought-provoking analysis of that world's prospects for political change. Nader Fergany turns to a single consequence of the Gulf Crisis that has had an impact throughout the Arab world and that is a particularly grave problem for several Arab states: the effect of the crisis on established patterns of labor migration. This is followed by Riad al Khouri's close examination of aspects of the context within which Jordan must function in the wake of the Gulf Crisis. As a non–oil-producing, regional, labor-exporting country, the Hashemite Kingdom can be expected to encounter conditions relevant to other, similar Arab countries. Utilizing a political economy approach, al Khouri particularly examines the social implications of the Gulf Crisis for movement toward more participatory politics in Jordan.

In Part 3 we focus directly on the political implications of the Gulf Crisis for the Arab world. Adeed Dawisha looks at the issue holistically and at its roots, seeking to determine whether the crisis can realistically be seen as a "determining event" in the region's fortunes. The remaining authors examine a range of specific, politically key questions being addressed in various ways by the contemporary Arab world. What is, or should be, the Arab image of self, and how should it be realized? How do, and should, Arabs relate among themselves at the regional level? What is the real meaning of security in today's Arab world; what are its structural implications? What can be expected of current hopes for the democratization of Arab states? What does the Palestinian issue imply for the Arab world in the wake of the Gulf Crisis? And, finally, what is the role of Islamic politics in the Arab world's future, and why does it exist?

Bassam Tibi evaluates the ideological underpinnings of pan-Arabist hopes for Arab unity in the light of the Gulf Crisis and reflects upon integration as an alternative, simultaneously analyzing the requisites of this latter goal. Ibrahim Awad looks closely at the Arab system in terms of its organizational infrastructure and suggests what the impact of the Gulf Crisis will be on the future of regional and subregional organization in the Arab world.

Bahgat Korany, whose careful appraisal of the relevance of orthodox strategic thought to today's Arab world would have equally merited his contribution's inclusion in Part 1, analyzes the empirical bases that will affect all strategic plans, whether Arab or non-Arab, for promoting security in that world. Mustafa El Sayyid critically examines calls for the Arab world's democratization against the backdrop of prevailing Arab political forces. Finally, implications of the Gulf Crisis for two issues that figured largely in earlier chapters—the Palestine problem and the significance of Islamist politics—are considered in depth by Ahmad Sidki Al-Dajani and François Burgat.

It is obvious that apart from the support of Palestinian nationalism and the desire to see Palestinian territory free from Israeli occupation, there is no single Palestinian view on the full range of questions raised by the Gulf Crisis. This enduring aspect of Palestinian political life was unchanged by the September 1993 agreement between the PLO and Israel on mutual recognition, limited autonomy for Gaza and Jericho, and further efforts to negotiate final peace. Yet, Al-Dajani, a prominent Palestinian scholar and activist, provides a comprehensive outlook that has deep resonance among Palestinians and others throughout the Arab world.

François Burgat brings a cool eye and careful research to the emotional question of Islamic currents in Arab politics. His analysis of the connection between nationalist and Islamic currents, and of its probable import for the Arab world, should be considered by anyone interested in the region's political future.

In Part 4, although we retain the book's primary focus on the Arab world, we also look at broader issues pertaining to the region's relations with non-Arab actors. The questions addressed have long-term perspectives. What does the post–Gulf Crisis situation in the Arab world imply for the future roles of external actors? To what extent can external actors shape the Arab world as an environment in which they must act? To what extent is the Arab world capable of trying to limit the impact of external actors?

Vitaly Naumkin looks specifically at Russia and the Commonwealth of Independent States (CIS) as possible factors in the Arab world now that the Soviet Union no longer exists. His analysis of a deeply transitional historical moment finds reason within that world to suggest that Russia and other parts of the former Soviet Union will not be permanently absent as important regional factors. Hossam T. El-Tawil then considers relations between the United States and the Arab world following the Gulf Crisis. Given U.S. power and Washington's record of applying a double standard in dealing with the Arab world on the one hand and Israel on the other, Tawil sees a danger of U.S. hegemony in the face of weak-willed Arab regimes.

Walid Kazziha focuses on the general situation in the Arab world, canvassing the main problems now facing the region and the possible role of external powers in furthering their resolution. He presents a strong argument that the United States has key responsibility for the region's future.

Somewhat in contrast, my own concluding chapter, "The Arab World and the Rest of the World," suggests that the region's internal dynamics and interaction with the broader international community now give the Arab world status as a potential threat to the non-Arab world. I recommend that recognition of this possibility by all concerned is the essential first step toward obviating the dangers it raises.

It should be clear that the reader will encounter a mixture of consensus and disagreement. Whether one considers this book part by part or (as is more advisable) in its totality, currents and crosscurrents of agreement and disagreement readily appear. At the same time, however, the very existence of differences of opinion among the authors inevitably reinforces an awareness of their basic agreement in important areas. Chief among these are the ties of consensus that give this book an underlying emphasis on the critical sociopolitical situation marking today's Arab world, on the need to understand this reality in its own right and to work realistically to minimize the suffering it implies, and on the need to consider realistically the limits that may constrain conscious political efforts to mold, shape, and direct political development and political developments in an area as vast and complex as the Arab world.

As Roger Owen stresses in Chapter 1, the real task is to understand that world within its global context. None of the contributors to this volume would disagree. None would claim at this point that his or her views are definitive expressions of Middle Eastern "truth." All would say that their views merit consideration. All would also say that if disagreements among them help engage a broader audience in thinking carefully about today's Arab world, this work will have served its purpose.

Notes

1. Victoria Brittain (ed.), *The Gulf Between Us: The Gulf War and Beyond* (London: Virago Press, 1991).

2. Haim Bresheeth and Niri Yuval-Davis (eds.), *The Gulf War and the New World Order* (London: Zed Books, 1991).

3. Charles A. Kimball, *Religion, Politics and Oil: The Volatile Mix in the Middle East* (Nashville: Abingdon Press, 1992); Kenneth L. Vaux, *Ethics and the Gulf War: Religion, Rhetoric, and Righteousness* (Boulder: Westview Press, 1992); Jean Bethke Elshtain, Stanley Hauerwas, Sari Nuseibeh, Michael Walzer, and George Weigel, *Reflections on the Morality of the Persian Gulf War: But Was It Just?* (New York: Doubleday, 1992).

Part 1
Understanding the Arab World After the Gulf Crisis

1

Reflections on the Meaning and Consequences of the Gulf Crisis

ROGER OWEN ⎯⎯⎯⎯⎯⎯⎯⎯⎯⎯⎯⎯⎯⎯⎯⎯⎯⎯⎯

It has been almost exactly thirty years since I went to Egypt to teach English in Cairo while working on my Oxford thesis. Of course, those were completely different times. Only ten years had passed since Gamal Abd-al Nasser and the Free Officers launched Egypt's revolution. Only six years had passed since Egypt's victory over the joint British-French-Israeli aggression that sparked the Suez Crisis.

President Nasser used that victory—a victory he deliberately portrayed as an Arab (rather than merely an Egyptian) victory—as a stimulus for his drive toward Arab unity, a campaign that culminated in the formation of the United Arab Republic (UAR) between Syria and Egypt in 1958. It is true that when I came to Egypt in 1962, some of the enthusiasm for such policies had waned a bit as a result of the breakup of this same UAR. But I also remember that pan-Arabist enthusiasm was rapidly rekindled during the unity talks held in Cairo in early 1963 with delegations from Syria and Iraq. It was a time of popular demonstrations and waving flags that sported four stars—one each, I suppose, for the members of the still larger union that suddenly seemed in sight, joining Egypt with Syria, Iraq, and what was then North Yemen.

We now live in less hopeful times. The Gulf War was a personal trauma for millions of people. Speaking only for myself, it was not quite as depressing a time as June 1967 when optimism gave way so suddenly to total defeat. Nevertheless, the atmosphere was nearly as gloomy—largely because of the time scale, which provided several months after Iraq's inva-

13

sion of Kuwait for everyone to ponder the death and destruction that so obviously lay ahead.

The outcome was so apparently inevitable that by January 1991, only a few minor questions remained to be answered. Would the Iraqis defend Kuwait City itself and thus force the coalition troops into a deadly process of house-to-house fighting? How much damage could Iraq inflict with its Scud missiles, perhaps armed with chemical warheads? What finally occurred was a triumphal progress in which we saw the war on television from only the victor's point of view. Each of us was left to make what we could of the awesome exhibition of U.S. power and the more fundamental questions it raised: Was the U.S. triumph inevitable? Could the United States continue to increase its global influence? Was there any way in which it could possibly be resisted?

It is difficult to know how to interpret the Gulf Crisis and its aftermath, how to give it larger meaning. The difficulty is increased by two factors. First, the crisis coincided almost exactly with the collapse of the Soviet Union and the realization that we were now living in a unipolar world. Second, concerning the war in the Gulf itself, events soon took an unexpected turn. The UN resolutions that bound the Allied Coalition together spoke only of the liberation of Kuwait and of the restoration of its legal government. But there was every reason to suppose that President George Bush sought the removal of Saddam Hussein. Instead, there occurred the Kurdish and Shi'ite insurrections and the survival of the Baghdad regime.

Other unexpected events soon followed. The Americans, having initially denied the link between Kuwait and Palestine, reversed themselves and put extraordinary effort into stage managing an Arab-Israeli peace conference. However, U.S. triumphalism quickly gave way to a period of deep introspection during which President Bush was challenged by a host of domestic contenders and, as I discovered during a visit to the University of Washington, General Norman Schwartzkopf soon found that he was the target of protests by students who regarded him as a less-than-welcome visitor to their campus. Meanwhile, General Colin Powell and his associates in the Pentagon perfected a method for preventing further U.S. military intervention in the Gulf: Long lists of questions about possible political consequences were drawn up, and clearly no new military initiatives—for example, against Iraqi positions near Kurdistan—would be countenanced until proper answers were obtained.

Turning to the Arab world's posture in the wake of the Gulf Crisis, I was surprised by the emir of Kuwait's long delay before returning to his liberated country. Nor did I anticipate the degree of vindictiveness the Gulf states displayed toward their local Palestinian—or, in the case of the Saudis, their Yemeni—populations. And only when I came to Cairo shortly after the Gulf War did I first appreciate the importance of the huge split that seemed to have developed between the Gulf regimes and those, such as the Egyptians and the Syrians, who had helped protect them.

Arab interpretations of these events have been eloquently proclaimed by others, such as Mohamed Hasanain Heikel. Professor Walid Khalidi has suggested that the Gulf War was the seventh of a series of landmark, and mostly tragic, events that have scarred the eastern half of the Arab world in the twentieth century, beginning with its division into separate states at the end of World War I. Each disaster, each *nakba,* he argues, revealed new levels of disintegration and impotence, leading to what is now a state of permanent political and governmental crisis.

The writers Halim Barakat and Kamal Abu Deeb refer with equal eloquence to a deep cultural crisis in an Arab world that is marked by growing fragmentation and individualism. If there is any hope for amelioration in the aftermath of the Gulf Crisis, they assert, it lies only in the fact that no illusions are left. Belief in the omniscience of leaders and leading parties has ended; only the unvarnished truth remains.[1]

Meaning and Consequences

Arab thinkers clearly see the Arab world as mired in an enduring crisis in the aftermath of the Gulf War. Yet, it seems to me that a crisis only exists when someone calls it a crisis, and outsiders such as myself should not join in this particular form of communal self-laceration. All I can offer is my personal perspective as someone who first came to the Middle East in 1956 and who has experienced most of its ups and downs since then, beginning, so it seemed to me, with the definite ups of independence and of the far-reaching plans for national development. It is from this perspective that I propose to look at the crisis of 1990–1991 and then to try to interpret it as an event whose importance stems—as is true of the 1956 Suez Crisis—from the way in which it drew back a curtain to reveal the movements of certain underlying changes that were already in train in the Middle East and in the world at large.

But first a word about my initial attempt at understanding, which was written just a few months after the fighting ended in Kuwait and was heavily influenced by Albert Hourani's wise insight after the Suez affair: although it was clear that things would never be the same, it would take some time before we could really see how they had changed.[2] Indeed, it seems to me that the impact of the Suez Crisis was felt most strongly in the late 1950s and that it was essentially exhausted with the breakup of the UAR in 1961. If this is so, then perhaps the essential features of the Gulf Crisis will reveal themselves in roughly the same short span of time.

As for the nature of the crisis, I took as my guide its likeness to an earthquake, with its epicenter in Kuwait and southern Iraq, where damage was the greatest, and its shock waves rippling out along existing fault lines of various kinds. These included the political fault lines—between Iraqis and Kurds, between the Gulf states and the rest of the Arab world, between pro-American and anti-American regimes; the ideological and religious fault lines—between Sunni and Shi'a, between those who supported Saudi Arabia's invitation to U.S. troops and those who opposed it; and, just as important, the moral fault lines—for example, the line between consistency and choice, in which some maintained the rights of all peoples to national self-determination whereas others sought to apply that right selectively.

The reverberations of all of this lasted quite a long time. Friends, families, associations, and parties were split over the issue, with few, it seems, being able to avoid the pressures to take a strong position one way or the other that were produced by the early commitment of U.S. troops.

Now, more than three years later, can we take a cooler view? What would this involve? In partly answering these questions, I explore two lines of thought I feel are necessary if we wish to come to terms with the crisis. These foci are the meaning and consequences of the Gulf Crisis. I propose to find in "meaning" the role of the crisis as a process of revelation whereas its "consequences" seem to me to relate most directly to the way in which it fitted so neatly into the changing patterns already visible in the wider world.

Let me start with this wider world. I think most of us would agree that we were witnessing not the birth of a new order but of something much better described as a Pax Americana. Washington is now the undisputed center of our world. Alternatives, whether viewed as other poles of power or as practices such as economic planning, have simply crumbled away. Meanwhile, under U.S. hegemony, the United Nations has reverted to what it was originally meant to be in 1945—a club of victors managing the world through the Security Council and the veto.

What does all of this mean? For one, it shows that a great disparity exists between the United States' undoubted military power and the question of its ability to continue managing an alliance system in which its economic rivals—Japan and the European Community (EC)—remain its political subordinates. Anyone visiting the United States is aware of how intensely all of this is being argued and, just as important, being felt.

Another central feature of the Pax Americana is the importance of what we might call *imperial attention*. Some countries and some regions of the world look more important than others when viewed through the Washington optic. This explains, for example, the differing U.S. reactions to the recent assaults on the democratic process in Peru and Algeria. Whereas there is a long-standing policy of U.S. support for political pluralism in Latin America, there is little concern for Algeria's section of North

Africa, which has no lobbies, no real interests, nothing to force the White House to react.

If this is so, then we all need to know what is happening in Washington and how to use its policies to our best advantage, or, if necessary, how to protect ourselves from those policies. This requires that other countries post their best diplomats to the United States. It also means listening to journalists and academics who understand one of the most complicated decisionmaking systems in the world. The United States is the only country, for example, in which the upper house of a parliament or a national assembly plays a more important role in foreign policy than the more popularly elected chamber.

All of this may seem too difficult to manage, but there is some comfort for the Arab states. In recent years, ambassadors from two very dissimilar regimes are credited with having played significant roles in Washington: the Iraqi ambassador of the mid-1980s, who promoted the famous tilt toward Baghdad, and Saudi Arabia's Prince Bandar, whose part in persuading his uncles to accept U.S. troops is now regarded as having been crucial.

I feel three consequences of the crisis for the Middle East itself are particularly significant. The first is Iraq's role as the object of a completely novel experiment in international intervention. This includes not only the UN-legislated reparations, sanctions, and program of weapons control but also the fact that at least some of these punitive measures were deliberately designed to get rid of Saddam Hussein and will apparently be lifted if and when he leaves office. Never before has the United Nations made such a distinction between a people and their president. The other form of intervention is that practiced by the United States and its allies without UN cover—for example, the safe haven policy designed to prevent direct Iraqi governmental control over the Kurds in the north.

The second consequence concerns the playing out of the larger U.S. program toward Middle East arms control, toward preventing nuclear proliferation, and toward the Palestinians. All of these were originally conceived as vital U.S. interests but only, it would seem, insofar as they stemmed from a recognition that a successful exercise of new U.S. hegemony demanded the removal of major causes of conflict within its heterogeneous group of Arab and Israeli allies. Seen from this perspective, there have been two U.S. successes. The first is the holding of the series of peace talks between Israel and its Arab neighbors. The second is the international acceptance of Washington's novel distinction between weapons of mass destruction and their delivery systems—which are to be curtailed—and ordinary weapons of national defense, which can be sold to Saudis or Israelis at will.

Finally, in the light of all that has been mentioned above, there is the basic question to be asked by peoples as well as regimes: How do we live best in this U.S.-dominated world? Here the good news, such as it is, is that Arabs, helped by their traumatic experience in the Gulf War, understood the realities of the post–Cold War world far more quickly than the Israelis, whose politicians—and, to judge from the elections held in 1992, much of whose citizenry—only slowly began to understand that the old bipolar world in which their state was born and flourished for so many years has vanished. Nevertheless, this may be small comfort to those, such as the Kurds and the Palestinians, for whom the degree of U.S. support has literally become a matter of life and death. The extent to which that support will be forthcoming remains unknown.

The other area in which the degree of U.S. involvement remains of vital importance to local rulers is the Gulf. Other Arab regimes are all being forced to make a choice. They can try to oppose Washington outright and face the consequences or they can, almost literally, jump into the pocket of the United States. Over time, other, more ideological forms of opposition will surely develop. I believe these are likely to take the initial form of joint efforts to avoid U.S. control over inventories of Arab military resources. But others think the crunch is more likely to come in the area of culture and human rights, where accusations of U.S. double standards will continue to move peoples and to stir strong passions.

The Middle East in the New World

My Welsh grandfathers, living in the dark coal-mining valleys of the South, would have approved the following text to be recommended to those who at this historical juncture wish the best for the Arab world and the Middle East: "I will lift up my eyes unto the hills." If we do this, if we look up and into the distance, not down at our own feet or, even worse, backward into the past, for inspiration, what do we see?

I argue that whenever we want to understand the new world in which we all live, we have to begin with what is most important—the relationship among the three great economic blocs, the United States, Japan, and Europe. Their fierce competition for hegemony will decide much of what happens elsewhere. Each has its own strengths and weaknesses. The United States remains the world's technological leader but is burdened with a huge budget deficit, poor schools (but good universities), and growing social disorder. Japan is more efficient and has a more docile labor force but lacks the outwardness and toleration of pluralism that facilitates a truly innovative society. Europe has all of the strengths and weaknesses of its own diversity, lacking a true common market but making up for this with its more eclectic and imaginative approach to social and educational affairs.

For anyone who cares about where the world is going, these are central realities from which projections must begin.

Turning to the Middle East, the most revolutionary proposal anyone can presently make is that there should be peace. Only true peace will allow the Arab peoples to turn away from reliance on large armies and powerful authoritarian movements and devote their resources and their imaginations to the two basics: democracy rather than dictatorship and development rather than debt. But we must also note that the end of the fighting that followed the Gulf Crisis produced a false peace. Washington's Gulf allies did not suddenly become more democratic. Then, too, regimes in both Tunisia and Algeria made serious mistakes in thinking they could take advantage of the splits generated by the Gulf Crisis within religious opposition forces in order to exclude Islamicists from systems of managed multiparty politics.

Finally, I turn briefly to Egypt. I feel, based on thirty years of observation, that Egypt's geographic position at the center of the Arab world provides an opportunity, not for Egyptian domination of the Arab world but for the exercise of beneficial influence based on a profound understanding of the region. For me, this possibility is highly visible because of various factors. For example, it is apparent in the way the sense of humiliation, felt so strongly by many Arabs after the Gulf Crisis but not so sharply in Egypt, is being balanced by a strong sense of history and reality. It can also be perceived in Egypt's tempered response to the problems posed by its three difficult neighbors—Israel, Sudan, and Libya. It can be seen in Egyptian awareness of the need for careful—some would say too much—internal direction during Egypt's difficult transition from a single-party to a multiparty system. Finally, it can be seen in Egypt's attempt to create a situation in which the state becomes the framework for political life rather than its hard-won prize.

From this I conclude that Cairo will also be a good vantage point from which to try to understand the Middle East's place in the new world of the Pax Americana tempered by fierce competition from Europe and Japan. It will also be a good place to observe Egypt's attempts to fit into that order. Egypt will have to make vital choices about alliances and even more vital choices about which of the major economic blocs it will associate with and what Arab partners it will accept.

I cannot stress too strongly the importance I give to the task of understanding the Arab world and the Middle East at this time. It is a challenge, particularly for those of us who are children of the Cold War and may not have the mental flexibility to live easily in our brave new world. Yet, the effort must be made. For me, this is the real meaning of the Gulf Crisis and, if the opportunities it provides for new thinking are taken, is its only real justification.

In world terms the crisis revealed certain basic forces at work that will make the twenty-first century quite different from the twentieth century. In Middle Eastern terms, it not only called attention to some of these forces but also gave them a powerful push in directions in which they were already going.

The good news is that the truth of all of this is now easier to see. The bad news is that morale in many parts of the Arab world is so low that people may lack the energy and will to make good use of what they can now see.

Perhaps the basic lesson here—particularly for those who are professional students of the area—is that we should leave regimes to struggle through the difficult currents of this new sea. Let us, some of the people, take up the much more exciting task of trying to understand what is occurring.

Notes

1. My remarks here are based on my understanding of presentations given by Walid Khalidi, Halim Barakat, and Kamal Abu Deeb at the 1992 Symposium on Arab Integration held at Georgetown University.

2. Roger Owen, "Epilogue: Making Sense of an Earthquake," in Victoria Brittain (ed.), *The Gulf Between Us: The Gulf War and Beyond* (London: Virago, 1991), pp. 159–178; Albert Hourani, "The Middle East and the Crisis of 1956," *Middle East Affairs* 1 (St. Antony's Papers, 4).

2

Scholarship and the Diplomatic Context of the Arab World After the Gulf War

L. CARL BROWN

Over three years have passed since Iraqi troops invaded neighboring Kuwait on August 2, 1990, and started the regional crisis that ended in the Gulf War. Yet, it is still too soon to demonstrate that the months of crisis and the weeks of war from August 1990 through February 1991, dramatic and traumatic as these events were, shocked the parties concerned into radically different policies and orientations. The Arab world, the Middle East, and the outside states concerned with the Middle East may well revert to old, familiar patterns of action and reaction.

Regardless of whether this bleak prognosis is true, the Gulf War did not reveal major faults in previous scholarly interpretations of Arab world politics and diplomacy. Neither scholars nor statesmen have discovered, as a result of the Gulf War, a hitherto ignored truth that can better explain the region and perhaps even lead to something approaching stability and peace.

In January 1991, shortly before the Gulf Crisis became the Gulf War, Walid Khalidi sought to distinguish the background causes from the particular causes of the confrontation. He began by evoking A.J.P. Taylor's assertion that wars can be compared to road accidents. The ultimate cause of such mishaps is the existence of automobiles and roads and the human propensity to move from place to place, but such a finding does little to explain any particular accident. This is also true for crises leading to war.[1] Thus, to confine the analysis to immediate causes, to say that the Gulf War came about because Saddam Hussein invaded Kuwait or George Bush organized a coalition to resist this aggression must strike us as true but woefully incomplete.

Over a century and a half ago, Alexis de Tocqueville addressed from a different perspective the same problem, which might be epitomized as simply our basic need to find causes for what occurs:

> I have come across men of letters who have written history without taking part in public affairs, and politicians who have concerned themselves with producing events without thinking about them. I have observed that the first are always inclined to find general causes, whereas the second, living in the midst of disconnected daily facts, are prone to imagine that everything is attributable to particular incidents, and that the wires they pull are the same as those that move the world.

Tocqueville then concluded with a sobering challenge to us all: "It is to be presumed that both are equally deceived."[2]

Yes, much more needs to be said concerning this particular war, concerning both its immediate causes and its results. Moreover, in the process of that examination, those in the scholarly community who were not "taking part" in the unfolding crisis should heed the cautions of Taylor and Tocqueville. In our search to clarify the big picture, we must not depict the flesh-and-blood actors who were involved as walking their way through their roles, scarcely perceiving the predetermined nature of their actions. To mention only two contingencies, Saddam Hussein's gamble and George Bush's memory of the 1930s did make a difference. Other leaders with other mind-sets would have brought about other results. Even so, there remains a historically shaped Middle Eastern context within which this crisis was played out. I address that larger context here.

Crisis and Consequence in the Middle East

"Whatever the denouement to Iraq's invasion of Kuwait—through war or diplomacy, confrontation or compromise—the political map of the Middle East is almost certain to be redrawn and many of the region's key issues redefined."[3] So wrote a perceptive observer, Robin Wright, early in the crisis. Few would have disagreed with her at the time, and the sense that this was a major turning point in modern Middle Eastern history was only increased as the standoff gave way to the air war, followed by the short ground war that crushed Iraqi forces.

And yet, nearly three years after this seemingly decisive military rout, an automobile bumper sticker in the recession-ridden United States reads "Saddam Hussein still has his job. How about you?" Saddam Hussein still rules in Iraq; that country has been neither dismembered nor democratized, and the same might be said for neighboring Kuwait. A promising peace conference has been held in Madrid, and so far, neither bilateral talks between Israel and the different Arab parties nor regionwide talks have ground to a halt. Yet, no breakthroughs have been achieved, either. It is difficult to demonstrate at this writing that either the political map or the key issues of the Middle East have been redefined, despite the new mutual recognition of Israel and the PLO.

Even that bumper sticker is something of a rarity on the American scene. The U.S. public that made Desert Storm a sort of national theater-in-the-round has moved on. The Gulf War seems fated to join such past dramas as the Iran-Contra affair or the U.S. invasion of Panama as an event vaguely remembered and seldom discussed. Although the *New York Times,* fulfilling its role as the national newspaper of record, continues dutifully to report on the follow-up to the Gulf War and to the peace process, most Americans are now more concerned about U.S. internal politics, the economy, and other domestic issues. To the extent that foreign policy still seizes U.S. attention, the commercial challenge from Japan or the rapidly unifying European Community or the breakup of the Soviet Union and of Yugoslavia account for the big stories.

U.S. inattention might be discounted if observers in the Middle East and beyond did not seem convinced that the United States is the most important actor in the world and that it must learn lessons from the Gulf War and take initiatives. This is the country that has won the dubious laurel of hegemon in the Middle East, if not in the world—or so assume both its friends and its foes. In any case, we might ask if Europe or East Asia (the so-called First World) offers a significantly different response. Surely, if ever there were a time for continental introspection, it would be in Europe, which is unifying in the West while dividing in the East.

Crises and wars are supposed to be the crucibles, melting earlier political arrangements and molding something radically new. This does not seem to occur in the modern Middle East. A short review of the past quarter century of Middle Eastern history demonstrates this stubborn resistance to systemic change, a pattern within which the aftermath of the Gulf Crisis may well fall.

Following the June 1967 war, for example, many seasoned observers foresaw prospects for a negotiated peace. If the optimal bargaining situation requires that everyone coming to the table should have something the other wants, then the Middle East after 11 June 1967 was seemingly ripe for a negotiated change. Before the Six Day War, the Arab confrontation states could support the Palestinian cause rhetorically or even with limited actions without risking major strategic interests. After that war, however, Israel had territorial assets (Sinai, the West Bank and Gaza, the Golan Heights) to offer Egypt, Syria, and Jordan. The latter three, even in the weakness of defeat, had the power to grant or withhold what Israel sought most—the kind of stable security that comes with fully elaborated peace and mutual recognition.

Moreover, in the few weeks leading up to the June War, the Western world lived through a sense of crisis similar to that following August 2, 1990. After the war came the meeting between President Lyndon Johnson and Prime Minister Kosygin, the extended UN debate throughout the summer of 1967, the Arab summit conference at Khartoum (with the notorious three "noes"), and finally, UN Security Council Resolution 242 advancing its "land for peace" formula. Cynics might say that over the years, UN Resolution 242 has become something of an incantation (or a mantra, to adopt a religiously neutral term), but no doors to peace have opened. Mention of later developments—the Jarring Mission(s), the War of Attrition, the Rogers Initiative—suffices to recall the flurry of activity that produced no breakthroughs.

The October–Ramadan–Yom Kippur War of 1973 was another crisis that at the time was deemed so intensive and far-reaching in impact as surely to provoke major changes. This war included the second-largest tank battle in history, that between Egyptian and Israeli forces in the sands of Sinai.[4] The war provoked a dangerous superpower standoff leading to the U.S. announcement of a limited nuclear alert. It also set in motion an effective Arab oil embargo that was felt immediately in sharp worldwide price rises and long lines at gas stations in the United States and elsewhere.

The immediate postwar period was equally dramatic. Secretary of State Henry Kissinger won world attention with his "shuttle diplomacy." Here again, however, the limited successes of disengagement agreements produced no momentum toward systemic change. It took Anwar al-Sadat's bold initiative of going to Israel four years after the 1973 war to get Egyptian-Israeli peace negotiations back on track. That step took place not in the storm of warfare but in the doldrums of "no war no peace," and the treaty itself came only after sixteen stormy months of negotiations capped by the hitherto unprecedented commitment of time and effort by a U.S. president, Jimmy Carter. Even this path-breaking treaty did not provide the impetus required for a generalized resolution of the Arab-Israeli confrontation.

The most long-lived and by far the most devastating Middle Eastern war in modern times, that between Iraq and Iran from 1980 to 1988, never quite managed a single, narrowly focused time of crisis such as those that characterized the June or October wars. It was a war neither superpower bloc seemed able to influence decisively. Or, to state the matter differently, it was a war the superpowers found they could live with, tilting now toward one side, now toward another—agreeing implicitly that the best outcome would be a stalemate, so why not just let the two sides wear themselves down fighting to a draw? A similar cynicism characterized the outlook of the neighboring Middle Eastern states.

The events of 1986–1988 that in the United States were dubbed the "Iran-Contra" affair, or "Irangate," followed the same vein. They amounted to moves to ensure that neither side won—or lost—on too large a scale. Moreover, except for the several examples of continuing human tragedy, such as the attack on the USS *Stark* and the downing of the Iranian airbus, the Iran-Contra affair could be dismissed as farce. We can well imagine the combination of disdain and disbelief with which historians a century from now will approach those bizarre developments. In any case, the terrible Iraq-Iran War wore on to its weary end without producing any apparent systemic change.

An intervening crisis—shorter in time and thus more capable of riveting regional and world attention—was the 1982 Israeli invasion of Lebanon. Here again, pundits were understandably inclined to see a crisis that should stimulate systemic change. On the one side could be seen an effort by certain Israeli leaders (personified by Ariel Sharon) to cut through all of the earlier checks and balances by destroying the military potential of the Palestinian Liberation Organization (PLO) and thereby discrediting the strategic option the PLO was seen as representing. This was coupled with the notion of a bold Israeli stroke to reconstruct regional balances radically by bringing into existence an Arab client state, a Christian "Zion," in the form of a Maronite-dominated Lebanon. The elusiveness of any such total victory on the ground, the assassination of Bashir Gemayel, the massacre of Sabra and Shatila, and bitter reaction in Israel to such Promethean shenanigans demonstrated the vast chasm separating system-shattering dreams and recalcitrant Middle Eastern reality.

The situation in Lebanon today is essentially a stalemate between Israel, exercising control in the south, and Syria, with substantial but indirect domination elsewhere. In the meantime, a fragile post–civil war government in Beirut holds tenaciously to political compromise and centrist policies. It can be assumed that the long-term aim of those now seeking to reconstruct a Lebanese state and society is to get both the Israelis and the Syrians to leave—probably by use of the persuasive argument to each that this is the best way to get the other out.

Many analysts, especially Arabs, noted that the Israeli invasion of Lebanon exposed the emptiness of pan-Arab rhetoric regarding Israel. As a foreign army besieged a major Arab capital, the Arab world—with the limited exception of Syria—watched in impotent agony. Surely, it was thought, the painful realization of the difference between rhetoric and reality would stimulate system-challenging initiatives on the Arab side. However, these were not forthcoming.

The United States, for its part, moved in, seeking to orchestrate a settlement. As in previous crises, the results were temporary. The Israeli siege of Beirut was lifted, PLO forces left Lebanon, the Reagan Plan was announced (thus recognizing the interrelatedness of Middle Eastern politics), and in May 1983, a U.S.-brokered Israeli-Lebanese agreement was signed. It was a conflict-resolution house built on sand, the futility of which was symbolized by the suicide bombing of the U.S. Marines quarters in Beirut in October 1983. U.S. troops soon "redeployed" outside of Lebanon. What Alexander Haig had earlier labeled a window of opportunity (that terrible Panglossian metaphor for making the best of what could have been avoided) proved to be yet another trompe l'oeil.

Much more could be said about these examples of earlier crises that were expected to lead to systemic change but did not, and other examples might readily be cited. At this point, however, it is more appropriate to address the argument that the Gulf War was really different in a fundamental way: The Cold War was over. The United States and the Soviet Union cooperated. Accordingly, the customary meshing of superpower and regional confrontations, leading to deadlock, did not prevail. This is a very important consideration that needs examination from several different perspectives.

The Impact of the Gulf Crisis

What difference, then, did it make that Iraq's invasion of Kuwait constituted the first post–Cold War crisis? First, it seems true beyond any reasonable doubt that this made possible the imposition of UN sanctions plus the ensuing UN authorization to use military action in forcing Iraqi withdrawal. Moreover, if the Cold War's impact on regional balances had still been operative, it is unlikely that Arab participation in the U.S.-led coalition against Iraq could have been realized. It is also unlikely that King Fahd would have agreed to accept U.S. and coalition ground troops in Saudi Arabia, even assuming that the United States would have pushed for this if Cold War reality had still prevailed.

Whether the upshot of the Iraqi invasion under Cold War conditions would have produced a replay of earlier (1961 and 1973) Iraqi actions or threats against Kuwait, or a successful absorption of Kuwait followed by regional balancing to counter enhanced Iraqi power, or some other concatenation of events will never be known and is not essential for present purposes.[5] Let us concede that the end of the Cold War clearly made Desert Storm possible. Did it do anything more?

We might begin by posing the question of whether the military results of Desert Storm have been decisive. Perhaps the most accurate current answer is that Saddam Hussein's immediate threat to his neighbors has been sharply reduced, but he and his regime still exist, and no territorial changes have been effected. Saddam Hussein's Iraq is much less likely to be quickly rearmed than were Egypt and Syria after the June 1967 war (another significant impact of the end of the Cold War). Yet, Iraq has sufficient population and natural resources to again play an important role in regional politics.

The Gulf War does not seem to have produced any fundamental regional realignments to this point. Turkey's concern about the Kurds has been, if anything, accentuated. This perhaps creates a certain tacit alliance between any governments ruling in Ankara and Baghdad. Saudi Arabia and, indeed, all of the Gulf Cooperation Council (GCC) states have been pushed to a more vulnerably overt reliance upon the U.S. protective shield. But can we realistically argue that the power wielders in Baghdad, Damascus, Cairo, or elsewhere were unaware of this ultimate political reality before August 2, 1990? Iran's relative power position has been enhanced enough to cause both Saudi Arabia and the GCC, as well as Turkey, to be disinclined to support the breakup of Iraq. Syria is strengthened, but not dramatically. In addition, any Syrian muscle flexing can provoke a compensating response from Israel or, in fact, from any of Syria's neighbors.

There has been much speculation about whether the end of the Cold War and Israel's awkward role (or lack of same) during the Gulf War has resulted in a major change in U.S.-Israeli relations. The United States, so this line of thought goes, no longer sees Israel as an asset—a "stationary aircraft carrier"—in the Middle Eastern arena of the Cold War. This is an interesting argument, but does it truly reflect U.S. strategic thinking regarding the Middle East from the 1940s to the present? A review of the record demonstrates many incidents or crises in which Israeli military actions have been seen by U.S. policymakers as a hindrance, not an asset. Examples include the February 1955 Israeli raid on Gaza (as well as the general Israeli policy of retaliation in force, which has prevailed since the days of Ben Gurion), the Anglo-French-Israeli collusion in attacking Egypt in 1956, Israeli dogfights with Soviet pilots operating in Egypt during the 1969–1970 War of Attrition, and the 1978 Israeli invasion of Lebanon, plus the 1982 invasion, if we assume that Secretary of State Alexander Haig's ambivalent position hardly represented administration policy.

Indeed, the one clear example of an Israeli military move taken in response to a U.S. request (instead of unilaterally) is the 1970 Black September incident, during which Israel, at U.S. urging, moved troops up to the Syrian border to deter Syrian intervention in King Hussein's military campaign against the PLO. As for other-than-military actions over the same period, the official U.S. perception has tended to see Israel as a state that takes everything from the United States except advice.[6] From a stiff-necked resistance to would-be U.S.-brokered peace arrangements in the early 1950s, to the long U.S.-Israeli standoff regarding further Israeli settlements in the West Bank, the record is filled with examples of sharply different tactical perspectives dividing the two parties. Significantly, this is especially true of the foreign policy establishments of the two states while being less so of their general publics and legislative branches.

All of this suggests that U.S.-Israeli relations (which are close and are a determining element in U.S. policy) are based on something other than the U.S. view of Israel as a strategic asset.[7] A review of the historical record suggests that considering Israel to be a strategic asset was largely a marginal, minority view until the Reagan years, when it became somewhat more respectable. Closer consideration of congressional reaction to the Bush administration's $10 billion loan guarantees to Israel indicates that the little attrition in congressional support for Israel that may have taken place can be attributed more to the unpopularity of foreign relations—especially foreign aid or loans—than to a post–Cold War reconsideration of Israel's strategic role.

A related line of inquiry asks whether the U.S.-led coalition, had it marched to Baghdad and created a military occupation regime in Iraq, could have set in motion genuine systemic changes. The prudent answer is that such decisive action might have done so, but two rejoinders are in order.[8] First, a military occupation regime might have produced an essentially benign result, as happened with the post-1945 U.S. occupation of Japan. However, in light of modern Middle Eastern history, a much less favorable result seems more likely. Such an occupation might have been no more stabilizing and institution-building than, say, the French mandate period in Syria. It might have been even worse.

Second, and of decisive importance for present purposes, such an occupation was never really a "thinkable" option. A major factor in this regard was President Bush's determination to avoid a Vietnamlike open-ended commitment (or a replay of the U.S. debacle in Lebanon). Moreover, Washington's Arab allies opposed the possibility of a U.S. occupation of Iraq (which is what it would have been, even with a UN fig leaf), knowing this would play into the hands of the many Arabs who insisted that the introduction of Western forces into the region heralded a new round of imperialism. A third consideration militating against a U.S. military presence in postwar Iraq was the virtual certainty of provoking an upsurge of guerrilla and terrorist actions sponsored by disaffected states. Finally, occupying Iraq would have increased pressures on the United States to somehow solve the Arab-Israeli confrontation to the satisfaction of all parties.

Although no resolution of major outstanding issues has taken place, the insistent claim remains that U.S. hegemony in the Middle East was demonstrated by the Gulf War and that Washington therefore has the power to broker—or even impose—a series of settlements in the area. According to this view, different parties may protest at such arm-twisting, but they are in no position to stop the U.S. juggernaut.

Again, there are two responses. First, even accepting that such an estimate of U.S. power in the Middle East is valid, there is no indication that the White House has either the strategic plan or the will for such an approach and even less indication that Congress would provide the necessary support. Second, a closer look at this presumed U.S. hegemony is in order. In addition to the historically documented ability of Middle Eastern regional clients to frustrate the plans of great-power patrons through some combination of delay, defiance, and duplicity (and while conceding that Russia, either with or without the other Soviet successor states, can hardly be a factor in the immediate future), the question remains of the extent to which the United States can impose its will on its European and East Asian allies.

It is true that Europe, especially Britain, has tended to follow U.S. leadership in this area, but Europe's effaced role in Middle Eastern diplomacy has been relatively cost free. It is, in a sense, the line of least resistance. That is, Europe maintains—indeed, strengthens—its position as a major Middle Eastern trading partner without the encumbrances of potentially costly political or military commitments. Moreover, it might be argued that the implicit condition for European effacement is the U.S. ability to keep Europe's commercial access to the Middle East (especially to the oil resource) effectively open. Signs of slight European independence that appear from time to time (such as during the 1973 October War or in the European Community's 1970 Venice Declaration regarding the Palestinians) demonstrate that U.S. leadership, even among North Atlantic Treaty Organization (NATO) allies, has its limits. Somewhat like the legendary French revolutionary leader rushing to join the crowd moving toward an already determined action, the United States is a hegemon only to the extent that it avoids steps that go too strongly against the wishes of those many states that are satisfied with the safety of maintaining a low profile in the Middle East's unpromising diplomatic environment.

Concerning Arab perceptions of themselves and others following the Gulf War, even those Arab states on the "winning side" could hardly take satisfaction from the outcome. An Arab solution to an Arab problem had not been forthcoming. The crisis revealed yet again the lack of Arab political unity. Enormous suffering was inflicted, most of all on Arabs—the people of Iraq, the Kuwaitis, Palestinians, and others caught in the maelstrom and since deprived of livelihood in the Gulf area. The previously somewhat papered-over cultural and political differences separating the Arab "haves" and "have nots" (which is almost exclusively the Arabs of the Arabian Peninsula against the others) were exposed for all Arabs and all the world to ponder.

Will the experiences of the Gulf War jolt the Arabs into taking steps that may lead to systemic changes? Here again, it seems to be too soon to tell. Some are already persuaded that the Arab world after the Gulf War will never be the same, and they present powerful arguments. However, similar predictions were presented following earlier wars and crises. For present purposes, we can say that the quiet—indeed, heroic—realism of the Palestinian leadership, in its negotiations at Madrid and Washington, suggests a possibly significant shift that could have repercussions throughout the region. Abba Eban's taunt (repeated in recent years more in sadness for all concerned than in dismissal of Israel's principal opponents) that the Palestinians have "never missed an opportunity to miss an opportunity" may have run its course.

Yet, this sign and others (such as hesitant Syrian willingness to pursue a U.S.-brokered peace process) must be set alongside many other circumstances that are appreciably less positive. Those who assert that the Arabs, in their disunity and, for many, recent defeat, now have no option but to end their quarrel with Israel and accept whatever terms may be offered would be well advised to review the historical record. Arab unwillingness to negotiate from demonstrable weakness was clearly illustrated after the crushing defeat of the June 1967 war.

It is also worth noting that the argument that only the Cold War made Arab rearmament after the June 1967 war possible can be called into question by evoking the Arab experience with the West after World War II and, again, following the Arab defeat in the 1948 war against Israel. In neither case was a generous outside patron at hand. Judged in strictly material terms, Arab prospects had seldom seemed weaker. Yet, in those very years, Western efforts to "line up" the Arabs failed miserably. A brief review of Anglo-Egyptian or Anglo-Iraqi relations during the decade after 1945 suffices to make the point.

In short, defeat, hopelessness, and anomie led more often to the extremist politics of rage than to the moderate politics of realism. This tends to play out in the Arab world as follows. Many, probably even most, Arab leaders recognize what is possible in diplomacy and are always disposed to consider, as intelligent political leaders should, practicing the art of the possible. Even so, with shaky legitimacy, a domestic public opinion embittered by past affronts and defeats, and always at least one regional opponent employing the demagogic cry of treason to the cause of Arabism against any statesman daring to offer too much realism, the leadership of the Arab world is strongly tempted to play it safe. That means not taking bold system-changing initiatives for peace or for war but instead offering mixed signals with a bit of both.[9] The irony and the tragedy is that this is, on balance, probably the least safe long-run policy for the Arab state system.

A final point remains: Time is almost certainly not on the side of system-challenging initiatives. The Gulf War, like all wars, crises, and bold initiatives, created for a short period a generalized sense of shock, disposing all to think the previously unthinkable. With the passage of time, however, what was once seen as extraordinarily threatening or promising becomes merely routine.

For all of these reasons, we must reluctantly conclude that it is simply too early to assert that the Gulf War has changed the rules of the game or even changed the perceptions of the players. Systemic breakthroughs may still come, but time is on the side of small steps along the well-worn diplomatic path.

Conclusion: Scholarship and Understanding the Middle East

My interpretation, arguing that the post–Gulf War Middle East is likely to offer more of the same, leads to the conclusion that existing scholarly interpretations or paradigms concerning Middle Eastern diplomacy and the Arab state system in its relations with the outside world have not been far from the mark. Of course, in a region afflicted with so many long-standing and unresolved political problems, advocacy scholarship has been rife. This is even more the case because the Middle East has consistently received more public attention in the West than has any other area of the Third World. From Western philhellenic championing of Greek independence in the 1820s to the fulminations of Gladstone and many others against alleged Ottoman misrule, or from the "desert romanticism" that embraced Lawrence of Arabia and the Arab Revolt or Morocco's Abd al-Krim to the Western support of Zionism and Israel (not to mention Greek-Turkish and Armenian-Turkish tensions, as seen in the West), there has been no lack of special pleading seeking to pass for history.[10]

Such pseudoscholarship aside, however, there is a respectable body of scholarly work depicting the diplomatic world of the Arabs in its regional and international context. To mention all of the authors, books, and articles and to place this development in its proper historiographical context must be left for another occasion. Here it is necessary only to establish that the interpretative frameworks produced over the past few decades to explain Arab diplomacy provide plausible and persuasive guides. They can, moreover, be used to interpret Arab diplomacy during and since the Gulf War. No new paradigm, no scholarly Copernican revolution is indicated.

During and after the Gulf War, one major argument to the contrary was that this crisis demonstrated just how divided the Arabs really were, where-as the "received wisdom" in the United States and the West had for too long posited a unified Arab world, unified at least against the outsider if not always among themselves. A quick survey of Western scholarship on this point—most of which is written in English—is illuminating.[11]

The Gulf War divided the Arab world, painfully so, and some observers argued that the breakup of Arab unity needs to be followed by an equivalent breakup of Western perceptions of a diplomatically significant Arab unity. Writing in the *Wall Street Journal* a year after the onset of the Gulf Crisis, Bernard Lewis insisted:

> One myth that is being reluctantly relinquished concerns the strength and effectiveness of pan-Arabism. . . . No one could dispute the passionate belief of the Arabs in their common cultural identity; few would question the hatred for the West that still dominates much of their public life. Yet neither the passion nor the hatred has provided a usable political force. Time and time again the pundits have warned that this or that action or policy would raise the whole Arab world in arms against us—but it did not happen. . . . The Gulf Crisis, which was essentially an inter-Arab conflict into which outsiders were drawn, finally demonstrated the falsity of this belief, except perhaps for the most obdurate of pundits and the most amnesiac of audiences.[12]

Yet, I would argue that it did not take the Gulf War to drive home an awareness that the existence of a very real and deep-seated Arab desire for unity has long gone hand in hand with Arab political fragmentation. Malcolm Kerr made this point in his classic *The Arab Cold War: Gamal Abd al-Nasir and His Rivals,* which first appeared in 1965. Fouad Ajami's oft-cited "The End of Pan-Arabism" made essentially the same point at the end of the 1970s.[13]

Indeed, as long ago as 1933, the hard-eyed but perceptive French specialist on the Arab world, Robert Montagne, observed, "One could say that the appeal to Arab unity appears as a kind of ideological reaction against local divisions and quarrels. The farther one is from [Arab unity] the more one invokes it."[14]

Moreover, although the U.S. and Western publics tend to lump all Arabs together, as most people everywhere do in categorizing and simplifying the reality of those far removed from them in physical and cultural space, the best scholarly literature has long emphasized the fissiparous nature of Arab and Middle Eastern politics. Patrick Seale's *The Struggle for Syria* made that point in 1965, the same year Kerr's *Arab Cold War* first appeared. Moreover, *The Struggle for Syria* stands as one of the few books in this field deemed worthy of being reissued a generation after it first appeared.[15] Nadav Safran's *Saudi Arabia: The Ceaseless Quest for Security* also stresses the multipolar nature of Arab and Middle Eastern politics, centering the story around Saudi Arabia instead of Syria.[16]

Further scholarly demonstration of this distinctive international relations subsystem, characterized by a penchant for countless making and breaking of diplomatic ties is found in a solid work—*The Origins of Alliances* by Stephen M. Walt—written not by an Arabist or an area expert but by a political scientist specializing in international relations.[17] My own *International Politics and the Middle East* seeks to present the same interpretation of fissiparous multipolarity while tracing the roots of this distinctive international relations subsystem to the beginnings of what historians have long labeled *the Eastern Question*. Many of the special studies concentrating on U.S. relations with the Arabs and the Middle East, such as those by William B. Quandt and Dan Tschirgi, reveal a clear-eyed view of Middle Eastern politics as a subsystem in which Machiavelli or, for that matter, Thucydides would feel at home.[18]

One could cite as well the many political science works that treat individual countries more than interstate politics (such as Michael Hudson's *Arab Politics*), the impressive revisionist literature on Israeli-Arab relations—especially in the crucial period just before and soon after the creation of Israel in 1948—or even the growing (in quantity and sophistication) historical literature on the rise and development of Arabism.[19]

In a word, if we leave aside poorly informed or polemical works, we can assert that students seeking to learn about Arab-style diplomacy, or statesmen seeking to move the Middle East toward more peaceful ways, do not lack adequate road maps and highway signs (to return to A.J.P. Taylor's metaphor with which we began). The unwary may, however, be misled by a few of the more glaringly inaccurate commercial billboards along the route, but that is a different problem.

Notes

1. Walid Khalidi, "Why Some Arabs Support Saddam," *Institute for Palestine Studies Occasional Paper* (January 1991), (Washington, D.C.: Institute for Palestine Studies, 1991).

2. Tocqueville's statement must strike a chord among scholars. It has been cited by Kenneth W. Thompson, *Understanding World Politics* (Notre Dame, IN: University of Notre Dame Press, 1975), p. 135; and Bruce Kuniholm, *The Origins of the Cold War in the Near East* (Princeton: Princeton University Press, 1980), and possibly by many others.

3. Robin Wright, "Unexplored Realities of the Persian Gulf Crisis," *Middle East Journal* 45, no. 1 (Winter 1991), p. 23.

4. The largest such battle took place between the Nazis and the Soviets in 1942. We must now add the massive confrontation of tanks in the roughly one hundred–hour ground war that brought Operation Desert Storm to an end. That two

such gigantic battles, using the most sophisticated military hardware available, took place in the desert wastes of the Middle East highlights the tragic distinctiveness of this region's recent politics. The two battles of 1973 and 1991, separated in time by a mere eighteen years, stand out as a far cry from the desert warfare along the Iraqi-Saudi border during the 1920s that John Bagot Glubb described in *War in the Desert* (New York: Norton, 1960).

5. "Counterfactual" scenarios *are,* however, important in historical study, especially in the kind that seeks to be relevant to policymakers. It really, in sum, amounts to nothing more than carefully reconstructing the options (actual and perceived—with the two never completely in accord) available to decisionmakers at any given time plus working out the likely results—again carefully reconstructed from the historical record—of those alternative choices.

6. These were reportedly the words of a Soviet ambassador to Syria concerning relations between the Soviet patron and its Syrian client. The argument that regional clients in the Middle East can often control the policy of their outside patrons as much as (if not more than) the other way around figures in my *International Politics and the Middle East: Old Rules, Dangerous Game* (Princeton: Princeton University Press, l984).

7. Examples of the opposing interpretation are Stephen L. Spiegel, "Israel as a Strategic Asset," *Commentary* (June 1983); and A.F.K. Organiski, *The $36 Billion Bargain: Strategy and Politics in U.S. Assistance to Israel* (New York: Columbia University Press, 1990).

8. Robert W. Tucker and David C. Hendrickson, in *The Imperial Temptation: The New World Order and America's Purpose* (New York: Council on Foreign Relations Press, 1992), argue that the Bush administration should have opted for economic sanctions rather than war, but once it had chosen the latter, it should have gone on to overthrow Saddam Hussein and establish a foreign military administration of Iraq. The latter part of the argument is heard in other, more hawkish, quarters without the careful eye for political reality Tucker and Hendrickson display.

9. Every U.S. diplomat has experienced realistic, "off-the-record" discussions with Arab political leaders set alongside public postures of a quite different orientation. Although hardly commendable diplomatic behavior, it is not so much reprehensible as merely understandable. It has been the plight of Middle Eastern political leadership ever since the intrusive Western state system penetrated the Middle East, resulting in the existence of states whose clear incapacity to check alien pressures has frustrated the development of domestic political legitimacy. At the same time, Middle Eastern political leaders have found themselves obliged to rely on one or another patron from that very system that oppresses them. Add to this the tendency to compensate for weak domestic acceptance by relying on strong state control (army, police, and intelligence services), which further undermines any sense of identity with the state, and the vicious circle is completed.

10. Abd al-Krim was a mountaineer, not a bedouin, and a Berber, not an Arab. Even so, inspired by Abd al-Krim's heroic stand against both Spanish and French colonial rule, Sigmund Romberg wrote a play entitled *The Desert Song.* Fictional films, just like bumper stickers, often reveal better than scholarly disquisitions the context of that elusive entity called *public opinion.* See on this subject my "Movies and the Middle East" in Bernard Lewis, Edmund Leites, and Margaret Case (eds.), *As Others See Us: Mutual Perceptions East and West,* a special double issue (Vols. 13 and 14, Fall 1985 and Spring 1986) of *Comparative Civilizations Review.*

11. It would be a great boon to have a solid historiographical study of scholar-

ly material in Arabic on this subject. As far as I am aware, nothing of the sort exists. This could also serve as a necessary step toward the production of a multiauthored work presenting the distinctive historiographical schools treating modern Middle Eastern diplomacy, both Middle Eastern and from outside the area.

12. "What Saddam Wrought," *Wall Street Journal,* August 2, 1991. Having cited and taken issue with this statement in another article ("Patterns Forged in Time: Middle Eastern Mindsets and the Gulf War," in *Political Psychology of the Gulf War,* Stanley Renshon (ed.), forthcoming, University of Pittsburgh Press), I believe a disclaimer against Bernard Lewis bashing is in order. I greatly admire and learn from his vast, wide-ranging scholarly work, even though we often disagree on matters that relate to contemporary public policy issues. Moreover, I concede that anyone, including an academician, writing in the opinion page of a newspaper is entitled to a difference in style and substance from what might be appropriate in a scholarly article or book. Even so, I feel he misstates reality on the point I raise.

13. Malcolm Kerr, *The Arab Cold War: Gamal Abd al-Nasir and His Rivals,* 3d ed. (Oxford: Oxford University Press, 1971); "The End of Pan-Arabism," *Foreign Affairs* 57, no. 2 (Winter 1978–1979).

14. Louis Jovelet (Robert Montagne), "L'Evolution sociale et politique des Pays Arabes (1930–1933)," *Revue des Etudes Islamiques* IV (1933), p. 473 (my translation from the French).

15. First published by Oxford University Press in 1965. Republished in Great Britain in 1986 (I. B. Tauris) and in the United States the following year (Yale University Press).

16. First published by Harvard University Press in 1985; reissued as a paperback by Cornell University Press in 1988.

17. Cornell University Press, 1987.

18. William B. Quandt, *Decade of Decisions: American Policy Toward the Arab-Israeli Conflict, 1967–1976* (Berkeley: University of California Press, 1977), plus his excellent in-depth case study, *Camp David: Peacemaking and Politics* (Washington, D.C.: Brookings Institution, 1986); Dan Tschirgi, *The American Search for Mideast Peace* (New York: Praeger, 1989).

19. Michael Hudson, *Arab Politics: The Search for Legitimacy* (New Haven: Yale University Press, 1980).

3

The Gulf Crisis, the Arab World, and Intellectual Models

NICHOLAS S. HOPKINS _____

One hopes that scholars, through their knowledge and imagination, can contribute to the peaceful resolution of disputes. Surely, the Middle East of the 1990s is in need of such hopes. In the following pages I therefore explore aspects of the broad and varied connection between the momentous events that occurred in the Middle East in 1990–1991 and intellectual frameworks within which students of the area try to understand the events and their implications. This seems a worthwhile task; if we accept that the normative goal of the scholar is to promote the use of reason over passion, of discourse and accommodation over violence, then it behooves both scholars and their intended audiences to be aware of the possibilities and limitations inherent in frequently used analytical tools.

Metaphors and Metaforce

On August 2, 1990, Iraq invaded Kuwait and shortly afterward annexed it. A coalition of countries—led by the United States—mobilized, reconquered (liberated) Kuwait, and largely destroyed Iraq. Three years later, little seems to have changed.

From the social science point of view, what sense can we make of this combination of events? Can we produce an argument that deals with what Max Weber called "adequate causation," or with "chance" causation, or even with causation? Given our knowledge of the societies and cultures of

37

the Arab world and of the relations that exist in the capitalist world system, can we "retrodict" the events?

In other words, do old theories apply? Are the events themselves sufficiently consistent with these theories that we are justified in holding to the latter, only dusting them off, as it were? Or were the events sufficiently novel that the old theories are undercut and destroyed and radical new interpretations are required? Or do the events show us that one theory, or set of theories, is valid and can be used to frame such events, whereas others are invalidated and must be discarded?

We need an explanation that lies deeper than the expressed motivations of the actors. One criterion of a sound theory is that it does not attempt to explain the particular by the general. That is, attempting to explain Baghdad's decision to invade Kuwait as simply a function of Iraqi or Arab values in itself explains nothing.

So far, most interpretations of the crisis have understandably been built around existing theories, some of which are little more than analogies (such as the precedent of Hitler's career, Munich 1938, or Vietnam). Political analysts have invoked events to demonstrate that their favorite theory has unique explanatory power. Most of these attempts have remained fairly close to the two grand events that cry out for an explanation: the invasion of Kuwait, and the resolution of the crisis through war. Early discussions focused on the first question, whereas more recent debates have centered on the second, particularly as more revelations come from Washington. More recently, some attention has been given to a third issue: the survival of the regime in Iraq.[1]

However, if one is to "explain" the invasion and the events surrounding it in other than personal terms (that is, by going beyond the demonization of Saddam Hussein and of Iraqis along with him), we must return to the social roots of the societies in question—Iraq, the Arab world, and the West. Yet, such an approach should not go to the other extreme of denying human intentionality altogether. One can argue that people make their history, but we should add that they make it from the raw material at hand. Put another way, actors always carry out their acts in a context that includes their memories of past events, their evaluations of those events, the concrete results of those events, and the pattern of interpersonal relations existing at any given moment. If past events cause present or future ones, it is through this complex set of filters.

There is, of course, an international political context that should be spelled out from the start. One main factor is the 1980–1988 war between Iraq and Iran, in which Iraq was widely seen as fighting off Iranian expansionism on behalf of the nearby Arab states and also of the West. Rightly or not, the metaphor preferred from the Iraqi point of view cast Iraq as the heroic gatekeeper defending Western civilization from barbarian invasions.

And, in fact, the West (the United States, France, Britain, Germany, and others), along with various Arab countries, largely supported Iraq during this period.

Another factor is the prolonged festering of the wound caused by the creation of Israel and the continuing oppression of the Palestinian Arabs in Israel and the Occupied Territories. This has long been widely perceived in the Arab world as symbolic of persistent Western colonialism and imperialism.

A third element of the overall context within which the Gulf Crisis unfolded was the Soviet Union's eclipse as a superpower, perhaps best represented by the collapse of the East German regime and the elimination of the Berlin Wall in November 1989. Although the actual dissolution of the Soviet Union came after the Gulf Crisis, the early signs of the old international order's demise were clear indications that the days when nonaligned countries could benefit from superpower rivalries had ended.

Let a Hundred Questions Bloom

At one level, current discussions of the Gulf Crisis are still about elementary facts: What did the Iraqis expect to gain by invading Kuwait? Were there "miscalculations" involved, and how can we account for this failure of judgment?[2] Why did the Kuwaitis miscalculate before August 2 (or did they), and how can this be explained? To what extent did the Americans or others have foreknowledge of Iraq's decision to attack Kuwait? What did U.S. Ambassadress April Glaspie really say to Saddam Hussein, and what difference did it make to the course of events in the summer of 1990? Was there a genuine chance for an "Arab solution" in early August of that year, and, if so, why did it not materialize? When did the Americans and their allies decide on military action, and was this an inevitable solution or the only possible solution, or did it even make sense in terms of the stated objectives? On a more abstract level: Are we dealing with tragic inevitability or political choice? Was the attitude expressed in early 1992 by the U.S. military (the Pentagon)—that the United States should maintain its status as sole superpower by slapping down any upstart rival before it could grow too big—already being acted out?

Some of these questions of "fact" will eventually be objects of historical research in the archives, in somewhat the same way aspects of the Suez invasion of 1956 and the Iraqi revolution of 1958 are now being probed. In other cases, the facts will doubtlessly remain elusive, either because records are not available or because the facts themselves prove too complicated to tie down with any degree of certainty.

This "factual" level quickly shades off into explicit political explanations, which are, in the end, so many kinds of narratives. What follows does not pretend to be a full categorization of proffered explanations, although it indicates something of the range of "causes" given for the Gulf Crisis.

- The invasion of Kuwait was the result of a particular megalomanical or adventurous personality (Saddam Hussein). Having kept Iraq at war against Iran for eight years, it became difficult for Saddam's regime to maintain the dynamic of Iraq's sociopolitical system by concentrating purely on internal issues. Legitimacy was pursued by crossing Kuwait's borders.
- The invasion was the result of a financial crisis in Iraq caused by the lopsided investment of oil revenues in guns rather than butter. The invasion can be explained by Iraq's need for resources at a time when oil money no longer covered the country's expenditures and foreign credit was drying up.
- The invasion and annexation of Kuwait were necessary to right a wrong committed by the colonial powers when they separated Kuwait from its rightful association with Iraq.
- The invasion reflected the antipathy of Arabs against the consumerist excesses of the sheikhs of the Gulf oil countries; those in the Arab world who supported the Iraqis were responding to Baghdad's defiance of the dominant West; Iraqis were acting on behalf of class allies elsewhere in the Arab world.
- The Iraqis were drawn into a trap set by the Americans, perhaps in collusion with the Kuwaitis and others, in order to destroy Iraqi power, not least because that power could be a threat to Israel.
- The war was really about control of oil, a war over resources.
- The war has to be understood against the background of the collapse of communism in Eastern Europe and the Soviet Union; recognition of the changed global balance of power is a necessary precondition for grasping the essence of what happened in the Gulf. The crisis was caused by the new post–Cold War global dynamics.
- Were it not for the racism and the power hunger of the Americans, the crisis would not have developed; it would have been solved amicably among Arabs in its initial stages.

Although some of these arguments seem fanciful, they are cited here to indicate a level of analysis that seeks causal explanations in the immediate events that comprised the crisis. From such a perspective, then, the invasion and subsequent war can thus be seen as being "about" Kuwait, Iraqi power, oil, or the protection of Israel.

Another level of analysis depends on somewhat more elaborate social science theories. For instance, should the war be interpreted as a nationalist conflict or a class conflict? In either case, there is the subsidiary question of whether there is a link among nations, states, and classes. Was there a religious dimension to the conflict? Can the war be explained by internal tensions and processes in Iraqi or Kuwaiti or Saudi society or, for that matter, in U.S. and other Western societies? Are some sociopolitical systems (which would have to be identified) inherently expansionist or aggressive? At the extreme, was the Gulf Crisis a natural expression of Arab values, of Arab or Western political culture, or of a basic conflict between them?[3] Alternatively, does an explanation of the war require a prior understanding of the dynamics of the world system and, in particular, of the different roles played by core and periphery states in that system? In other words, is there a comprehensive model of "struggle for power" or international political process that would adequately account for the events of 1990–1991?

How long can countries that produce a key resource (oil) be maintained in political dependency on others? When can upstream countries assert themselves vis-à-vis the downstream ones? Is the willingness of the West to resort to force a manifestation of racism, of a tendency to regard Third World societies as inferior others? Are we dealing, as the ideologues would have it, with a quarrel between democracy and authoritarian dictatorship?

Can the politics that produced the Gulf Crisis be understood purely in terms of a struggle over oil or Palestine, or should we seek social and cultural explanations? To some extent this comes down to deciding how to handle individual motivations and goals.

Can we learn something from the unfolding of the crisis that will help us better control crises and prevent or avoid warfare? After all, as Hisham Sharabi wrote in another context: "Experience has shown that military approaches have never solved political problems and that repression and coercion, whether applied from within or from without, can bring only temporary stability and will in the end lead to collapse and unpredictable consequences."[4]

Political Sociology

There can be no definitive answer to one, let alone all, of these questions at this point. I explore two lines of reasoning, one drawn from political sociology and the other from political anthropology. From the point of view of political sociology, I first examine Iraqi society and then place it in the context of Arab society. Following this, I explore some of the major implications of assessing the Gulf Crisis through the use of political anthropology. This requires a holistic approach in which the world is the unit of analysis.

Adhering to the principle that there are links among the nature of a society, its political culture, and its form of political organization, political sociology suggests that the government of Iraq is somehow an expression of Iraqi society. This, of course, raises the possibility that fundamental sources of the Gulf Crisis may be found in the nature of the relationship between society and state, not only in Iraq but also in the structures of other main protagonists in the crisis.

What can we say about Iraqi society? First, the country is one of the successor states of the Ottoman Empire, created in its present boundaries after World War I as part of the division of the Arab territories of that empire between France and Britain. The boundaries were always somewhat controversial, whether with Kuwait, with the new Turkey, or with Syria.[5] Once the boundaries were more or less established, it turned out that inside those boundaries was some raw material that was fairly unpromising for a new state.[6] There was considerable ethnic (religious and linguistic) variety, most notably the distinction among Kurds, Sunni Arabs, and Shi'a Arabs. But there were also other religious minorities, Christians of various kinds, Jews, Yezidis, Sabaeans, certain quasi-schismatic Muslim sects, and linguistic minorities. There were also Armenians as well as groups distinguished by distinctive life-styles (bedouins and marsh Arabs).[7] The society was overwhelmingly rural and was dominated by major "tribal" leaders.

The country was ruled by the British, who had conquered it from the Ottomans. There was some resistance to this rule, especially from Shi'a religious leaders in the south and from the Kurds.[8] When London imposed a Hashemite king, Faisal, in 1921, the challenge facing the new monarch was to weld this heterogeneous material into a single unit. His effort was cut short by his premature death in 1933. Iraqi politics continued to be rather turbulent.

In 1958, the monarchy was overthrown and replaced by a military government under Abdul-Karim Qassem. Whether this was simply a coup or whether it marked the beginning of a social revolution is still debated.[9] Politically, the period was characterized by the rise and fall of the Iraqi Communist Party and by a debate between Iraqi nationalism and pan-Arabism.[10] Qassem was overthrown in 1963 by the first Baath regime. Six months later, a military takeover resulted in the presidency of the two Aref brothers, which lasted for five years. A second Baath coup followed in 1968, and the Baath have ruled in Baghdad ever since.

Notwithstanding all of this, Iraq's underlying ethnic tensions have remained the same.[11] Essentially, the ruling elite in Republican Iraq has come from the small Sunni towns of northwest Iraq. Kurds and Shi'a have had only marginal, although variable, shares in central political power.[12] Social and political conditions characterizing Iraq's smaller minorities have also remained essentially the same, except for the departure of virtually all Jews from the country.

In other respects, however, Iraqi society has changed a good deal—let us say in the period between 1958 and 1990 or, in other words, within approximately a generation. The society has changed from predominantly rural, if not tribal, to overwhelmingly urban. Iraq's population is now nearly 70 percent urban, much higher than countries that would appear to be comparable, such as Syria, Egypt, and the Maghreb countries—all of which are around 50 percent urban. Iraq also qualifies as a "hydrocarbon society,"[13] which John Davis argues are those in which over 90 percent of national revenues come from petroleum. He includes Brunei, Libya, the United Arab Emirates (UAE), Kuwait, Saudi Arabia, Oman, and perhaps Qatar. Although Iraq is not on Davis's list, over 90 percent of its export income came from the sale of petroleum and petroleum products (99 percent in 1979, according to figures published by the American Educational Trust), and much of its bureaucracy has been organized around this industry. Both the income of individuals and the generosity of the state came to depend on oil revenue. With the growth of the oil industry and the burgeoning of oil revenues, there was a concurrent expansion of the bureaucracy, and thus of waged employment, as the basis for the organization of society. The emphasis on discipline, on timekeeping, and on other aspects of bureaucratic life also turns up in the teachings of the Baath Party. During the 1980s, more of an entrepreneurial private sector emerged.[14]

Since the second Baath coup in 1968, Baghdad has undertaken serious efforts to develop Iraq's human resources. Large strides have been made in the extension of literacy (combined, however, with severe limitations on the production of written texts, such as controls on typewriters, computer printers, photocopy machines, and the like). The literacy rate in 1987 was 70 percent (compared to Egypt's 44 percent in 1988).[15] Despite human rights abuses, Iraq has seen an artistic renaissance. Indeed, the UN Development Program's (UNDP's) 1990 "Human Development Report" ranked Iraq seventy-sixth from the bottom of 130 countries on the Human Development Index (HDI). This was the highest rating of any non–city-state Arab country and was preceded only by the UAE (seventy-seventh from the bottom) and Kuwait (eighty-eighth) and followed by Saudi Arabia (sixty-fourth) and Egypt (forty-fifth). Finally, it has been clear since the Gulf War that the Iraqi technical and scientific establishment has become fairly sophisticated.

Su'ad Joseph has detailed Iraq's somewhat ambivalent official policy toward women. On the one hand, the government has been tempted to treat women as individuals outside the family context, perhaps to weaken the family as the intermediary organization between the state and the individual. On the other, it has recognized that its desire to see a rapidly rising Iraqi birthrate requires the family framework.[16]

In recent years, Baghdad's willingness to confront existing Iraqi social institutions has attracted the attention and won the approval of certain French intellectuals. Jacques Berque, for example, saw in Iraq a push toward modernization that echoed of "Jacobinism" and the French Revolution, involving the concerted use of state power to impose a unitary state and to build the foundations for a new social order and political culture:

> This is one of the most dynamic and creative states in the Arab world. . . . The Iraqi Baath has managed to modernize while remaining faithful to its roots. This is certainly the most lively of the socialisms which are characteristic of the Arab world . . . Iraq is at the stage of a Jacobin republic which brings progress at the point of a bayonet. This is a plebeian dictatorship, as was Nasserism. In a country surrounded by misery and by the enemy, and in a phase of building, it is hard to escape having a Committee of Public Safety. This is reminiscent of our French revolution, so let us not purse our lips. (author's translation)[17]

The other side of this coin is the near elimination of civil society, even including interference in family life through programs directed at women or youth.[18] Yet, were we to depend on a limited range of indicators—literacy and occupational structure, for instance—Iraq could be considered a relatively modern society, probably more suggestive of the future of the Arab world than are the oil states of the Gulf. But the question remains whether, as Isam al-Khafaji maintains, Iraqi modernization is actually no more than a veneer covering a fundamentally tribal society.[19]

There is no question that Iraqi politics has its rough side. The establishment of Baath power after 1968 was marked by a brutal power struggle, and it could be argued that this was little different from the periods before and after.[20] Dissension is not tolerated, and discipline is maintained by the use of fear. People are constantly called upon to reaffirm their loyalty to the regime. The treatment of the two main "minority" groups, the Shi'a and the Kurds, has relied heavily on force.

Despite this, as Amazia Baram points out, under the Baath there was initially a considerable renewal of upper-middle-level cadres in the government and in Parliament. He also indicates that the social background of these cadres over the years has been declining: from upper class to upper-middle class, to middle class, to a combination of lower-middle class and lower class backgrounds in the 1980s.[21]

Having become something of a hydrocarbon society by the 1980s, Iraq—like its neighbors to the south—took on characteristics of a "rentier state"; that is, a state that distributes income to citizens rather than taxing them to generate its own income. It has been argued that in such states, rulers are less dependent on public opinion because they do not require legitimacy in order to collect revenue.[22] One implication is that such states easily fall into authoritarian political patterns.

Much of the income that accrued directly to Iraq's Baath regime was used for military expenditures—to a far greater extent than was true of other Arab rentier states.[23] However, in other respects, Iraq's political economy appeared to have had social consequences similar to those experienced by other Arab oil-producing states. Thus, Iraq became a net importer of labor. Moreover, as in other petroleum countries—Algeria, for example—oil drove out agriculture, and by the 1980s, Iraq was highly dependent on food imports. Alan Richards and John Waterbury quote U.S. Department of Agriculture figures to show that in 1981, Iraq imported 53 percent of its cereals, 96 percent of its vegetable oil, and 56 percent of its meat.[24]

Keeping in mind the changes past decades have seen in Iraq's social matrix, what can we say of the country's political culture? Anthropological accounts of traditional Iraqi rural society stress the role of hierarchy, status concerns, deference, and patron-client links between people of different social levels.[25] Some accounts of this "traditional" politics sound similar to the description of the Swat Pathans given by Fredrik Barth and criticized and extended by Talal Asad and Charles Lindholm.[26] In this kind of a system, people start with different endowments of land and other resources, but a critical factor is skill in building coalitions. The more successful politicians are those who possess this skill and who are also temperamentally able to engage in "encounters" in which they mobilize coalitions to overcome opponents through force or bluff.

But it is uncertain how widespread this kind of politics is in today's Iraq. The changing life conditions in Iraq may have produced something closer to a class situation, as Hanna Batatu argues.[27] This possibility seems enhanced by the destruction of agriculture, the ensuing migration from rural areas, and the growth of cities.[28] The logic of the creation of state and party power has entailed the breakdown of any aspect of civil society that stands between state power and the individual, including perhaps family.[29] Despite this relative absence of civil society, most (very imperfect) accounts of Iraqi politics at the center suggest that it is highly personal.

If we assume on the one hand that Iraq has become a society dominated by state power and on the other that the class basis of power has drifted downward, does this mean conflict and rivalry between Iraq and its southern neighbors can be interpreted along class lines? Another way of looking at the issue is this: If a fairly close relation exists between Iraqi society and the Iraqi state, then presumably the evolution of the state does not strongly depend on the individual persons involved. This would also imply that the state could not change without some change in the society as well. But does this mean that the government of Iraq is somehow inevitable? Michael Hudson points to the paradox that Iraq has usually engaged in robust pan-Arab rhetoric yet has often failed to get along with other Arab countries.[30]

To what extent is this linked to the interaction of local-internal factors and inter-Arab or international ones? Does Iraq "need" a strongman to hold a fissiparous country together? Perhaps, if it has a strongman for this reason, this colors interstate relations. Or has Iraq gone far enough along the road toward creating a bureaucratic party-state based on individual responsibility and upward mobility that the system would be sustained even if personalities change?

The Nature of Gulf Society

The hydrocarbon societies of the Gulf and the Arabian Peninsula have a distinctive, not to say unique, social configuration.[31] Following Fuad I. Khuri's work on Bahrain, we can note that the politically dominant sector here is the tribal elite, including the royal family.[32] Next to these are various other Arabic-speaking and Persian-speaking groups that have been present for various lengths of time. In Bahrain, the contrast is between Arabic-speaking Sunni, who are "tribal," and Arabic-speaking Shi'a, who are "peasants." In this situation, following colonialism and the discovery of oil, a bureaucracy has emerged, often manned largely by outsiders. In fact, throughout the Gulf and the Arabian Peninsula, the presence of outsiders (guest workers) is a major factor. By and large the traditional rulers, with the help of the colonial powers and the oil companies, have made the transition to rulers of contemporary states.

In some of these societies it is possible to speak of an internal and an external proletariat, a double proletariat.[33] The indigenous lower class, so to speak, is often set off and stigmatized for being of Shi'a or some other contrasting origin. The imported lower class of workers from other Arab countries, the Indian subcontinent, and so on, forms the second proletariat. The system makes use of ethnic and linguistic divisions among these workers to control them.

Within the elite there have often been political currents as well, as in the case of Kuwait, where Shafeeq Ghabra has shown that since the 1960s, voluntary associations have played a certain political role.[34] Some of these associations reflect pan-Arabist values, others Islamist or professional interests. Khuri similarly analyzes the different political currents in Bahrain in the 1970s, distinguishing an Arab nationalist-leftist trend, a "religionist" trend, and a business-oriented middle. Khuri argues that leaders of the ministates of the Arabian Gulf face two main problems: whether (and how) to merge with each other to create a larger unit and, second, how to assimilate the foreign labor force. He does not think the Gulf regimes are capable of solving these problems; thus, Khuri implicitly concludes that the Gulf ministates are politically unstable.[35] One could add that the geopolitical situation is out of balance: Here are tremendously wealthy countries with fairly small populations. How are they going to defend themselves and their wealth from more powerful neighbors (Iran, Iraq, Egypt, and perhaps others)? Because (except perhaps for Saudi Arabia) they cannot hope to compete with these countries in terms of sheer military power, they have to make alliances—either with some neighbors against others or with distant countries (the United States, Britain) against near neighbors. Alternatively, they can rely on mercenaries of various kinds. All of these solutions are fairly unstable.

Can we conclude that the conflict between Iraq and its southern neighbors is essentially a class conflict between a proletarian Iraq and the tribal chiefs (or aristocratic oil families) of the Gulf and the peninsula? Certainly, accounts of the personal relations between the Iraqi delegates to pan-Arab conferences and their colleagues from these countries suggest something of the sort. But is this enough?

Perhaps the class argument would be strengthened were it extended to the support given to Iraq and to Saddam Hussein during the Gulf Crisis by many individuals throughout the Arab world. From what I could see of the reaction of Tunisians to the crisis in September-October 1990, this hypothesis would be supported. It is remarkable that the basic pattern of reaction was established very early. Although in September 1990 Tunisian intellectuals tried to persuade me that popular reaction in their country resulted from the arrival of U.S. troops in Saudi Arabia, it seems that it had already taken shape in the first day or two after the invasion—well before the troops were sent. Perhaps it is relevant that Tunisia resembles Iraq in having a strong secular state that bestrides the society, leaving little room for civil society. Under such circumstances, was Tunisian "street" support of Saddam Hussein rooted in a type of class affinity—a manifestation of street alienation from the secular, pro-Western, autocratic Tunisian regime?

Based on such reactions, we could argue that the Gulf Crisis highlighted a class division in the Arab world. Paradoxically, this could be taken as a sign of Arab unity, because if class divisions run across different Arab countries, this suggests that the latter form part of a single society.

Iraq and Algeria Compared

If class relationships are of central importance to the Arab world's regional and domestic politics, and therefore to an understanding of the Gulf Crisis and its implications, comparisons between Iraq and other Arab states might be illuminating. For example, a comparison of Iraq and Algeria seems to indicate possible general sociological trends that are exceedingly relevant politically, despite the fact that there are many differences between the two states.

Algeria became independent in 1962, after a devastating war of independence and lengthy colonial subjugation. Iraq has been going through considerable political turmoil since leaving the Ottoman sphere. During the 1960s and 1970s, both countries went through a period of socialism that particularly affected rural social organization and land tenure. In the 1980s, both moved away from this. We can argue that in both countries, the socialist project undercut traditional rural structures and led to the migration of many rural people to the cities (and from Algeria to Europe). Both countries also have high population growth rates, in part because they have not considered themselves to be overpopulated (as Egypt, Tunisia, and Morocco do). High urban growth rates, due to natural increase and migration, have caused social problems in both countries. Both have also become overwhelmingly dependent on oil and petroleum products as exports to compensate for their heavy imports, including food imports.

It is possible to argue, as Eric J. Hooglund did regarding Iran, that the migration of uprooted rural people to cities is a major input into the political equation.[36] The rural migrants in Algeria have been major supporters of the FIS (Front Islamique du Salut, the main Islamic party); in Iraq they have been recruited into the Baath Party. In each case they represent a lower class or a lower-middle class of rural origin in the midst of a highly urbanized society.

The underlying point here is that a sociological approach to understanding the Gulf Crisis enhances the attraction of class analysis as a means of intellectually penetrating the Arab world's political dynamics. At the microlevel—that of the individual Arab state—the nature of the relationship between rulers and ruled, between society and state, is highlighted. At the macrolevel—that of the Arab world—a related but more complex sort of relationship between "haves" and "have nots" may perhaps be glimpsed. At this macrolevel, local elites, such as those comprising Iraq's Baathist regime, may perhaps stand as the vanguard of a regional proletariat, sharing with regional non-elites a common sense of alienation from the area's dominating political currents. Comparisons between Iraq and other Arab societies, such as that sketched above, would have to be pursued in far greater depth and detail than is possible here to fathom the full potential of a sociological approach to Arab politics.

Political Anthropology: A Holistic Approach

Another line of analysis for attempting to understand the causes and implications of the Gulf Crisis differs markedly from the sociological approach by eschewing the assumption that fundamental explanations are to be found in the sociopolitical contexts of individual Arab countries, the Arab world, or external actors. Political anthropology, in contrast, suggests that understanding the Gulf Crisis requires an overall analysis of the process of breach, redressment, and reconciliation.

Anthropology characteristically seeks a holistic approach. In the case of the Gulf Crisis, this basically amounts to considering the world as a system. There is nothing startling in this, because the United Nations, to take but one indicator, was centrally involved. However, the point needs to be deepened.

Whether the root issue at stake in the Gulf Crisis was access to oil (or pricing of oil), Palestine, or Western unease over growing Iraqi military powers, the crisis itself can be seen as arising from the use of brute force in the pursuit of power. In fact, it can be seen as a conflict between two chieftains, one of whom (Saddam Hussein) was asserting power in a way that challenged the other (George Bush); the encounter led to a showdown, in which each chieftain mobilized maximum support. From this perspective, the Gulf Crisis was a matter of politics in an arena that encompassed most of the world.

Anthropologists often remark casually on similarities between political conflict in acephalous societies and in the international arena. An analytic method developed by Marc J. Swartz, Victor W. Turner, and Arthur Tuden in 1966 took this insight seriously, suggesting that it is "equally applicable to factional struggles in Indian and African villages and to major international 'trouble cases,' such as the Suez and the Cuban crises."[37]

The approach is, at bottom, related to the broad spectrum of Conflict Theory. It distinguishes several stages that mark political confrontations. Some years after working with his colleagues on this approach, Turner independently developed a slightly different analytical construct,[38] which warrants attention in the present context.

According to Turner, prior to an actual "breach of the peace" comes the "mobilization of political capital" (Phase 1). During this phase, contestants try to build up their resources, especially political support, by reinforcing what already exists and by trying to subvert support that might be committed to the "other side." In Phase 2, a crisis is precipitated by one side or the other: "Breach of the peace is usually heralded or signaled by breaching a norm that is considered binding on *all* members of the political field."[39] It would be convenient in this case to take the invasion of Kuwait by Iraq as such a breach. This breach of the peace then leads to a "crisis" (Phase 3)—a "turning point in the relations between components on a political field."[40] A somewhat amorphous "political field" then becomes a more precise "arena" in which the parties involved resolve themselves into two parties. Previously existing rivalries among members of each side are suspended until the crisis is resolved. One mechanism through which the crisis is addressed is "countervailing tendencies" (Phase 4) based on "multiple cross-cutting conflicts of loyalty and allegiance."[41] The evocation of general values to which all can subscribe plays a key role at this point. Within Turner's framework, various efforts to find an "Arab solution" to the Gulf Crisis by those who had links to both sides, such as the Palestinians, fall into place here, as do the efforts of those who argued that humane values (such as avoiding human injury through "collateral damage") should be given political priority.

Turner's next theoretical phase (Phase 5) involves the "deployment of adjustive or redressive mechanisms," in which various parties try to act as arbitrators, mediators, or simply intermediaries in order to "restore the semblance of a peaceful state of relationships."[42] In other words, whereas in Phase 4 those with links to both sides try to establish a framework of values that would enable the contestants to restore the peace, in Phase 5 outsiders try to reduce the differences between the contestants through some form of negotiation. In the Gulf Crisis, efforts of both kinds were clearly visible between August 1990 and January 1991 and in fact, continue to some extent.

Within this framework, the final phase of the Gulf Crisis (Phase 6) has not yet occurred. Phase 6 requires not only the restoration of peace but also—along with the "reestablishment of relations between the contending parties or . . . a social recognition of irreparable schism"—a reordering of the political field:

> The nature and intensity of the relations between parts, and the structure of the total field, will have changed. Oppositions will have become alliances, and vice versa. Asymmetric relations will have become symmetric relations. High status will have become low status and vice versa. New power will have been channeled into new authority and old authority defenestrated. Closeness will have become distance, and vice versa. Formerly integral parts will have segmented; formerly independent parts will have fused. Some parts will no longer belong in the field, and others will have entered it. Institutionalized relationships will have become informal; social regularities will have become irregularities. New norms will have been generated during the attempts to redress conflict; old norms will have fallen into disrepute.[43]

By the winter of 1992, various Arab states gave visible signs of hoping that Iraq might be reintegrated into the community of nations. So far, however, the U.S.-UN-dominant combine has shown little interest, arguing that no steps toward this end can be taken until Baghdad complies fully with all aspects of the cease-fire agreement upon which the end of the Gulf War was predicated (or perhaps for as long as the Iraqi leadership remains unchanged). But in general, it seems we are clearly still on the threshold of

Phase 6, and relations among the various actors in the field are still being sorted out.

What the schema of Swartz, Turner, and Tuden does not allow for is the use (or the threat of the use) of force. This can in some senses be present in any stage—as a technique to mobilize support, for instance, or, obviously, as the breach of the peace, or because outside arbitrators or "umpires" use force to impose a settlement on the primary contestants, as well as when efforts to negotiate a settlement break down.

Talcott Parsons pointed out that the use of force can be very effective in achieving particular goals but that it cannot compete with consent or legitimacy in long-term effectiveness: "A power system in which the only negative sanction is the threat of force is a very primitive one which cannot function to mediate a complex system of organizational coordination—it is far too blunt an instrument."[44] In the case at hand, there were two principal moments in which force was used: the invasion and occupation of Kuwait and the war against Iraq. From this point of view, the two together, or only the first, could be taken as the "breach of the peace." If the two are taken together, then we are only now in the subsequent phases.

Clearly, from the point of view of resolving a conflict, the use of force is a particularly aggravating feature—although exactly how it will be understood may vary from one cultural setting to another. In itself, the use of force does not constitute going outside established patterns of political conflict. But there are understandings, as well as arguments, about what constitutes "fair" and "unfair" use of violence. The introduction of unfair force changes the nature of political confrontation from a "game" to a "fight": Beyond a certain point, "politics ceases to be a competition and becomes a fight, in which the objective (we cannot call it a prize, as we can in a game) is not to defeat the opposition in an orderly 'sporting' contest, but to destroy one 'game' and establish a different set of rules."[45] It should be noted that from this point of view, a "fight" is not necessarily violent; it suffices that the goal is to change the rules.

F. G. Bailey points out that any "political structure" contains rules defining prizes (or objectives), personnel and leadership (who can compete), competition (distinction between fair and unfair tactics), and control: what rules to follow when a rule has been broken. "A political structure, like a game, operates within limits set by agreed rules, which specify prizes, say how teams may be formed and led, lay down lawful and unlawful tactics, and sometimes appoint a referee with authority to see that rules are observed."[46]

How does all of this apply to the Gulf Crisis? Certainly, much effort was made to mobilize supporters, although this occurred mostly after the breach of the peace. Iraq attempted to appeal to Arab masses throughout the region, not so much on grounds of a valid historic right to Kuwait as that the real objective was the liberation of Palestine, coupled with suggestions that income from oil should be more widely distributed. In Bailey's terms, Iraq's efforts to forge a "team" combined "moral" appeals (the Palestine issue) and "contract" (if the Iraqis were to prevail, there might be more wealth to distribute). The U.S.-UN coalition used a similar combination of "moral" appeal (the invasion and annexation of Kuwait was contrary to international law and should be resisted) and "contract" (benefits would be extended to Arab members of the international coalition) appeals. An additional version of "moral" appeal was the identification of Iraq and Saddam Hussein with Nazi Germany and Hitler and the U.S.-UN coalition with the "civilized world." The fact that such appeals often degenerated into common racism and disdain for the "uncivilized" is another story.

Continual efforts were made to define "legitimate" personnel and leaders: The notion that the conflict should be settled among Arabs, for instance, tried to rule out non-Arab participants. The idea that non-Muslim soldiers should not be allowed on Saudi territory had a similar objective. One complex issue was the role of the Israelis: Whether either side considered them a legitimate contestant or team member was highly ambivalent. Iraqis argued that Israel was a legitimate team member—on the other side. The implication, of course, was that some members of the other side were on the wrong side and should switch. Clearly, one of the Iraqi problems was that they had not mobilized their supporters (they had not canvassed them to discover their willingness to be supporters), so they apparently were taken aback by the reaction of the Soviet Union and perhaps by such Arab countries as Egypt.

The Gulf Crisis also spawned much discussion about "fair" and "unfair" tactics or, more accurately, claims that the other side was using, or could use, unfair tactics. This began on the anti-Iraqi coalition's side, with outcries against Iraq's taking Western hostages. It continued with charges of Iraqi pillage in Kuwait and predictions that Iraq would resort to the use of poison gas and chemical and biological warfare, as well as probably engage in deliberate environmental damage. There were also hints that Baghdad might resort to nuclear warfare.

Apocalyptic imagery was taken up by Iraqi spokesmen with outcries against the use of embargoes and blockades that might cause harm to non-combatants, especially small children, and the use of extended and intensive bombing, especially of targets that might be considered civilian—such as bomb shelters and power stations. Toward the end, with the war having produced a rout on the Iraqi side, the Iraqis simply charged that the extent of violence was unfair.

The implication of the pronouncements emanating from both sides was that there were (or should be) normative rules about fair and unfair tactics.

However, because there was no agreement among the various participants on rules of violence, the only result was that each side charged the other with having violated presumed norms.[47]

When applied to the Gulf Crisis, the analysis of the dynamics of conflict holds some promise of being more than an intellectual exercise. In a region of the world where hostilities tend to remain close to the surface of political interaction, a holistic understanding of conflict dynamics may be useful and possibly even vital. Perhaps the advantage of the approach suggested by Turner, Bailey, and others is to force familiar material into unfamiliar categories and thus incite us to fresh thoughts. If participants to a dispute can place the moves of their opponents into a theoretical framework, it may help them to resolve the dispute together instead of prolonging it by impetuous action.

Conclusion

I began this essay with the proposition that a better understanding of the nature of human disputes will contribute to peace and hence to our ability to focus our efforts on long-range problems, such as material well-being, development, or ecological sustainability. This understanding can exist at different levels; I have stressed the kinds of understanding that can come from an analysis—in terms of political sociology or political economy—of Iraq, its neighbors, and its rivals, as well as that which can come from an understanding of the dynamics of dispute. The assumption here is that understanding eventually has to be achieved in theoretical terms; it is not simply a matter of measuring the momentary position of one side vis-à-vis the other. Thus we need to scrutinize disputes such as the one that broke out when Iraq invaded Kuwait, to see what lessons there are for a theoretically sophisticated social science and, conversely, what insights a theoretically inclined social science can bring to the debate.

What theory or combination of theories best derives from or explains the crisis remains to be seen. There is presently no sign of a new paradigm, which is all the more reason to keep alive the ongoing debate over the causes and implications of the Gulf Crisis.

Notes

1. Faleh Abd al-Jabber, "Why the Uprisings Failed," *Middle East Report* 22, no. 3 (May-June 1992), pp. 2–14.
2. Mohamed Heikal, "A Time of Strangeness," *Al-Ahram Weekly,* April 2–8,

1992, p. 5. (Extract from *Illusions of Triumph: An Arab View of the Gulf War* [London: Harper Collins, 1992].)

3. Youssef M. Ibrahim, "'New Order' Discounts Arabs," *International Herald Tribune,* April 6, 1992, p. 1.

4. Hisham Sharabi, "The Poor Rich Arabs," in Ibrahim Ibrahim (ed.), *Arab Resources: The Transformation of a Society* (London: Croom Helm, 1983), p. 304.

5. See Feroz Ahmad, "A Note on the International Status of Kuwait Before November, 1914," *International Journal of Middle East Studies* 24 (1992), pp. 181–185; and Eliezer Tauber, "The Struggle for Dayr al-Zur: The Determination of Borders Between Syria and Iraq," *International Journal of Middle East Studies* 23, no. 3 (1991), pp. 361–385.

6. Pierre-Jean Luizard, "L'improbable democratie en Irak: le piege d l'Etat-nation," *Egypte-Monde Arabe,* no. 4 (1990), pp. 47–85.

7. S. M. Salim, *Marsh Dwellers of the Euphrates Delta* (London: Athlone Press, 1962), London School of Economics Monographs on Social Anthropology, no. 23.

8. Pierre-Jean Luizard, *La formation d l'Irak contemporain: le role politique des ulemas chiites à la fin de domination ottomane et au moment de la creation de l'Etat irakien* (Paris: Editions du Centre National de la Recherche Scientifique, 1991).

9. Robert A. Fernea and William Roger Louis (eds.), *The Iraqi Revolution of 1958: The Old Social Classes Revisited* (London: I. B. Tauris, 1991).

10. On communism in Iraq, see Hanna Batatu, *The Old Social Classes and the Revolutionary Movements of Iraq: A Study of Iraq's Old Landed and Commercial Classes and of Its Communists, Ba'thists, and Free Officers* (Princeton: Princeton University Press, 1978).

11. Isam al-Khafaji, "State Terror and the Degradation of Politics in Iraq," *Middle East Report* 22, no. 3 (May–June 1992), pp. 15–21.

12. Hanna Batatu, "Iraq's Underground Shi'a Movements: Characteristics, Causes, and Prospects," *Middle East Journal* 35, no. 4 (1981), pp. 578–594.

13. John Davis, *Libyan Politics: Tribe and Revolution* (Berkeley: University of California Press, 1987).

14. Robert Springborg, "Baathism in Practice: Agriculture, Politics, and Political Culture in Syria and Iraq," *Middle Eastern Studies,* no. 17 (1991), pp. 191–209; Kirin Aziz Chaudhry, "On the Way to Market: Economic Liberalization and Iraq's Invasion of Kuwait," *Middle East Report,* no. 170 (May–June 1991), pp. 14–23.

15. Actually, the UNDP/HDI gives Iraq's literacy rate as 89 percent in 1985. See *The Economist,* May 26, 1990, p. 81.

16. Su'ad Joseph, "Elite Strategies for State-Building: Women, Family, Religion and State in Iraq and Lebanon," in Deniz Kandiyoti (ed.), *Women, Islam and the State* (London: Macmillan, 1991), pp. 176–200.

17. From an interview with Jacques Berque, reprinted in *Le Temps Hebdo* (Tunis), September 24, 1990, from *L'evenement du jeudi.*

18. On Iraq's policies toward youth, see Su'ad Joseph, "Ruling Elites and the Young: A Comparison of Iraq and Lebanon," in Laurence O. Michalak and Jeswald W. Salacuse (eds.), *Social Legislation in the Contemporary Middle East* (Berkeley: University of California Institute of International Studies, 1986), pp. 191–237.

19. Al-Khafaji, "State Terror."

20. Majid Khadduri, *Socialist Iraq: A Study in Iraqi Politics Since 1968* (Washington, D.C.: Middle East Institute, 1978).

21. Amazia Baram, "The Ruling Political Elite in Ba'thi Iraq, 1968–1986: The Changing Features of a Collective Profile," *International Journal of Middle East Studies* 21, no. 4 (1989), pp. 447–493. See also, David Pool, "From Elite to Class: The Transformation of Iraqi Political Leadership," in Abbas Kelidar (ed.), *The Integration of Modern Iraq* (London: Croom Helm, 1979), pp. 63–87.

22. Davis, *Libyan Politics,* pp. 15–19.

23. In 1984, for example, Iraq devoted a substantial 42 percent of its gross national product (GNP) to military expenditures. By 1989–1990, despite the end of the Iraq-Iran War, 32 percent of the country's GNP was devoted to military purposes. By contrast, during the latter period the percentages of GNP devoted to defense needs by Saudi Arabia, Libya, Kuwait, Bahrain, and Algeria were, respectively, 12.8, 11.1, 5.2, 4.1, and 3.0. See *PC Globe,* Inc.: Tempe, AZ, 1990.

24. Alan Richards and John Waterbury, *A Political Economy of the Middle East* (Boulder: Westview Press, 1990), p. 144.

25. See, for example, Salim, *Marsh Dwellers*; Robert A. Fernea, *Shaykh and Effendi: Changing Patterns of Authority the El Shabana of Southern Iraq* (Cambridge: Harvard University Press, 1970); and Amal Rassam, "Al-taba'iyya: Power, Patronage and Marginal Groups in Northern Iraq," in Ernest Gellner and John Waterbury (eds.), *Patrons and Clients* (London: Duckworth, 1977), pp. 157–166.

26. Fredrik Barth, *Political Leadership Among Swat Pathans* (London: Athlone Press, 1959), London School of Economics Monographs on Social Anthropology, no. 19. See also, Fredrik Barth, "Swat Pathans Reconsidered," in Fredrik Barth, *Collected Essays on Pathans: Selected Essays of Fredrik Barth,* Vol. 2 (London: Routledge and Kegan Paul, 1981), pp. 121–181; Talal Asad, "Market Model, Class Structure and Consent: A Reconsideration of Swat Political Organization," *Man,* no. 7 (1972), pp. 74–94; and Charles Lindholm, *Generosity and Jealousy: The Swat Pukhtun of Northern Pakistan* (New York: Columbia University Press, 1982).

27. Batatu, *The Old Social Classes.*

28. See Robert Springborg, "Baathism in Practice: Agriculture, Politics, and Political Culture," *Middle Eastern Studies* no. 17 (1981), pp. 191–209; Eugen Wirth, "Agrarreform und Laendliche Abwanderung im Irak: Sozialer Wandel und Wirtschaftliche Dynamik in Einer 'Sozialistisher Gesellschaft' mit Freiraeumen fuer Privatinitiativ," *Erdkunde,* no. 36 (1982), pp. 188–198.

29. See the comments on "gelding" in Ernest Gellner, *Nations and Nationalism* (Ithaca: Cornell University Press, 1983), p. 15.

30. Michael Hudson, *Arab Politics: The Search for Legitimacy* (New Haven: Yale University Press, 1977), p. 279.

31. Soraya Altorki and Donald P. Cole, *Arabian Oasis City: The Transformation of 'Unayzah* (Austin: University of Texas Press, 1989).

32. Fuad I. Khuri, *Tribe and State in Bahrain: The Transformation of Social and Political Authority in an Arab State* (Chicago: University of Chicago Press, 1980).

33. Nicholas S. Hopkins, "Class and the State in Rural Arab Communities," in Adeed Dawisha and I. W. Zartman (eds.), *Beyond Coercion: The Durability of the Arab State* (London: Croom Helm, 1988), pp. 239–259.

34. Shafeeq Ghabra, "Voluntary Associations in Kuwait: The Foundation of a New System?" *Middle East Journal* 45, no. 2 (Spring, 1991), pp. 199–215.

35. Khuri, *Tribe and State in Bahrain,* pp. 244–247.

36. Eric J. Hooglund, *Land and Revolution in Iran, 1960–1980* (Austin: University of Texas Press, 1982).

37. Marc J. Swartz, Victor W. Turner, and Arthur Tuden, *Political Anthropology* (Chicago: Aldine, 1966), p. 38.

38. Victor Turner, *Dramas, Fields, and Metaphors: Symbolic Action in Human Society* (Ithaca: Cornell University Press, 1974).

39. Ibid., p. 33.

40. Ibid., p. 33.

41. Ibid., p. 35.

42. Ibid., p. 36.

43. Ibid., p. 37.

44. Talcott Parsons, *Sociological Theory and Modern Society* (New York: Free Press, 1967), p. 313.

45. F. G. Bailey, *Stratagems and Spoils: A Social Anthropology of Politics* (Oxford: Basil Blackwell, 1969), p. 1.

46. Ibid., pp. 32–33.

47. Hisham H. Ahmed, "Iraq's Conduct of the Gulf Crisis: A Critical Assessment," *Arab Studies Quarterly* 13 (1991), pp. 11–35.

4

The Need for an Alternative Construction of Knowledge

CYNTHIA NELSON

During the conference at which preliminary drafts of the chapters forming this volume were reviewed, I was struck by the absence of women—both from the roster of contributing authors and from the list of issues to be addressed. The situation was not, I found, rooted in any desire or decision on the part of conference organizers to boycott women. In fact, three women scholars had been invited to participate but proved unable to do so. In any case, upon learning of my concern, the organizers invited me to take the more active role of writing this chapter rather than limit myself to chairing a panel, as I was originally asked to do. I accepted with alacrity—because if questions are to be raised regarding the implications of the Gulf Crisis for existing analytical approaches to an understanding of the Middle East, the issue of women should be directly confronted.

Because women constitute at least half of the human race and have always shared this world and its catastrophes with men, their frequent invisibility in scholarly accounts of historical events appears startling and cries out for explanation. This is particularly true in the context of an undertaking designed to explore the impact of the Gulf Crisis on the Middle East.

The appalling destruction of community infrastructures and environments, the increase in malnutrition and disease—especially among women and children—and the displacement and resettlement of hundreds of thousands of civilians in the aftermath of the Gulf War have heavily affected women. Their response to these catastrophes amply demonstrates that they are not passive objects. The search for security and identity, the demand for political reform and democratization, and the sharing in reconstruction and development are as much the concerns of women as of men. Yet it seems that *men's experiences* and *men's voices* have constructed the knowledge by which we try to understand the implications of this crisis, not only for the peoples of the Arab region but also for those intellectuals (Arab or Western) whose task it is to analyze and explain such phenomena.

The invisibility of women and the eclipsing of women's voices in this male-dominated discourse reflect a fundamental problematique within the sociology of knowledge.

> Although women, like men, are and always have been actors and agents in history [meaning the unrecorded past as recollected by human beings], they nevertheless have been kept from contributing to History-making [meaning the recorded and interpreted past]. Although women are essential and central to creating society and to building civilization, they have been kept from knowing their History and from interpreting history, either their own or that of men. Women have been systematically excluded from the enterprise of creating symbol systems, philosophies, science, and law. Women have not only been educationally deprived throughout historical time in every known society, they have been excluded from theory-formulation.[1]

Although I do not know the specific reasons the three women scholars invited to contribute to this volume were unable to do so, the real problem of women's exclusion (Arab women, in the present context) from "theory-building" rests on a more fundamental epistemological level: *how social science is thought—its methods, conceptual schemes, and theories.* And I would like to render problematic the unexamined presuppositions about the praxis of social science in the Arab world, particularly in the aftermath of the Gulf Crisis. My point is not to argue that more women should be added to academic conference panels, as one might appoint the token woman to a cabinet of ministers and think power sharing has taken place. Nor do I suggest that women should be conceptualized primarily as victims of the sex-gender system (although women have been victimized by patriarchy). Rather, I call for a critical examination of assumptions about whose voices are heard and whose authority counts in the construction of scientific knowledge of the Arab world, particularly after the Gulf War of 1990–1991. Only through such a critique may we move away from the split vision of social reality that comes from our patriarchal past and that still dominates mainstream social science. The movement must be toward a more comprehensive double vision, such as that reflected in contemporary feminist scholarship. Only by achieving this can we hope to arrive at an alternative to the prevailing patriarchal episteme and its concomitant political agenda.

Toward a Feminist Epistemology

One of the most important "discoveries" of the women's movement is that as women, we had been living in an intellectual, cultural, and political world from whose making we had been almost entirely excluded and in which we had been recognized as no more than marginal voices. The consequence of this discovery has been the emergence of a serious critique of mainstream social science. One of the most influential voices in this critique is that of Dorothy Smith, who states:

> In writing a feminist critique and an alternative to standard sociology, I am doing more than a work for specialists. A sociology is a systematically developed consciousness of society and social relations. The "established" sociology that has been built up over some fifty to eighty years in North America (depending on when you choose to date its beginnings) gives us a consciousness that looks at society, social relations, and people's lives as if we could stand outside them, ignoring the particular local places in the everyday in which we live our lives. It claims objectivity not on the basis of its capacity to speak truthfully, but in terms of its specific capacity to exclude the presence and experience of particular subjectivities. Nonetheless they are there, and must be.[2]

Smith's argument for "a women's perspective as radical critique" is premised on the recognition of two fundamental givens of social life.[3] The first is the existence of a disjunction between how women find and experience the world (beginning, although not ending, with their place in society) and the concepts and theoretical schemes available in which to think about this experience. The second given is that the two worlds and the two bases of knowledge and experience do not stand in an equal relationship: The world as constituted by men stands in authority over that of women. The combined effect of these two fundamental factors is a generalized assumption that male experience is universal experience. The concepts and terms in which the world of men is thought are imposed as those in which women must think of their world. The methods, conceptual schemes, and theories that have been based on—and built up within—the male social universe are presented as universal paradigms for "thinking scientifically."

Many critics, feminist and otherwise, have challenged this intellectual state of affairs on firm epistemological grounds, describing it as resting on one of the most subjective, value-laden biases underlying the praxis of mainstream social science. In Charles Taylor's words:

> The profound bias of mainstream social scientists in favor of the empiricist conception of knowledge and social science makes it inevitable that they should accept the verification model of political science and the categorical principles that this entails. This means, in turn, that a study of our

civilization in terms of its intersubjective and common meanings is ruled out. Rather this whole level of study is made invisible.[4]

In a provocative article published in 1977, one feminist critic drew attention to the epistemological problem inherent in this verification model of knowledge:

> Problems presented by questions of biases or values cannot be dealt with simply by admitting, as mainstream political sciences long ago began doing, to one's bias and claiming to set these biases to the side for purposes of research. This response does not touch the heart of the matter, namely, the epistemology which requires the severance of fact from value. The problem is more complex and fundamental than any charge of bias! *It is that every explanatory theory of politics supports a particular set of normative conclusions.* To have an explanatory theory, the analyst must adopt a framework linked, implicitly if not explicitly, to notions of human nature and human purposes. This framework sets the boundaries of the phenomena to be investigated. Some factors of social life will be incorporated, and others will be expunged from view before research begins. The framework gears the choices, celebrates some interests, excludes others and precludes seeing the political world under an alternative characterization.[5]

Crisis and Rethinking

Crisis usually forces us to rethink situations. This should be as true for social scientists reflecting upon the aftermath of the Gulf Crisis as it is for those men and women of the Arab world whose lives were affected in so many ways by the invasion of Kuwait and its repercussions. We need to reflect upon those paradigms that have been uncritically accepted as the only mode of knowing. If this means a challenge to mainstream social science, so be it. In an "Open Letter to the Sixteenth Annual Symposium of the Center for Contemporary Arab Studies," Professor Tareq Ismael expressed his feelings of intellectual anguish and impotency in the face of the Gulf Crisis:

> We are trapped somewhere between Saddam Hussein's *1984* and Henry Kissinger's *Brave New World* on the road to President George Bush's New World Order. On a trail of destruction that leads from Palestine through Baghdad, this road has all the signposts of the future. *What do we do with our knowledge?* Add to the jingoism and benefit our careers; ignore it, and protect our careers; challenge it and risk our careers? As experts and specialists, *what role do we play in history?*

If we are to rethink the implications of the Gulf Crisis and its aftermath for the women and men of the Arab region, we need an alternative epistemology that starts not from the "relations of ruling," a standpoint that sees societies and social relations from the perspective of ruling structures and the men who rule.[6] Rather, what is required is a standpoint based on women's perspective.

However, this is not a call for the imposition of a Western feminist perspective as the prism through which to experience and understand the situation of Arab women. On the contrary, whether the social scientist is Arab or Western, whether the discourse takes place in the harem or in the household, in the marketplace or the mosque—wherever women go about the business of living their lives—it is women's situation and experience that constitute the basis of social inquiry. Although such a sociology would not be exclusively for, or done by, women, it should begin from the analysis and critique originating in their situation.

> If we begin from the world as we actually experience it, it is at least possible to see that we are located and that what we know of the other is conditional upon that location as part of a relation comprehending the other's location also. There are and must be different experiences of the world and different bases of experience. We must not do away with them by taking advantage of our privileged speaking to construct a sociological version which we then impose upon them as reality. We may not rewrite the other's world or impose upon it a conceptual framework which extracts from it what fits ours. Our conceptual procedures should be capable of explicating and analyzing the properties of their experienced world rather than administering it. Their reality, their varieties of experience, must be an unconditional datum.[7]

Once the sociologist becomes aware of how her world is put together as a practical everyday matter and of how her relations are shaped by its concrete conditions, she is led to the discovery that she cannot understand the nature of her experience by staying within its ordinary boundaries of assumptions and knowledge. It is impossible to account for one's directly experienced world, or how it is related to the worlds others directly experience, by remaining within the boundaries of the former. The problem is one of discovering how our directly experienced world is organized and mediated for us *prior to our participation as knowers*. Accounting for that initial "knowledge," and the social organization that sets it up for us, necessarily leads us back to an analysis of the total socioeconomic order. The structures that underlie and generate our own directly experienced world are social structures, and they bring us into unseen relations with others. Their experience is necessarily different from ours. Thus, attempting to analyze and account for our directly experienced world necessitates positing others whose experience is different and, therefore, requires us to focus on the total socioeconomic order "in back" of those experiences.

Through this act of rendering our everyday world problematic, we

women social scientists (Arab or Western) may discover clues that will
help us understand the social and political processes that contribute to our
own oppression and thereby expose those very structures or "relations of
ruling." What women do with that knowledge draws us closer to what
Gerda Lerner describes as the "dialectic of women's history":

> The contradiction between women's centrality and active role in creating
> society and their marginality in the meaning-giving process of interpreta-
> tion and explanation has been a dynamic force, causing women to struggle
> against their condition . . . in that process of struggle at *certain historic
> moments, the contradictions in their relationship to society and to histori-
> cal process are brought into the consciousness of women.* This coming
> into consciousness of women becomes the dialectical force moving them
> into action to change their condition and to enter into a new relationship
> to male-dominated society. (emphasis added)[8]

Speculations and Implications

What are the implications for our understanding of the Gulf Crisis and its
aftermath if we apply social science from the standpoint of women's perspective? The most obvious implication is the need to reexamine accepted
wisdom regarding what constitutes politics. What has traditionally been
described as politics in mainstream Arab political science, as with its
Western counterpart, tends to factor women out of the activity and for
many years has excluded the questions raised by Arab feminists. The Arab
world is rich with examples of women who experience various forms of
oppression and who resist and struggle to change their lot. Such experiences are generally relegated by the current dominant mind-set of most
observers to a sphere outside organized political activity and are dismissed
as "private troubles." Alternatively, when Arab women seek a voice of
their own in defining the politics of the Middle East, they meet largely with
ridicule, exclusion, or ostracism as a form of punishment for assuming the
right to interpret their own role in society or, worse, daring to rewrite the
script.

Nowhere is this more clearly exemplified than in the total eclipsing
from serious analytic concern of the several incidents of women's acts of
resistance during the Gulf Crisis and its aftermath. Where are the interpretations or analyses that attempt to "explain" why the women of Saudi
Arabia decided at that particular historical moment to apply for licenses to
drive their own cars? And why was this demand perceived as such a stark
threat by the Saudi Arabian regime? Where are the attempts to incorporate
into mainstream Arab social science explanations of Kuwaiti women's participation in the resistance to the Iraqi occupation? Where are the empirical

studies focusing on those Arab women agitating to change the situations of ruling within their own societies in the wake of the Gulf Crisis? How do Arab women relate to the processes of liberalization and democratization that are occurring in the Arab world? Indeed, what does the discussion of political reform or democratization mean without defining women's role in the process? If there is to be a full and human understanding of the labels *political reform* and *democratization,* men and women must share not only in the construction of that knowledge but also in changing the conditions that contribute to their own oppression.

A women's perspective as radical critique offers alternative criteria for defining political activities and issues, because by its very nature it thrusts directly to the center of discourse issues that have been previously declared private or nonpolitical. A women's perspective faces a double challenge: to struggle not only against political policies, structures, and arrangements but also against prevailing definitions of politics and modes of political explanation. A women's perspective is necessary to liberate us from the present concepts and methods of thinking within mainstream social science that reconstruct us as objects. As Smith points out, "To learn how to know society and sociology is to take on the view of ruling and view society and social relations in terms of perspectives, interests and relevances of men active in relation of rulings. It is to know ourselves thus."[9]

The peculiar eclipsing of a women's perspective from the discourse concerned with the various implications of the Gulf Crisis helps obscure, and therefore preserve, the detrimental sociopolitical effects of women's oppression in both the Western and the Arab worlds. This weakens both societies' abilities to cope with the myriad challenges that face us all in the aftermath of the Gulf War. As women social scientists, Arab or Western, we have to situate ourselves within this "world" we are trying to understand. We have to rethink the relationship between the knower and the known and recognize that women's place is not a separate sphere or domain but a position within social existence generally; that men's experience cannot speak for women's experience. A truly liberated social science needs the stereoscopic vision a women's perspective as radical critique can offer. A social scientist (or anyone else, for that matter) who denies to the majority of women, minorities, and the poor a central role in politics because he or she clings to established concepts that ignore the political realities of those not already ensconced within the existing system of rewards and benefits is not engaged in some mere reflection or neutral description. He or she is providing normative justification for an extant way of life. This failing must be avoided if social scientists are truly to understand and help explain societies on which they focus their attention. Although this assertion applies generally, it seems particularly relevant to today's Middle East.

Notes

1. Gerda Lerner, *The Creation of Patriarchy* (New York: Oxford University Press, 1986), p. 5.

2. Dorothy Smith, *The Everyday World as Problematic: A Feminist Sociology* (Boston: Northeastern University Press, 1987), p. 2.

3. Dorothy Smith, "A Women's Perspective as Radical Critique," in Sandra Harding (ed.), *Feminism and Methodology* (Bloomington: Indiana University Press, 1987), pp. 84–96.

4. Charles Taylor, "Interpretation and the Sciences of Men," in Paul Rabinow and William M. Sullivan (eds.), *Interpretive Social Science: A Second Look* (Berkeley: University of California Press, 1987), p. 63.

5. Jean Bethke Elshtain, "Methodological Sophistication and Conceptual Confusion: Critique of Mainstream Political Science," in Julia A. Sherman and Evelyen T. Black (ed.), *The Prism of Sex: Essays in the Sociology of Knowledge* (Madison: University of Wisconsin Press, 1977), p. 242.

6. This concept grasps power, organization, direction, and regulation as more pervasively structured than can be expressed in traditional concepts provided by the discourses of power. Smith, *Everyday World*, p. 3.

7. Smith, "Women's Perspective," pp. 2–3.

8. Lerner, *Creation of Patriarchy*, p. 5.

9. Smith, *Everyday World*, pp. 2–3.

Part 2
Economic and Social Issues

5

Oil Wealth in the Arab World: Whence, to Whom, and Whither?

ALAN RICHARDS

During the Gulf Crisis, Iraqi spokesmen made much of the fact that oil revenues accrued mainly to Arab Gulf states, whose combined populations were less than 15 million. Cast in the context of propagandistic simplification, Iraq's point was to blame the Arab world's economic, social, and political ills on the greed and self-indulgence of key oil-producing regimes in the Gulf.

In this chapter I briefly examine the nature of Arab oil wealth and its impact on the Arab world at large in the years prior to the Gulf Crisis. An effort is also made to identify economic and political implications of that experience for the future of the Arab world.

The vicissitudes of oil wealth have dominated Arab political economies since the early 1970s. Economic and political forces interacted in complex, still hotly debated ways to generate a historically unprecedented transfer of wealth from oil consumers to oil producers during the 1970s and early 1980s. The resulting oil boom transformed the political economy of the Middle East, as oil exporters acquired and spent vast sums and hired millions of workers from poor countries. The resulting flows of capital and labor often dominated the economies of the poorer Arab states. The oil price increase also interacted with a renewed sense of pride after Egypt's respectable showing in the 1973 October War to generate considerable self-confidence throughout the Arab world. Some Arab thinkers proclaimed that the region would experience a renaissance, transformed by oil wealth that would guarantee a prosperous future.

However, oil provided a slippery path to wealth and power: The oil boom was doomed to be relatively short-lived, and the flood of foreign exchange undermined both industry and agriculture—the only long-term roads to sustainable development. The economic essence of the oil boom was rent collection: capturing the difference between the very low cost of production and the cost of production of the next-best alternative. The Organization of the Petroleum Exporting Countries (OPEC) could garner these rents, partly because of demand conditions, partly because of political shocks, and partly because of the actions of one critical producer—Saudi Arabia. But because of consumer responsiveness over the longer run, and because of the increasing entry of non-OPEC producers, OPEC could maintain high prices only by seeing its market share decline.

Similarly, within OPEC, one country—Saudi Arabia—played the role of "swing producer," reducing its output in a vain attempt to hold up prices. As the Saudis did so, their market share fell. It became increasingly obvious to the Saudi government that its national interest was ill served by higher oil prices: The government opened the taps in the summer of 1986, and oil prices collapsed.

In retrospect, the oil boom was a historically unique, conjunctural event—the outcome of unrelated, interacting forces. As such, it is unlikely to be repeated, which is not to say that the long-run trend of oil prices may not be upward. I am merely guessing that a repetition in the near future of the heady days of the oil boom is unlikely.

The absence of a rerun of the oil boom years may not be bad for Arab economies. The oil (and remittance) boom shifted profitability away from internationally traded goods, such as farm and factory products, toward services, whether public or private. This phenomenon, known to economists as the Dutch Disease, was superimposed upon state-led, import-substituting industrialization (ISI) strategies inherited from the 1950s and 1960s. Dutch Disease on top of state-led ISI effectively blocked sustainable industrialization.

There are roughly 55 million more Arabs today than there were in 1980. Roughly speaking, during the 1980s the Arab world "added an Egypt" to its population. This implies that oil wealth will not solve the region's problems. Only internationally competitive industry can provide the jobs and the foreign exchange that are necessary to improve living standards in a sustainable way.

The worst legacy of the oil boom is not that the benefits were not widely shared but that they *were* widely shared: Labor exporters as well as oil producers caught the Dutch Disease, leaving the Arab world poorly equipped to face the challenge of an increasingly competitive international economy. Solving this problem has the highest priority for economic policymakers.

Oil Wealth: Whence It Came

Oil revenues are rents.[1] Economic rent is the difference between the market price of a good or a factor of production and its opportunity cost. For example, in the Gulf today, the market price of oil is about $18 per barrel, whereas the cost of producing that barrel is about $0.75–$1.00. Oil rents per barrel are accordingly about $17.00–$17.25; put differently, over 90 percent of today's oil price is rent. Such rents can be captured because the next-best alternative technology for producing the energy equivalent of oil is far more expensive than oil extraction in the Gulf. Gulf producers also enjoy cost advantages over non-OPEC producers: For example, it costs roughly $8 to produce a barrel of oil in the North Sea. Rents can also be captured because consumers are very insensitive to oil price increases in the short run—short-run demand elasticities for oil are quite low, with estimates ranging from –0.2 to –0.4 (that is, a 10 percent increase in price reduces quantity demanded by only 2–4 percent).[2]

The first oil shock of 1973 was the outcome of complex forces. The story has been told often and is only sketched here. During the late 1960s and early 1970s, international oil companies had been slowly ceding power over oil prices to national governments. The outbreak of the October War greatly accelerated this process. When President Richard Nixon decided to resupply Israel, the Saudis declared an oil boycott. Although the boycott was ineffective in reducing the oil supply to the United States (because oil companies simply reallocated international supplies), it combined with the uncertainty created by the war to generate near-panic conditions in the spot (auction) market. The shah of Iran, among others, tested the waters by holding oil auctions to see what the market would bear. The answer was roughly $20.00 per barrel. The Saudis disliked this high price, but they bargained within OPEC—now the sole determinant of OPEC-country prices—and agreed on a consensus price of $11.65 per barrel. Although the overall context mattered, the behavior of Saudi Arabia was crucial in generating the first oil shock.

A massive transfer of resources to oil-producing countries ensued, which promptly launched unprecedented development plans and projects. Stagflation in the West reduced the demand for oil, leading to a gradual erosion of real oil prices. Europe and Japan passed the price increases on to their consumers and raised taxes on oil. The United States, paralyzed by squabbling over the distribution of pain, did nothing: U.S. imports of OPEC oil as a percentage of consumption continued to grow, coming to just under 50 percent in 1979.

The second oil shock (1979), like the first, was the outcome of a complex interaction of political and economic factors. The Iranian Revolution withdrew approximately 2 million barrels per day (mbd) from the market when oil workers in Abadan struck. Initially, however, the gap was filled by Saudi Arabia, which increased its production to roughly 10 mbd. The Saudis sought to restrain price increases, which they believed were not in their long-run interest. However, in April 1979, they cut back production to around 8 mbd. Historians continue to debate whether this decision was the result, as the Saudis argued, of technical difficulties in maintaining production so close to capacity or of Saudi dissatisfaction with the U.S.-brokered Camp David Agreements between Egypt and Israel. In any case, the decision set the stage for another round of panic buying in the spot market, which pushed nominal prices over $25 per barrel. The resulting transfer of rents was even more massive than that of 1974, and the spending of the Gulf states grew accordingly.

But "rent booms" are not forever. For oil, as for most commodities, consumers are more responsive in the long run: The long-run demand elasticity for oil (perhaps −1.25) is more than twice that of the short run. The demand for oil is what economists call a *derived demand:* We want oil not for its own sake but because it helps us move around, heat our homes, generate electricity, and so forth. The impact of price on consumption, accordingly, is mediated by consuming countries' investment in capital stock—if the oil price increases, consumers install energy-saving technologies, which they do not necessarily remove when the oil price falls. Take, for example, automobiles in the United States. Average automobile efficiency rose by 30 percent from 1973 to 1985, but the average fuel efficiency of a new 1985 car was 85 percent higher than that of a new car in 1973.[3] Over time, capital stock slowly comes to embody fuel-saving technologies.

Consequently, when the United States finally deregulated domestic oil prices and passed the increases along to consumers in 1979, demand declined. This was particularly the case because the prices of the second oil shock had crashed through the rent ceiling: Oil prices were now close to, or even above, the cost of a variety of alternative energy technologies for some end uses. By the mid 1980s, Organization for Economic Cooperation and Development (OECD) countries were using only 70 percent as much energy per unit of GNP as they had in 1973.

Oil sales by non-OPEC producers increased available supplies and thereby compounded the problem for OPEC. OPEC could maintain high prices only by reducing its market share, which fell from 63 percent in 1979 to 38 percent in 1983. These developments exacerbated the internal cartel problem of cheating. Because OPEC lacked formal mechanisms to detect and deter cheating, in practice OPEC prices were maintained by Saudi Arabia's acting as a residual supplier. But the consequences for Saudi Arabia were the same as those for OPEC as a whole: Residual suppliers lose market share. Saudi Arabia's market share fell from 21 percent in

1980 to 8.5 percent in 1985. The Saudis saw their revenues decline, even as they made extensive commitments to development projects.

Saudi Arabia never had a strong interest in high oil prices. The country has a small population and very large reserves of oil. Its best strategy is to maximize the long-run payoff from these reserves, which requires moderate, only gradually increasing, oil prices. It is particularly important for the Saudis to avoid precipitously higher prices, because these will stimulate energy conservation, thereby reducing the long-run benefits of their immense reserves. We could argue that the first two oil shocks, which Saudi actions caused, were, in the first case, the result of overwhelming political pressure and, in the second, of a combination of political pressure and miscalculation.

The third oil shock, like the first two, was also the result of Saudi action. Faced with a shrinking market share and declining revenues and much annoyed by the incessant cheating of other oil producers, the Saudis decided to increase their market share and send a message to other producers. They opened the taps in July and August 1986, which promptly drove prices down to under $10 per barrel. Some analysts argue that the Saudis were actually sending three messages: one to their fellow producers (quit cheating; we can take losses better than you can), one to OECD investors in energy conservation technology (we can drive down prices and push you to the wall), and one to the Iranian regime, which was then engaged in a major military push in Iraq's Faw Peninsula (stop the Faw Offensive or we will bankrupt you). As in the first two oil shocks, a confluence of political and economic factors set the stage for the leading actor—Saudi Arabia—to make the decisive move. The oil boom ended, as it had begun, with decisions taken in Riyadh.

The lessons of this thumbnail sketch of the modern economic history of international oil policies can be summarized as follows: (1) The long-run impacts of the first two oil shocks on demand are still being felt; (2) Saudi Arabia is the critical player on the supply side for any sharp short-run change in price, because only that country has the capacity to cause significant fluctuations in international supplies (from 3 to 10 mbd); (3) so long as Saudi decisions are based on its own national interests, economic considerations will dictate price moderation; (4) political forces in the region can alter this economic calculus, as occurred in 1973–1974 and 1978–1979; and (5) there has been much learning by both producers and consumers. At least 50 percent of world oil reserves still lie in the Gulf area, and short-run demand functions are still highly inelastic. The possibility of short-run shocks is real, but no country with a long-term vision (such as Saudi Arabia) will want such shocks.

Oil Wealth: Where It Went

Facile rhetoric to the contrary notwithstanding, the benefits of the oil boom were rather widely shared through the mechanisms of labor migration and remittances and, less spectacularly, through aid flows. The collapse of oil prices in the mid-1980s and their continued stagnation have had effects that parallel those of the previous era of the oil boom: The pain, like the gain, was also widely shared. Oil wealth also had important negative, as well as positive, effects—a fact that suggests that opportunities, as well as difficulties, lie ahead should relatively moderate oil prices persist.

I have already mentioned the emphasis Iraqi propagandists gave during the Gulf Crisis to the fact that the bulk of Middle East oil revenues flowed into small Gulf states with minuscule populations (the Iraqis failed to note that their own country depended almost entirely on oil for foreign exchange, which was squandered on military hardware of dubious utility). This charge overlooked the main mechanisms for sharing wealth in the Arab world: labor migration and remittances. Estimates of the size of the labor and capital flows are varied; however, it seems that by 1985, 4 million to 8 million Arab workers were employed in the Gulf states. These workers sent back remittances officially valued at over $10 billion in 1985; because these figures show only sums officially recorded through the banking system, they grossly underestimate actual flows—especially in countries (such as Egypt before 1987) in which the official exchange rate was seriously overvalued. Several countries—Egypt, Jordan, and the Yemen Arab Republic—became especially dependent on remittances as a source of foreign exchange. From 1973 to 1987, remittances covered 30 percent of Egypt's and Jordan's imports and 60 percent of the YAR's imports. In 1984, remittances exceeded all commodity exports from Jordan and Egypt; figures for the YAR are unavailable, but the same was undoubtedly true in that country.

Remittances became a crucial part of national income in the poorer Arab countries and were the main mechanism by which oil wealth was shared. Participation by the poor in labor migration was widespread: roughly one of three rural Egyptian men had worked abroad at some point during the boom years.[4]

We should also note that labor emigration and remittances had other effects. The emigration of unskilled labor led to a dramatic increase in the wages of those who remained behind: In Egyptian agriculture the real wage rose around 350 percent from 1970 to 1985.[5] Similar phenomena occurred elsewhere. This labor market effect meant that the benefits of oil wealth were even more widely shared than figures on remittances suggest. It also implied that as a consequence of unskilled labor migration, the oil boom reduced poverty. Egyptian evidence is consistent with this statement: The percentage of Egyptians living in poverty dropped between 1973 and 1983—during the height of the oil boom.[6]

A secondary mechanism for sharing wealth was official development assistance (ODA) from the Gulf states. The image of "stingy Gulfis," although widespread, does not withstand comparative analysis. From 1973 to 1987, Arab donors gave out over $100 billion in ODA.[7] Gulf states' ODA comprised about 7 percent of their GNP in 1973, 5 percent in 1978, roughly 1 percent in 1985, and less than 1 percent (0.95 percent) in 1987. Perhaps the image of niggardliness comes from the relative decline of ODA over time. However, we should note that two states did somewhat better— Kuwait and Saudi Arabia, whose aid is shown in Table 5.1.

Table 5.1 Aid as a Percentage of GNP—Kuwait and Saudi Arabia

Year	Kuwait	Saudi Arabia
1973	8.34	14.61
1980	3.40	4.85
1983	3.83	2.69
1986	2.91	4.66
1987	1.23	4.04

Source: Pierre van den Boogaerde, "The Composition and Distribution of Financial Assistance from Arab Countries and Arab Regional Institutions" (Washington, D.C.: International Monetary Fund, Middle East Department Working Paper WP/90/67, July 1990).

By comparison, wealthy Western countries and Japan donated 0.347 percent of their GNP to ODA of all types during the same period. By international standards, Kuwait and Saudi Arabia were models of generosity.

These ODA transfers were often highly significant for recipient countries. Consider aid as a percentage of investment from 1973 to 1987: Jordan, 58.2 percent; YAR, 27.1 percent; Syria, 24.8 percent; Mauritania, 64.3 percent; and Sudan, 36.2 percent.[8] Aid and remittances together exceeded all investment in Jordan and the YAR and represented over 50 percent of all investment in Sudan and Mauritania. The charge that oil wealth was not shared cannot be sustained.

The image of shared wealth was, and is, not the dominant perception in the Arab world, perhaps largely because of the enormous disparity in per capita incomes that remains between the oil-exporting countries of the Gulf and other regional states. However, the inequality of per capita incomes across Arab countries declined between 1970 and 1989.[9] Income distribution within countries is far less certain, but there is little doubt that, to the extent unskilled labor participated in migration to the Gulf, absolute poverty declined—at least during the period of the oil boom.

Perhaps another reason for the widespread perception that oil wealth was not shared is the persistence of poverty in many Arab countries. A recent World Bank study estimates that about one-third of Arabs are "poor."[10] The absolute gap between the standards of living of the rich and the poor remains very large. In politics, perceptions usually speak louder than realities.

Several conclusions emerge from this brief review of the mechanisms of sharing oil wealth: (1) Oil wealth was not bottled up in oil-exporting states but rather was partially shared through remittances and ODA. (2) The indirect impact of labor emigration by way of labor markets for unskilled workers was at least as important as the direct impact of the emigration in reducing poverty and, less certainly, in reducing inequality. (3) From an international comparative perspective, Arab Gulf states—particularly Saudi Arabia and Kuwait—have been among the world's most generous donors. (4) Remittances and ODA constituted a substantial fraction of incomes, trade, and investment in poorer Arab countries. (5) Inequality among Arab states declined during the oil boom. (6) Since the oil price decline, poverty has likely begun to rise in most Arab countries, most seriously in the labor-exporting countries and even more seriously in those countries such as the YAR, Jordan, and Sudan whose leaders were perceived to have backed Saddam during the Gulf War, even as their economies were overwhelmingly dependent on Gulf ODA and workers' remittances. Rarely has so much been squandered so quickly by so few for so little.

Oil Wealth: Where Is It Going?

Part of the problem with the oil boom for poorer Arab countries was precisely that the oil wealth was shared; accordingly, countries such as Egypt, Yemen, and Jordan caught the Dutch Disease, which has limited their international competitiveness in traded goods. This is a serious problem, because only these sectors can provide jobs for the new generation of young people. Arab states are saddled with heavy debts (a total of around $116 billion, excluding Iraq) and face an international economy that is more intensely competitive than ever, as China, Vietnam, Thailand, and Indonesia replace Korea and Taiwan as producers of labor-intensive manufactures. Arab states' wage structures have been greatly distorted by the infusion of oil rents. Now that these rents have greatly declined, the countries are poorly placed to compete.

In short, unless oil prices rebound, the Arab states' economic future must lie with increasingly competitive manufacturing, not only because of the need to create jobs but also because of the need to import food. Rhetoric notwithstanding, the climate prevents food self-sufficiency for most Arab countries. Even in Egypt, the water constraint is tightening. Arab countries must export in order to eat.[11]

The necessity of competing in world markets requires an increased role for the private sector and reformed, more efficient government—in sum, structural adjustment. The necessity of structural adjustment, in turn, will likely require increased democracy, because it is very difficult to impose painful but necessary economic changes in any sustainable way without broad political participation. If there is no repetition of the oil boom, with its shared wealth and shared Dutch Disease, then the hope of the Arab world lies in accelerating the pace of economic and political reform.

Might the oil boom return? The long-run path of real oil prices should, according to economic theory, be upward: Oil is, after all, a depletable natural resource. But the oil boom era, both for good and ill, was really the result of sharp, discontinuous changes. Could such oil shocks recur? Perhaps, but as long as Saudi Arabia acts in its own national interest, a rerun of 1974 or 1979 is unlikely. Should the oil of that country be controlled by someone else, with a different, shorter time horizon, then a short-run oil price shock could be generated. Avoiding such an eventuality was one of the main reasons the United States went to war against Iraq in 1991. As long as the United States retains this commitment (and the resources and willingness to back it up), and as long as Saudi Arabia remains an independent decisionmaker, a repeat of the first two oil shocks is unlikely.

But remember, recent history suggests that blindfolded orangutans throwing darts at random numbers have outperformed economists in predicting the future path of oil prices.

Notes

1. This section draws heavily on Alan Richards and John Waterbury, *A Political Economy of the Middle East* (Boulder and Cairo: Westview Press and American University in Cairo Press, 1990).

2. See Geoffrey Heal and Graciela Chichiilnisky, *Oil and the International Economy* (Oxford: Clarendon, 1991).

3. Ibid.

4. Richard H. Adams, Jr., *The Effects of International Remittances on Poverty, Inequality, and Development in Rural Egypt* (Washington, D.C.: IFPRI Research Report, no. 86, 1991); Richards and Waterbury, *Political Economy of the Middle East*.

5. Alan Richards, "Agricultural Employment, Wages, and Government Policy in Egypt During and After the Oil Boom," in Heba Handoussa and Gilian

Potter (eds.), *Labor Absorption and Structural Adjustment: Egypt in the 1990s* (Cairo: American University in Cairo Press, for the International Labour Organization, 1991).

6. Karima Korayim, *The Impact of Economic Adjustment Policies on the Vulnerable Families and Children in Egypt* (Cairo: Third World Fund and UNICEF, 1987).

7. Nemat Shafik, "Has Labor Migration Promoted Economic Integration in the Middle East?" Unpublished paper presented at the seventeenth annual Symposium of the Center for Contemporary Arab Studies, Georgetown University, Washington, D.C., April 1992.

8. Pierre van den Boogaerde, "The Composition and Distribution of Financial Assistance from Arab Countries and Arab Regional Institutions" (Washington, D.C.: International Monetary Fund, Middle East Department Working Paper WP/90/67), July 1990.

9. Shafik, "Has Labor Migration Promoted Economic Integration?"

10. Ibid.

11. Richards, "Agricultural Employment."

6

Arab Elites and Societies After the Gulf Crisis

SAAD EDDIN IBRAHIM ⎯⎯⎯⎯⎯⎯⎯⎯⎯⎯⎯⎯⎯⎯⎯⎯⎯⎯⎯⎯

The Gulf Crisis seriously eroded the legitimacy of Arab ruling elites. It exposed their incompetence in managing inter-Arab conflicts and at the same time emphasized their important, although poorly filled, role in defending their national territories. During the crisis many observers reiterated the proposition that "the Arab world will never be the same." Along these lines, some contended that the unprecedented cleavage caused by the crisis would require several decades to heal. Others wishfully predicted that many, if not all, existing regimes would be swept away unless they were radically reformed. There were further predictions bearing on the redistribution of wealth in the Arab world, the Palestine issue, the spread of religious extremism, and the possibility of rapid democratization.

More than three years after the onset of the Gulf Crisis, nearly all Arab ruling elites are still entrenched in power. Interelite relations seem to have reverted to their old modalities. To be sure, there are some changes, although it is yet uncertain whether these are merely cosmetic or, on the other hand, embryonic trends toward major structural transformations of the Arab order. In this chapter I examine the implications of such changes for processes of democratization in the Arab world.

Sociological Roots of the Erosion of Regime Legitimacy in the Arab World

Most Arab regimes had been discredited in the eyes of the populations they govern even before the 1990–1991 Gulf Crisis. The discrediting process started in 1967, when the mightiest Arab army suffered a crushing defeat at the hands of Israel. The process was briefly reversed in 1973 because of the respectable Arab performance in the October War, but it resumed with the Lebanese Civil War, which broke out in 1975. The process was given further momentum by inter-Arab cleavages stemming from President Anwar al-Sadat's visit to Israel in 1977, his signing of the Camp David Accords in 1978, and the Egyptian-Israeli Peace Treaty of 1979. Other inter-Arab ruptures—over the Iran-Iraq War that began in 1980 and over the helplessness of Arab regimes when Israel invaded Lebanon in 1982 and forced the Palestine Liberation Organization (PLO) from Beirut—had the same effect.

Dramatic as they were, external defeats have not been the only phenomena discrediting Arab regimes. Their domestic performance has also been a major factor. In non–oil-producing Arab countries, in the 1970s and 1980s, continuous population and urban growth occurred without matching economic growth in real terms. The 1950s and 1960s strategy of import substitution reached its upper ceiling by the early 1970s. In the following two decades, food imports rose steadily—from $2 billion to $20 billion annually. At the same time, the Arab external debt rose from less than $5 billion in 1970 to about $200 billion in 1990. The ability of most Arab states to subsidize food, provide services, and generate sufficient jobs for new entrants to the labor force steadily diminished. Many gains achieved in the three decades following independence and the ascendancy of so-called revolutionary Arab regimes had bottomed out.

Even regimes in the oil-rich countries were having problems by the mid-1980s—at least five years before the Gulf Crisis. Much of the windfall oil revenues of the 1970s was quickly depleted, either because of external regional adventures—such as those embarked upon by Iraq, Libya, and Algeria—or, as frequently happened in the Gulf states, because of corruption and wasteful public spending. With the sharp decline of oil prices after 1983, some of these countries were quickly joining the ranks of economically strained non–oil-producing Arab states.

Thus, when the Gulf Crisis broke out, all Arab regimes were already experiencing a serious erosion of legitimacy. The implicit social contract forged by elites in the 1950s had been predicated on a trade-off between genuine political participation and socioeconomic-nationalist gains: The former was to be sacrificed to the latter. The 1967 defeat was a dramatic early sign that this trade-off was no longer viable. Although for a short while after 1973 it looked as if the formula might be restored, the subsequent march of events clearly showed such hopes were false. Restoration of it is now sociologically untenable; efforts to sustain the trade-off as the basis of Arab political organization would be politically costly.

For one thing, new socioeconomic formations cannot be tamed by the formula of the 1950s and 1960s—that is, by romantic pan-Arabism, anti-imperialism, anti-Zionism, and socialism. These new socioeconomic formations include the New Middle Class (NMC), the Modern Working Class (MWC), and the urban lumpen proletariat (ULP). The first two grew quickly and steadily between 1950 and 1970. The ULP developed steadily and rapidly in the years after 1970.

The growth of these formations was not uniform in all Arab countries. Generally, all three appeared on the social landscape of the northern tier of the Arab world (Egypt, North Africa, and the Fertile Crescent) at least twenty to thirty years earlier than in countries of the southern tier (Sudan, Somalia, Mauritania, and the Arabian Peninsula). Of these formations, the ULP is yet to appear in homegrown form in the oil-rich Gulf states—and what did exist of it in those countries was made up of poor expatriates. From the 1980s on, the ULP proved the most flammable social sector in Arab countries.

No longer able to honor the terms of the social contract forged in the 1950s and 1960s, and unable to tame the new socioeconomic formations by means of the old political discourse, Arab ruling elites resorted either to mounting coercive repression at home or to risky adventurism abroad. Saddam Hussein's regime in Iraq has done both since 1980. It scored an all-time high in the use of such tactics on August 2, 1990, when it invaded Kuwait.

The unfolding of the ensuing crisis has been amply told and retold, and there is no need to recount the details here. It suffices to reiterate one prediction made during the crisis: that democratization of the Arab world would be among its outcomes. This prognosis was based on the proposition that the Gulf Crisis was as much an internal regime crisis as it was a regional and international crisis.

Regime Maintenance Prior to the Gulf Crisis

During the few years immediately preceding the Gulf Crisis, several Arab regimes were acutely sensing a mounting loss of internal legitimacy. This was often expressed in violent confrontations between regimes and one or more of the major socioeconomic formations—the NMC, the MWC, and the ULP. The upper rungs of the NMC engaged regimes in battles over basic freedoms, human rights, and democracy; the lower rungs employed Islamic activism in battling established elites. The MWC opted more for strikes or other forms of work slowdowns and industrial sabotage. The ULP resorted to "street politics," such as random eruptions of demonstrations, rioting, and looting. Regardless of which formation started a confrontation, and however its discontent was expressed, the other—equally alienated—socioeconomic formations would join in to advance their own demands.

During the 1980s, we observe the phenomenon just described taking place in Egypt (1981, 1986), the Sudan (1985), Tunisia (1984, 1988), Morocco (1984, 1988, 1990), Algeria (1988), Jordan (1989), Kuwait (1989, 1990), Mauritania (1986, 1988), Somalia (1985–1990), and South Yemen (1986–1990). Ruling elites in all of these countries responded to growing expressions of discontent with promises of economic and political reforms. Some began to honor such promises before the outbreak of the Gulf Crisis; others took advantage of the crisis to abandon or delay honoring the promises.

Jordan, Yemen, and Algeria embarked upon serious democratization processes prior to the Gulf Crisis. In all three, national or municipal elections were held between 1987 and 1990, with few complaints regarding their integrity. The fact that antiregime Islamic candidates performed well and captured more seats than expected added credibility to the process. The fact that these democratically elected bodies swayed all three countries into supporting despotic Saddam Hussein during the Gulf Crisis has understandably perplexed Western observers who espoused democratization in the Third World. However, that irony is to be pondered on its own.

A few years before the crisis, Tunisia also peacefully changed its top leadership (from Bourguiba to Ben-Jadid), doing so without undergoing a regime change. The new leadership promised political reforms to secular opposition parties but continued to deny legitimacy to the Islamic *Nahda* Party. A series of bloody confrontations took place between the regime and *Nahda* Party supporters in late 1989 and early 1990. The Gulf Crisis, on which all Tunisian parties agreed, froze the confrontations between the regime and the Islamists for nearly a year. However, unrest has since resumed.

Other secular opposition parties in Tunisia have continued to have misgivings over the regime's domination by one party. However, when they consider the Islamists, they have found this to be the lesser of two evils.

The limited democratization in Egypt and Morocco that began several years before the outbreak of the Gulf Crisis has not progressed further in the wake of the Gulf War. In the Sudan, a serious setback to the democratization process occurred prior to the Gulf Crisis, when the military—supported by Dr. Hassan Tourabi's Islamic Front—seized power. In Mauritania, Somalia, and Djibouti, mounting ethnic and tribal conflicts were kept under control during the Gulf Crisis.

In the countries either directly or closely involved in the Gulf Crisis— Iraq, Syria, and the six Gulf states—the affair gave ruling elites a "legitimate" excuse to delay moves—if any had been intended—toward democratization. The exiled Kuwaiti ruling elite made firm commitments to resume democracy after "liberation." Saudi Arabia's King Fahd promised to establish the long-awaited (for thirty years) Shura (consultative) Council, but this promise also hinged on Kuwait's liberation.

Moves Toward Democratization

After the Gulf Crisis, a full year passed before some, although not all, Arab elites showed a real inclination to move toward serious participatory politics. It was obvious that something must be done in this regard. One positive outcome of the Gulf Crisis was the unprecedented political mobilization of Arab masses. Popular expressions of support for one or the other Arab side in the crisis were not always in accord with the official stands of ruling elites, which had the effect of breaking the "wall of fear" of many Arabs vis-à-vis existing regimes. Iraqis may be a dramatic case in point. The Shi'a in the south and the Kurds in the north rose in arms against the regime of Saddam Hussein. However, we can argue that they were emboldened by Baghdad's crushing defeat and the prospect of aid from the victorious allies. But even the "triumphant" Gulf elites faced mounting demands by their populations for more political participation.

In the immediate aftermath of the Gulf War, around five hundred leading Saudis from outside the royal family signed a petition to King Fahd asking for sociopolitical reforms. Three months before the war, a small group of Saudi women had staged a motorcade demonstration in defiance of discriminatory practices barring them from driving. Leaflets and cassette-taped messages circulated underground, criticizing the royal family for ineptness in defending the country—despite massive military spending—and for its reliance on non-Muslims for the task. More accountability was demanded.

Popular criticism was even harsher in Kuwait. An immediate demand, to which the ruling elite bowed, was that several cabinet members held responsible for the swift collapse of the Kuwaiti defenses during the invasion be removed from office. The emir of Kuwait also had to pledge a specific date for free parliamentary elections and restoration of the 1963 constitution, which had been suspended since 1986.

Since the Gulf War, democratization has unfolded slowly and reluctantly in a score of Arab countries and has been set back in others. I next present a sketch of the Arab world as it stood in 1992 and as it appears likely to develop in the near future.

On the positive side, Mauritania reinstituted a multiparty system, held presidential elections—in which the incumbent defeated three other candidates and gained over 61 percent of the votes—and then held parliamentary elections in March 1992. The leading party also won a comfortable majority. The elections were boycotted by several major opposition parties amid charges of rigging. More serious than these charges was the pattern of voting in both the presidential and parliamentary contests. The ethnic cleavage was obvious and disturbing. The ruling party mobilized the support of Arab and Arabized Mauritanians in rural and northern areas of the country.

Opponents mobilized black Mauritanians in the capital and the southern areas of the country. Such a division, if not wisely contained, could threaten not only the nascent democracy but also the country as a whole.

In Yemen, shortly after the unification of the North and South in March 1992, the regime (made up of an alliance of the two single parties that had previously ruled in the two Yemens) announced its intention to introduce a multiparty system and a full-fledged democracy. An interim period not to exceed thirty months was to culminate in open, free parliamentary elections. The Gulf Crisis threatened to cast doubts on this commitment. But as of early 1992, the regime seemed intent on honoring its promise, and by spring a democratic environment was flourishing. This was shown by the sprouting of forty-six political parties and organizations. The number of daily and weekly newspapers and magazines multiplied several times. In all, ninety-three such publications existed, fewer than one-fourth of which were governmental or semiofficial (that is, published by one of the two ruling parties). Any observer visiting Yemen in the first half of 1992 would have been impressed by the open atmosphere in which opinions and criticism were freely expressed without fear of retribution. Parliamentary elections were scheduled for late 1992.

However, there are some justifiable apprehensions about the future of democratization in Yemen. The existence of too many parties could badly fragment the Yemeni polity. Mounting incidents of violence, especially against persons associated with one of the partners in the ruling alliance— the Socialist Party—threaten the entire experiment.

In Jordan, King Hussein pressed ahead with his country's march toward democracy shortly after the Gulf War. Early in 1992, the Hashemite monarch terminated the application of emergency laws that had been in effect since the 1967 June War. This was followed in July by reinstitution of the multiparty system that had been suspended for thirty-five years. By the fall of 1992, Jordan's parliament had passed a new law lifting previous restrictions on the country's press. Together, these measures indicate that Jordan's democratization is on an upward trajectory. Many observers contend that King Hussein's effort to expedite the democratization process is part of a strategy to atone for his support of Saddam Hussein during the Gulf Crisis and to strengthen his hand in the Middle East peace talks that started at the Madrid Conference in late 1991.

In Saudi Arabia, long-awaited political reforms were finally announced by King Fahd in March 1992—exactly a year after the end of the Gulf War. Although modest by Western (or even Third World) standards, the reforms represented a giant step in the political evolution of the puritanically Islamic desert kingdom. They formalized the country's system of governance, provided for a system of local government in the Saudi provinces, and established a Consultative Council (*Majlis Al-Shura*). This last is by far the most important reform. Composed of sixty members, who are chosen by the king, the *Shura* Council is designed to perform all activities usually associated with parliaments, except for that of enacting laws. In other words, the council can initiate debates and discussions on all public matters, question members of the executive branch, and recommend new laws and policies to the cabinet, which forwards such suggestions to the king. The king is invested with the power of lawmaking, "within the bounds of the Islamic Shari'a." In the fall of 1992, King Fahd named the president and members of the *Shura* Council.

Many Saudi intellectuals understandably think these measures are insufficient. Petitions circulated during the summer of 1992 calling for more and deeper reform. These were published in the Arab press outside the kingdom. Proregime elements countered with a press campaign of their own. Paid advertisements in newspapers that published the petitions reprimanded the petitioners and commended King Fahd for his wise, gradualist approach.

We should note that even this practice—the "politics of petition"—is new to the Saudis. The fact that none of the petitioning critics is known to have been arrested, interrogated, or jailed also testifies to a markedly enlarged margin of political tolerance in the conservative kingdom. Observers note that such developments are functions of the delayed impact of the Gulf Crisis and the growth of free, open debate in three key neighbors: Yemen, Jordan, and Kuwait. Many of these debates are televised and therefore are seen by average Saudi citizens. Even the sultanate of Oman, a fourth neighbor, has announced plans to transform its own appointed consultative council into an elected body. If Saudi Arabia is to maintain its leading role on the Arabian Peninsula and its leadership in the Gulf Cooperation Council, it may not be able to afford lagging far behind its neighbors in terms of democratization.

Lebanon and Kuwait enjoy longer democratic traditions. Beset by long internal strife and persisting external threats, Lebanon had not conducted parliamentary elections since 1972. But thanks to the 1989 Ta'ef Agreement, and to regional and international efforts, a modicum of relative stability allowed the Lebanese in 1992 to hold their first parliamentary elections in twenty years. These were also the first elections in which a new formula was used to distribute parliamentary seats among Lebanon's six main communal groups.

Most Maronite Christians boycotted the elections on grounds that Syria retained a military presence in much of the country in violation of the Ta'ef Agreement. Nevertheless, the Lebanese government, under Syrian tutelage, disregarded Maronite objections and proceeded with the three scheduled rounds of elections. A striking feature of the outcome was the impressive showing by Islamist forces, both Shi'a and Sunni. It was also notable that several long-standing traditional Lebanese leaders were not reelected.

Lebanon's new government, headed by a newcomer to the country's political life, billionaire businessman Rafik al-Hariry, took office in October 1992. Despite tremendous obstacles ahead and the many challenges of rebuilding the country after nearly seventeen years of civil war, Lebanon's democracy seems to be back on track.

In Kuwait, the resumption of parliamentary life under the reinstituted 1963 constitution took place on time, as promised by the royal family. A heated and spirited campaign was carried out in the summer and fall of 1992. Elections were held in October, with few or no complaints about irregularities. Several new members won seats in Kuwait's National Assembly. Again, Sunni and Shi'a Islamist forces won nearly one-third of the total seats.

The significance of the Kuwaiti election is that it was the first to be held after the traumatic experience of Iraq's invasion, as well as the first since the 1986 suspension of the representative body that had been elected under the 1963 constitution. The election, therefore, was a victory for Kuwait's democratic forces, which had opposed both the 1986 dissolution of the National Assembly and the regime's tampering with the 1963 constitution. Moreover, the regime's failure to avert the Iraqi invasion combined with revelations of ineptness before and during the Gulf Crisis allowed democratic forces to extract significant concessions, including the appointment of six elected members of parliament to the cabinet. If there has been a single clear-cut positive effect of the Gulf Crisis, it is the unequivocal resumption of Kuwaiti democracy. This will certainly resonate throughout the rest of the Gulf.

Iraq, having existed as an authoritarian state for three decades, has emerged from the Gulf Crisis as a tragic mixed case. Being the immediate cause of the crisis, and having been badly defeated by the U.S.-led international coalition, Saddam Hussein's regime was substantially weakened. It was challenged internally by Kurds in the north, the Shi'a community in the south, and a score of attempted coups d'etat in the center. Nevertheless, the regime has doggedly clung to power in Baghdad and in the center of the country.

Thanks to the Western-protected zone in the north, Kurdish opposition parties have been able to set up democratically elected bodies to administer "liberated areas" and to negotiate with the Baghdad regime for a possible settlement allowing for self-rule. By the fall of 1992, Saddam Hussein's reluctance to meet some of their basic demands induced Kurdish leaders to rally other Iraqi opposition groups to the support of a national united front dedicated to ousting the regime in Baghdad. The effort is clearly backed by the United States and other Western powers, which in the summer of 1992 declared a No-Fly Zone in southern Iraq to reduce military pressure on Shi'a rebels. The Shi'a may well emulate their Kurdish counterparts by setting up some kind of interim home rule. Thus, although Iraq as a whole is still licking its massive and deep wounds, partial democratization appears to be being born—albeit by way of the political equivalent of a cesarean section.

Obstacles to Democratization

Despite advances in Arab democratization after the Gulf Crisis, there have also been major reversals, the most dramatic of which came in Algeria. Tunisia and Egypt have also had some difficult moments in their zigzagging democratization processes.

After 1988, Algeria appeared to be experiencing a real transition from autocratic to democratic rule. Following nearly thirty years of one-party rule by the National Liberation Front (FLN), and in the aftermath of widespread rioting in the fall of 1988, the regime of President Chadli Ben-Jadid embarked upon a series of political reforms. A multiparty system was introduced in 1989, under which municipal elections were held in 1990, shortly before the Gulf Crisis erupted. Of the many parties that competed in those elections, the Islamic Salvation Front (FIS) emerged as the most threatening to the FLN. It scored victories in about 50 percent of Algeria's municipalities.

National parliamentary elections were scheduled for the summer of 1991. In the interim, around fifty parties prepared to compete for office. However, internal divisions within the ruling FLN, along with the FIS's insistence that electoral rules be modified and its resort to militant confrontations with the government, led to the postponement of national elections for several months and to the arrest of some FIS leaders. When the first round of elections was finally held in late December 1991, the FIS gained a landslide victory, winning over 300 of 599 contested seats. The secular, Berber-based Front of Social Forces won only 25 seats, and only 16 seats went to the ruling FLN.

About 250 parliamentary seats were at stake in a runoff second round of elections scheduled for mid-January 1991. With its decisive victory in the first round, the FIS was destined to form the government regardless of the outcome of the second-round voting. This prospect alarmed many important anti-FIS forces—particularly the army, the Berbers, organized women's groups, and the ruling FLN. Their apprehensions were reinforced by some FIS statements regarding possible changes in Algeria's sociocultural life.

On January 11, a few days before the elections were to be held, President Ben-Jadid resigned, the army took power, a provisional presidential council was established, and an interim head of state—Mohamed Bou-Dief—was appointed. The democratic experiment in Algeria was aborted. The country was to witness the widespread arrests of FIS leaders and a streak of violent confrontations between FIS supporters and government forces. The interim president, an elderly statesman and former freedom fighter, paid with his life at the end of June 1992, the tragic victim of assassination. By early 1993, the future of Algerian democracy looked dim.

In Tunisia, a multiparty system has been operational since President Zain Al-Abdeen Ben Ali came to power in 1988. However, the same ruling party continues to monopolize power, although it engages in democratic rhetoric and interacts with secular opposition parties. Meanwhile, the regime has been forceful in isolating and oppressing supporters of the Islamic *Nahda* Party and other Islamic militants; thus, gross violations of human rights have been reported by Amnesty International and Middle East Watch. The regime has not only been oblivious to such criticism but has gone a step further by curbing the activities of the Tunisian League for Human Rights (TLHR), making it illegal to combine memberships in the TLHR and in any political party. By July 1992, the TLHR found it impossible to operate and dissolved itself. This represented a serious setback to both Tunisia's democratization process and the country's development of civil society.

Egypt's regime has continued to muddle through in the aftermath of the Gulf Crisis, with little, if any, change leading to further democratization. Although the press enjoys a reasonable margin of freedom, and three new political parties have been established by court order, little else has happened to render the system truly more participatory. Meanwhile, new bouts of violent confrontations with Islamic groups broke out in 1991 and 1992. Ominous among the incidents of violence were the assassination of a notable secular thinker, Dr. Farag Fouda, and sectarian strife in Upper Egypt. The regime has reacted by engaging in more of its old practices: tighter security measures and additional antiterrorist laws.

The regimes of Syria, Iraq, and the Sudan have shown no discernible change in their established autocratic methods. Whatever impact the Gulf Crisis may have had on them is still to unfold. They seem to have taken advantage of other pressing events to deflect attention from democratization.

Syria, for example, conducted another presidential plebiscite in early 1992. The outcome put Hafez al-Asad in office for six more years, with the usual "four nines" (99.99 percent) majority. Having mended his fences with the West, Egypt, and the oil-rich Arabs during the Gulf Crisis, al-Asad was under no particular regional or international pressure to change his ways of governance. With his Baathist rival in Iraq weakened and isolated, his forthcomingness in the Middle East peace talks endearing him to Washington for the time being, and aid from the Gulf and Syria's new oil discoveries filling his coffers, al-Asad has been able to present a stronger case than ever before—if he needed one at all—to the home front.

Some optimists contend that al-Asad may initiate some democratic measures in preparation for concluding a peace agreement with Israel. This contention is based on an analogy with policies of the late Egyptian president, Anwar al-Sadat. The argument is as follows: Now that al-Asad has repaired relations with the West, initiated an open-door economic policy (although using a much more gradual and subtle approach than did Sadat), and started negotiating with Israel, it is only a matter of time before he introduces controlled democratization. Such a step may be prudent in preventing or reducing the harmful effects of hostile propaganda by internal and regional detractors.

In Libya, the Qaddafi regime has been embroiled with the West over the Lockerbie Pan Am incident since the fall of 1991. The sanctions and the brewing confrontation with the United States and Great Britain have allowed the regime to mobilize Libyan public opinion behind Qaddafi. The opposition, fragmented from the start, has essentially been silenced both at home and abroad.

In the Sudan, Omar al-Beshir's military regime, backed by the Islamic Front, has broken out of its internal, regional, and international isolation since the Gulf Crisis. Bridges were hurriedly extended to Libya and Iran, which for reasons of their own responded with financial and military aid. The Sudanese regime has used this aid to pressure rebels in the south. Lacking havens in Ethiopia after the collapse of the Marxist Mengisto government in 1991, and suffering serious internal divisions, the South Sudanese rebels were dealt several military blows by the Khartoum regime. The Sudanese regime has tightened its grip on the home front and even felt bold enough to escalate an old border dispute with Egypt over the small town of Halayeb. Much of the vocal northern Sudanese opposition now operates from Cairo and London, although with little prospect of overthrowing the military-Islamic dictatorship in the foreseeable future.

In Iraq, Saddam Hussein's regime has retained its tight hold in a much reduced area—the center of the country. Defeated in the Gulf War, and still under military-economic siege, the regime has nevertheless been able to force de facto allegiance from its Arab-Sunni citizens, who see no better prospect in sight. Their growing discontent has been skillfully directed toward the West. Their fear of being dominated by an Iranian-backed Shi'a majority has forced them into acquiescence.

Like its Sudanese counterpart, the vocal Arab-Sunni Iraqi opposition is generally heard more in Damascus, Riyadh, London, and Washington than in Baghdad. However, a broad coalition of anti-Saddam forces—composed of Sunni, Shi'a, and Kurdish notables—is slowly emerging and is backed by Syria, Saudi Arabia, and the United States. It is evolving a vision of a federated democratic Iraq—a state that will reflect the legitimate aspirations of various ethnic groups while preserving the country's integrity.

Conclusion

Two years after the end of the Gulf Crisis, nearly all Arab regimes are still in power. Only two presidents—Algeria's Ben-Jadid and Somalia's Siad Beri—have been forced from office. But the surface resilience of most Arab regimes is undermined by growing dissent, most of which is militantly expressed by Islamic activism. This is forcing Arab regimes to adopt new strategies for survival.

Coercion, long a favored survival strategy by most regimes, has been stretched to the limits of diminishing returns. It has already led to the tragic disintegration of Iraq and Somalia and to quasi-guerrilla warfare in Algeria and parts of Egypt. One of the latent outcomes of the Gulf Crisis was not only the political mobilization of urban masses but also their diminishing fears of the coercive power of Arab regimes. The fact that hundreds of Arab volunteers returned home from Afghanistan and that many are Islamic activists reinforces this development.

Another established survival strategy for Arab regimes is to contrive a crisis or take advantage of a real one. However, at best this gives regimes a short respite from internal pressure. This strategy too is reaching the point of diminishing returns.

A relatively novel strategy in the Arab world is symbolic, or token, power-sharing with selected opposition groups. Here, the regime identifies its most dangerous rival and then tries to isolate it through a combination of coercive and accommodating measures. Islamic militancy is a prime example of a movement that in most cases has been targeted for coercive measures—witness the examples of Tunisia, Algeria, Jordan, and Egypt. In such cases, ruling elites typically dangle the prospect of power-sharing before other secular opposition groups in the hope of neutralizing them, if not winning their outright support. Although many such secular opposition groups may seriously distrust existing regimes, their deeper fears of Islamic militancy tend to drive them into accommodation with the regime. In practice, this usually wins them only a few seats in parliament or a few cabinet portfolios.

Nonetheless, this last survival strategy offers the best hope for a transition from autocratic to democratic rule in the Arab world with a minimum of instability and bloodshed. Token or symbolic though it may be, it creates a three-way bargaining situation. The more the regime perceives the threat of Islamist opposition, the more it will be inclined to allow real power-sharing by secular opposition parties. The more secular opposition parties perceive the regime's offer as still too little, the more they will be inclined either to bargain for a greater share or to gamble on entering into alliances with Islamic activists. And the more these activists perceive that regimes are willing to enter into real power-sharing, the more they may be willing to enter into the democratic process through real accommodation with secular forces.

It is notable that in some Arab countries, Islamic activists have shown willingness to compete with ruling elites by entering into alliances with secular opposition parties. A case in point is Egypt's Muslim Brothers. In 1984, this group entered into a coalition with Egypt's foremost secular liberal party, the Wafd. Later, in 1987, it did the same with the Labour Socialist Party.

Meanwhile, organizations that constitute civil society are playing a growing role in the political arenas of a score of Arab countries. Professional associations and organized interest groups, nominally nonpartisan, are increasingly being politicized. Elections held by Kuwait's Chamber of Commerce in the spring of 1992 attracted much public attention as a harbinger of the upcoming parliamentary elections. Egypt's medical, engineering, and lawyers' associations have been politicized, with the Muslim Brothers dominating in the outcomes of such elections during 1992. The same has been happening in Jordan.

The worldwide wave of democratization is also furthering the opening of Arab politics. So is the eminent role played by international and Arab human rights advocates, such as Amnesty International, Middle East Watch, and the Arab Organization for Human Rights. These groups are making the coercive impulses of ruling Arab elites increasingly difficult to act out.

Thus, although the Gulf Crisis may not have led to a democratic revolution in the Arab world, it has definitely contributed to a marked reduction in the viability and practice of Arab authoritarianism.

7

Arab Labor Migration
and the Gulf Crisis

NADER FERGANY ⎯⎯⎯⎯⎯⎯⎯⎯⎯⎯⎯⎯⎯⎯⎯⎯⎯

The impact of the Gulf Crisis cannot be properly understood without reference to inter-Arab migration, as well as to the socioeconomic context in
which it takes place. In this chapter I sketch the Arab migration system,
then present salient features of the precrisis inter-Arab migration process
before dealing with the impact of the Gulf Crisis on regional labor migration.

The Arab Labor Migration System

Arab countries interact within a complex migration system. First, there is
the "brain drain," through which Arab countries lose a significant segment
of highly qualified workers to the world's developed countries. Running
counter to this is the persistent stream of highly qualified and skilled workers that countries of the region receive, usually temporarily, in conjunction
with modernization projects that are launched and run by Western actors.
This is a privileged migration stream because of the lavish compensation
for moving into "hardship" posts and because of its participants' ability to
join rigid class societies at or near the top of the social ladder.

In contrast, millions of Arab migrants to Europe are underprivileged in
their host societies, and their plight is mounting. The vast majority of Arab
workers in Europe come from the Maghreb countries and are concentrated
in France. Although a small minority of Arab migrants to Europe are highly
qualified professionals, the remainder are unskilled and semiskilled workers who join the weaker segment of the local labor market, as well as the
lower rungs of the social ladder. These migrants and their dependents are

frequently confined to physical, sociocultural, and political ghettos and are subject to harassment and discrimination that heighten in times of economic recession.

There is also the labor migration stream of Palestinians who work in Israel. Although small in number, this group is significant in political terms and bears important implications for the future of the region as a whole.

However, the most consequential labor migration process in the region has put millions of Arabs to work, on a temporary basis, in the Gulf labor market.

Countries of Employment

The use of expatriate labor in the oil-rich Arab countries is not a recent phenomenon. Prior to the era of oil wealth, major portions of the Gulf region contained minorities from various non-Arab nationalities, and the emirates of the region had been receiving technical aid missions—especially in education and health—from more advanced Arab countries. Large-scale exploitation of oil reserves in these countries began around the middle of this century under the aegis of Western firms that brought non-Arab labor to this vital sector of economic activity.

With the rise in oil revenues, the demand for labor rose to proportions that could not be supplied locally. It was natural that professional labor for government, public services, and construction be recruited from the traditional Arab and Western sources of technical aid. Distribution of oil revenues to nationals produced unprecedented wealth and helped create a strong commercial elite. Strong demand for cheap and docile labor in private commerce and personal services also materialized, and this was met initially by expatriates from the subcontinent.

Expatriate labor in the oil-rich countries experienced a quantum jump in response to rises in the price of oil after 1973. Oil revenues increased twenty-five-fold over the next seven years. The ensuing economic boom generated demands for similar proportions of expatriate labor. Although it is estimated that the expatriate labor force in the Gulf states did not exceed 750,000 in 1970, its size doubled by 1975—and probably surpassed 5 million by the early 1980s. These are spectacular increases, particularly when set against the small populations of the host societies. During this period of phenomenal growth, the share of Asian labor increased steadily, and a new, more highly skilled and better organized stream of East Asian labor was developed.

By the early 1980s, expatriates constituted the majority of the labor force in countries of the Gulf Cooperation Council (GCC), exceeding 80 percent of the total labor force in some. Non-Arab labor in the Gulf grew to about 1.5 million workers, representing more than one-third of all expatriate labor. Although expatriate labor was mostly Arab in Kuwait and Saudi Arabia, Asians dominated the labor forces of the other GCC countries. Kuwait had the largest Palestinian population of all of the Gulf labor-importing countries. Reliable estimates indicate that Saudi Arabia hosted nearly a million Yemeni workers by the onset of the Gulf Crisis. Both the Palestinians in Kuwait and the Yemenis in Saudi Arabia enjoyed long-term residence, and the latter were exempt from some of the restrictions on expatriate labor.

The collapse of oil prices in the early 1980s reduced revenues considerably. However, contrary to expectations, the flow of expatriate labor to the Gulf region did not diminish, although the growth rate of expatriate communities slowed and the proportion of non-Arabs continued to rise.

Two major issues characterized the articulation of expatriate labor with the economies of the GCC. Host countries ensured that expatriate labor remained temporary and that it was isolated from the national socioeconomic fabric. Second, a discrimination-resentment syndrome ultimately conditioned relationships among elements of the local populations and the guest workers in these countries. An elaborate system of discrimination in work and living conditions developed against expatriate labor, with its actual impact depending upon the expatriates' ethnic origin and social status. Not surprisingly, expatriates' reactions were marked by quiet resentment—which, of course, was measured so as not to endanger their residence and employment prospects.

But nationals also resented expatriates, particularly those who rose to positions of influence within government or business. Resentment was also directed toward prominent expatriate communities of long standing that were considered to play decisive economic roles. The outstanding example of this phenomenon is the case of Palestinians in Kuwait.

As host countries, Iraq and Jordan have always been special cases. Although entry to the rich GCC countries was tightly controlled, Iraq adopted a policy of free entry and treated Arabs as Iraqis. This policy especially attracted semiskilled and unskilled Egyptians who could not find employment opportunities in GCC countries. Iraq became the largest recipient of Egyptian migrants in the 1980s, when its civilian labor force was largely mobilized on the war front with Iran.

Migration to Iraq was never a particularly positive experience. Work and living conditions were unsatisfactory, and financial returns were limited. The situation worsened with the imposition of foreign exchange restrictions that reduced or delayed transfers of remittances by Egyptian workers.

In addition, tensions between Iraqis returning from the front to civilian life and the large Egyptian work force sometimes led to major outbreaks of violence as the Iraq-Iran War drew to a close.

Being a major labor exporter itself, Jordan enjoyed a boom that was fueled largely by remittances from GCC countries until the early 1980s. During that period, Jordan opened its doors freely to a strand of Egyptian labor similar to that which was going to Iraq. However, when the local labor market hit a slump in the early 1980s, Jordan adopted a more restrictive labor policy.

In the view of Egyptian migrants, Iraq and Jordan were the worst countries of employment, because of limited financial accumulation and harsh working and living conditions.[1] It is interesting—and telling—that the most trying times for Egyptian migrants in Iraq and Jordan coincided with the period during which the three countries were partners in the Arab Cooperation Council.

Although Libya played some role as a receiving country, especially for Egyptian and Tunisian migrants in the past, employment opportunities there remained erratic and declined considerably during the 1980s.

Countries of Origin

Labor migration is always fueled by self-interest. Arab migrants, and the regimes that encouraged them to seek employment beyond national borders during the 1970s and 1980s, were no exceptions to this rule. The basic aim of individuals and governments in countries of origin was to claim a share of the oil revenues in order to ameliorate economic difficulties at home.

Countries of the Arab East entered the migration stream to oil-rich countries in varying degrees. Jordan (including Palestinians), Yemen, and Egypt were prominent entrants, Egypt in terms of absolute numbers and the other two by virtue of providing large proportions of the labor force. Jordanians and Palestinians were predominantly skilled workers and professionals; Yemenis were mostly unskilled and semiskilled; and Egyptian migrants spanned the spectrum of skills and occupations.

Labor migration quickly became a significant feature of the socioeconomic structures of countries of origin and led to consequences the extent of which depended on the magnitude of the phenomenon and on the socioeconomic context. Many migrants secured levels of financial accumulation that helped ease their personal economic difficulties. However, this did not necessarily contribute to a significant process of social innovation and economic growth in their home countries. Governments became dependent on remittances as an easy source of hard currency. Workers' remittances grew to represent a significant source of revenue.

In addition to the instability of remittances, however, the policy frameworks within which labor migration took place did not help the full potential benefits of remittances to be reaped at the macro level. Thus, the phenomenon tended to reinforce negative economic repercussions such as inflation, speculation in hard currency, and dependence on imports. Moreover, dependence on remittances, coupled with the relative weakness of governments of the sending countries, engendered an opportunistic stand on the part of those governments that often compromised the interests of their nationals working abroad.

In short, although individual migrants behaved in an economically rational manner in response to conditions of hardship in their countries, the governments that were responsible for economic crises in the first place in countries of origin continued to function in ways that sustained a gap between individual benefit and collective welfare. In the second half of the 1980s, a combination of economic recession and a net return of migrants in response to the economic slowdown in countries of destination, as well as forced return due to the end of the Iraq-Iran War (in the case of Egypt), contributed to the growth of organic unemployment in countries of origin.

The Arab Regulatory Framework

Despite the existence of a formidable body of international institutions and legal instruments, labor migration in the Arab region has been regulated on terms set by countries of employment. This is a feature of a buyers' market. When the supply of a commodity greatly exceeds demand, buyers dictate their terms. This has essentially been the character of the Gulf labor market since the mid-1970s.[2]

We would hope that the set of specific policies and proposals being pursued in Europe to improve the conditions of Arab migrants in accordance with international standards can be adopted, with obvious modifications, as desired objectives for regulating migration in the Gulf labor market. But that is probably a distant hope given the present Arab environment.

Impact of the Gulf Crisis

The chain of events that began with Iraq's invasion of Kuwait in August 1990 was to have grave consequences for Arab labor migration, some immediate and others long term. The most immediate consequence of the Gulf Crisis was the dislocation of large numbers of migrants from their countries of residence. It is estimated that more than 700,000 Egyptians returned from Iraq, Jordan, and Kuwait. Over 800,000 Yemenis were essentially expelled from Saudi Arabia and other Gulf countries. The government of Jordan estimates that approximately 200,000 nationals and Jordanian passport holders returned from the Gulf. An additional 150,000 Palestinians are estimated to have left Kuwait and other Gulf emirates during the crisis. Significant numbers of Iraqi and Sudanese migrants were also forced to leave their employment and residences in GCC countries. In all, about 2 million Arab expatriate workers and their dependents were removed from their residences in Kuwait, other GCC countries, Iraq, and Jordan during the crisis. These people either returned to their countries of origin or went to third countries.

For obvious reasons, the uprooting of the Palestinians from the Gulf, especially Kuwait, was a humanitarian calamity. Although Palestinian and other expatriate workers did not enjoy permanent residence, this was in itself a major shortcoming of migration to GCC countries. The length of service and residence of most Palestinians in the Gulf would have qualified them for permanent residence, if not citizenship, in most places.

The sudden, massive, and sometimes brutal removal of Palestinians from the Gulf cannot be justified, even by the claim of collaboration with invading Iraqi forces. If a minority of Palestinians collaborated with the Iraqi occupation, another minority fought in the ranks of the resistance. Some gave their lives fighting the invaders. Most simply suffered along with their Kuwaiti neighbors. An extremely vulnerable group of Palestinians caught in this quagmire consisted of nearly stateless individuals who carried travel documents, usually Egyptian, that did not even give them the right to enter the countries that had issued the documents.

We should note that the massive return from the Gulf entailed great losses for all migrants and their communities of origin. Under normal conditions, returning migrants bring accumulated savings and personal belongings that soften their reentry. This was not possible during the crisis. Although former employees of the government of Kuwait were compensated, the compensation did not cover all damages incurred. Most of those employed by the private sector were even less fortunate. In the case of countries such as Egypt, Jordan, and Yemen, the crisis-induced massive influx of returnees exacerbated the already severe recession, increased foreign exchange bottlenecks, and added to open unemployment. The loss of a significant part of the stream of remittances means these difficulties will continue.

It is probably too early to assess fully the long-term impact of the Gulf Crisis. However, one conclusion is possible: The Gulf labor market has been basically transformed in terms of both size and composition for a long time to come. This will have far-reaching consequences for all countries involved.

Iraq and Jordan have effectively been removed from the list of receiving countries of the Gulf labor market, at least for the next few years. The two countries suffered dire economic conditions stemming from the devastation brought about in Iraq by war and the blockade and in Jordan by the loss of regional export markets, remittances, and sources of aid.

This is an especially severe blow to the economically deprived stratum of Egyptian migrant workers. Jordan and Iraq hosted at least 700,000 Egyptian workers prior to the invasion. At present, the most plausible estimates place the number of Egyptians in Iraq at around 100,000. Many of these have established interests in Iraq, and some have little reason to return to Egypt, despite the hardships of living in Iraq, the difficulties of communication, the problem of transferring remittances, and even—until recently—the absence of an Egyptian interest section in Baghdad to tend to consular needs.

The fragility of the social structures of the GCC countries, particularly the small emirates, was brought to the fore and even intensified by the crisis. Tensions between local populations and expatriate workers have been accentuated along the lines of sides taken during the crisis. The resulting social rift is not limited to the traditional expatriate-nonexpatriate division. A new split has evolved among nonexpatriates in Kuwait between those who left and those who stayed during the Iraqi occupation.

But there is more to the resulting social fissure. In Kuwait, nonexpatriates consisted of a mixture of two grades of nationals, and a third category comprised persons without nationality. This third category has earned a place in history by introducing a new word to the English language— *bidoun,* literally meaning *without*—to describe this singular relationship with a state, a relationship by which a person without a declared nationality qualified to serve in the army and security forces and derived some benefits of nationality but could not become a national. In the past, these benefits tempted people to renounce their nationalities and present themselves as bidouns. Many of the hundreds of thousands of bidouns were lifetime residents of the emirate, although they remained strictly stateless. From a position of relative prominence in Kuwait, the bidouns have been reduced to a form of diaspora. They must now undergo severe security tests in order to have some place in Kuwaiti society. Even so, their position in postwar Kuwait is not comparable to their previous status.

Kuwait, having been at the center of the storm that swept the region, has also taken the lead in reshaping its expatriate labor policy. In doing so, it gives priority to two considerations: security and the attainment of a more "favorable" population and labor force composition. The drastic reduction of the precrisis 400,000-member Palestinian community to only about 50,000 by early 1992 is the clearest example of this new policy, which aims at reducing the total population to about half its preinvasion size—excluding nationals of countries that did not join the coalition against

Iraq—and even further ensuring the temporary character of expatriate labor.

Within this framework, Kuwait's current reconstruction effort points to a sluggish recovery, dominance of Western firms, and capital-intensive technology. This course is likely to prove detrimental to Kuwait in light of the fundamental role expatriates, especially the long-standing Palestinian community, once played in the socioeconomic life of the emirate. More significantly, this policy will probably be recessionary, on the one hand, and, on the other, will not increase demand for Arab labor in Kuwait. On the contrary, the tendency seems to be to reinforce the previous relative preference for non-Arab labor. For example, one year after the liberation of Kuwait, the number of Egyptian workers there had not reached the preinvasion level, despite the needs imposed by reconstruction efforts.

Other GCC countries have followed Kuwait's example, although perhaps not as drastically. It is unfortunate that policy responses in the area of labor migration and residence have meant reinforcing the worst modalities of precrisis migration—that is, an increasing reliance on non-Arab labor and a cementing of the temporary status and isolation of expatriate labor. As a result of these developments, labor-exporting Arab countries, including those who joined the anti-Iraq coalition, obviously face the prospect of reduced demand in the Gulf market.

To take Egypt as a case in point, the capacity of Kuwait to absorb expatriate labor is unlikely to grow drastically in the near future, and even if it does, it cannot ultimately absorb hundreds of thousands more Egyptian migrants. Egyptians cannot replace Yemenis in Saudi Arabia to any large extent. As petty traders and manual workers of traditional standing, Yemenis played a unique role in Saudi Arabia, one that has cultural and political underpinnings Egyptians cannot easily replicate. Further, the Saudi-Yemeni rift caused by the invasion of Kuwait will probably be one of the first crisis-related political estrangements to be repaired.

Even a surge of reconstruction in Iraq will probably not entail a rise in demand for Egyptian labor. Two considerations underlie this conclusion. The first is that large construction projects in Iraq were normally carried out by foreign firms using non-Arab labor. The second is the legacy of hostility that arose between the two governments during the Gulf Crisis.

But apart from probable enduring limitations on employment opportunities in Iraq, Egyptian would-be emigrant workers face other, equally unhappy prospects. Libya's post–Gulf Crisis attempt to effect a rapprochement with Cairo and Tunis raised expectations that quickly proved false. It is doubtful that the Libyan economy can accommodate significant numbers of expatriate laborers in the near future. Finally, talk of the availability of markets for Egyptian labor in Africa is baseless.

The diminishing prospects for exporting labor only darken an already grim environment marked by deepening economic stagnation and mounting unemployment. These conditions are expected to deteriorate even further in some cases as a result of structural adjustment programs. Egypt is a prime example in this regard, despite the generous treatment it received from the international financial community as a result of its role in the crisis.

The end result of all of this will almost certainly be a further reduction in the bargaining power of countries of origin, heightening the buyers' market for employers in the oil-rich Gulf states. This development carries negative implications for the welfare of expatriate labor in the Gulf.

Notes

1. Nader Fergany, *Sa'ia Waraa' Alrizq* (In pursuit of livelihood) (Beirut: Center for Arab Unity Studies, 1988).

2. Nader Fergany, *Roh'al fi Ard al-Arab* (Travelers in the land of the Arabs) (Beirut: Center for Arab Unity Studies, 1987).

8

The Political Economy of Jordan: Democratization and the Gulf Crisis

RIAD AL KHOURI

In this chapter I explore the political economy of Jordan, focusing on the period after 1987, with democratization as a major theme. I also attempt to assess Jordan's economic prospects and chances of democratization in light of the 1990–1991 Gulf Crisis.

Within a framework that links economics and politics, this is a study in political economy. Such a combined approach is desirable because economics and politics are inseparable in the real world. Moreover, many from both North and South "now argue that there is a relationship between the economic system and the nature and extent of democracy."[1]

In particular, many in the North have their own version of political economy, in which an attempt is made to extend orthodox neoclassical economic analysis of markets into the political arena. The "economics of politics" has thus emerged. But "there are two important limitations to this approach. The first is that the political sphere is, by its nature, quite different in structure and function from that of the market."[2] The arguments of this approach work by analogy: "Competition" for votes is "like" competition for profits in markets. But this analogy reduces political phenomena to market forms, and the distinctive features of political structures and practices are lost. The economics of politics becomes the dissolution of political analysis into an economic theory of market behavior.

The second limitation is that the economic theories and methods used reflect and perpetuate "the ideological assumptions of classical liberalism."[3] The approach of orthodox economics is therefore subjective and individualistic. The individualistic approach of classic liberalism is unsatis-

101

factory because it often has little conception of society as a system, except as a mere aggregate of individual components. Its method survives in economics partly because "individualistic assumptions tend to lead to market-based policy conclusions."[4] The proliferation in the North of the practice and ideology of private enterprise helps explain the vitality of this approach.

To understand the interaction of economics and politics, a theory of socioeconomic systems as a whole is required. But this has been slow to develop and promises to be even slower in the wake of the launching of the New World Order. Meanwhile, efforts such as the present one must get by as best they can, leading—one hopes—to the fashioning of a proper theoretical framework in the near future.[5]

Before proceeding, I must make my personal view clear, as a Jordanian working in the private sector. I firmly believe in both democracy and economic liberalism. But this does not imply that the two are inextricably bound in the Third World in general or in Jordan in particular nor that democracy and liberalism should be applied immediately to eliminate all of our problems.

Keeping this caveat in mind, we can examine an idea that is popular in the North but one that may not necessarily be relevant to Jordan. The words are Milton Friedman's, and although we may or may not agree with them, we ignore him at our peril:

> Economic arrangements play a dual role in the promotion of a free society. . . . Freedom in economic arrangements is itself a component of freedom broadly understood, so economic freedom is an end in itself . . . economic freedom is also an indispensable means toward the achievement of political freedom.[6]

Friedman continues:

> Viewed as a means to the end of political freedom, economic arrangements are important because of their effect on the concentration or dispersion of power. The kind of economic organization that provides economic freedom directly, namely, competitive capitalism, also promotes political freedom because it separates economic power from political power and in this way enables the one to offset the other. . . . I know of no example in time or place of a society that has been marked by a large measure of political freedom, and that has not also used something comparable to a free market to organize the bulk of economic activity.[7]

Friedman then affirms that the existence of a free market does not eliminate the need for government, which is essential both as a forum for determining the rules of the game and as a referee to enforce those rules.

What the market does is to reduce greatly the range of issues that must be decided through political means, and thereby to minimize the extent to which government need participate directly in the game. The characteristic feature of action through political channels is that it tends to require or enforce substantial conformity. The great advantage of the market, on the other hand, is that it permits wide diversity. It is, in political terms, a system of proportional representation. Each man can vote, as it were, for the color of tie he wants to get; he does not have to see what color the majority wants and then, if he is in the minority, submit. It is this feature of the market that we refer to when we say that the market provides economic freedom. But this characteristic also has implications that go far beyond the narrowly economic. Political freedom means the absence of coercion of a man by his fellow men. The fundamental threat to freedom is power to coerce, be it in the hands of a monarch, a dictator, an oligarchy, or a monetary majority. The preservation of freedom requires the elimination of such concentration of power to the fullest possible extent and the dispersal and distribution of whatever power cannot be eliminated—a system of checks and balances. By removing the organization of economic activity from the control of political authority, the market eliminates this source of coercive power. It enables economic strength to be a check to political power rather than a reinforcement.[8]

These and similar ideas underpin much of the world's economics and politics. Whether such thoughts can be invoked to help liberalize Jordan both economically and politically remains to be seen. But one thing is certain: Jordan is changing, and as usual, theory will have to take a back seat to political and economic developments in the real world. Change in the wake of the Gulf Crisis is not slow and promises to accelerate. This has been true throughout the region, and Jordan is no exception.

Background

Because Jordan is both small and new, its political economy is quickly summarized. The state was created in the early 1920s in the wake of the collapse of the Ottoman Empire. Its territory is small, as is its rapidly growing population. The country is poor in both water and energy.

In such a difficult setting, the government assumed a preponderant economic role, characterized by interference in or ownership of enterprises in practically every sector; the biggest (and some of the most successful) businesses were held fully or in part by the government (which has always been the country's largest employer). At the same time, a lively private sector developed alongside the public sector—although as a junior partner.

Jordan's strategic geographic position has rendered it susceptible to regional tensions. Waves of refugees from Palestine and elsewhere have at times destabilized the economy. But the country has managed to handle these two factors well—obtaining a fair amount of foreign aid by playing upon its strategic role, and integrating Palestinians into its economy.

From the mid-1970s to the early 1980s, the country enjoyed a period of strong growth, a rising standard of living, and political stability. Regional oil wealth spilled over into Jordan, generating hopes that the kingdom would leave the ranks of the developing world and turn into a newly industrialized country. The oil price decline ended these illusions, and by 1987 Jordan was well into recession. In December of that year, the outbreak of the Palestinian intifada deepened the Jordanian fear of destabilization, although this was mixed with pride in the Palestinian struggle.

Meanwhile, the economic downturn continued, and internal and external political pressures mounted, compounded by the intifada. On July 31, 1988, King Hussein announced Jordan's disengagement from the West Bank.

The king had finally concluded that a role for Jordan as the prime impetus in promoting Arab-Israeli peace talks was too ambitious an undertaking for a country that lacked influence even in dealing with the Palestine Liberation Organization (PLO). Jordan now set its sights realistically: It remained an active player in regional peace efforts but no longer sought a leading role.

In the spring of 1988, the interaction of a regional slump with local factors triggered a foreign exchange crisis. The Jordanian dinar fell. This was met with measures that failed to restore full or substantial confidence and even exacerbated the capital outflow.

The dinar declined in value against the U.S. dollar throughout the summer and early autumn of 1988. Faced with a severe shortage of foreign exchange and with debt repayment problems, the government introduced measures to cut imports, boost exports, and curb consumer demand.

Prime Minister Zaid Rifai soon announced that the government would adopt an austerity budget for 1989, cutting infrastructural and other project spending. But there was little scope for a squeeze, because approximately 60 percent of the budget was accounted for by salaries, pensions, defense, and internal security—all of which were, and are, regarded as sacrosanct.

Thus, the budget announced on December 31, 1988, projected a growing deficit. The finance minister attributed the situation to the failure of Arab countries, except for Saudi Arabia, to honor financial commitments under a decade-old Baghdad Summit resolution. This only added to the feeling of crisis. Jordan defaulted on its first scheduled debt payment of 1989. The country had become another Third World debtor unable to meet its financial commitments.

In return for the economic sacrifices demanded by the government as it struggled with the country's economic problems, Jordanians began to call for a greater say in decisions affecting their daily lives and to seek the accountability of public officials. Public unrest was exacerbated by the fact that the lower house of Jordan's parliament, a sounding board for grievances, had been dissolved in July 1988. Then, too, accusations of a news blackout vis-à-vis the intifada also emerged. People were now openly calling for change, whether political or economic. Whatever other motives were behind these outbursts, no such public articulation of grievances had been seen in Jordan for some time.[9]

The Crisis of 1989

The rapid devaluation of the Jordanian dinar that began in 1988, coupled with the April 1989 announcement of cuts in subsidies on certain basic items (called for as part of the Jordanian government's agreement with the International Monetary Fund [IMF]), precipitated serious riots. The unrest was a spontaneous reaction to what were viewed as unbearable price increases, and it came against the background of growing political malaise and general economic deterioration.

The rioters denounced the austerity measures and demanded the resignation of Prime Minister Rifai. Riots broke out in towns and villages in the southern part of the country, a region that traditionally formed the backbone of East Bank support for the regime. This was a stark reflection of the extent of frustration among loyalists. One of the most significant documents to emerge was a petition submitted by a group from the city of Karak demanding the resignation of Rifai, a change in existing electoral laws, punishment of officials for corruption, an end to austerity measures, and greater democratization.

The economic crisis underlying these disturbances had been mounting for many months. External debt, unemployment, and corruption went unchecked. Living standards were deteriorating. Because it had no intention of lifting the austerity reforms, the regime needed to strengthen its legitimacy through a measure of public participation in decisions affecting resource allocation. It therefore concluded that the country could not be controlled with the techniques utilized in the 1960s and 1970s. To maintain continuity, the regime had to share power with the people. Many were unwilling to tighten their belts to pay for an economic crisis they felt was the result of widespread corruption. The king dismissed Rifai in late April and again promised to allow general parliamentary elections—the first since 1967.

Democratization

Jordan's earlier experience with political liberalization goes back a few decades. Elections were held in the early and mid-1950s, but the process came to a halt following a 1957 coup attempt, after which martial law was imposed and political parties were banned. These restrictions were eventually eased, but the 1967 Arab-Israeli War and the occupation of the West Bank prompted the reimposition of martial law and the suspension of general parliamentary elections. The government pointed out that holding kingdomwide elections was impossible when part of the country was under occupation and argued that elections for the East Bank alone would have constituted acquiescence to the occupation.

Nonetheless, the dislocation caused by the 1967 war allowed a brief period of more open political activity in Jordan. However, this ended abruptly with the civil conflict of 1970–1971 and the subsequent departure of Palestinian resistance organizations from the country.

Following this internal conflict and the 1973 Arab-Israeli War, the king suspended parliament in 1974, and opportunities for political expression and participation were restricted for nearly a decade. Instead, the National Consultative Council (NCC) was formed in 1978 and assumed, in principle, the role of parliament. But the decisions of the NCC were not binding.

By the early 1980s, the status quo began to break down because of a variety of social, economic, and political factors. The presence of a growing, educated, and affluent middle class in Jordan's politicized environment, combined with regional developments—such as the signing of the Egyptian-Israeli peace treaty in 1979, the Israeli invasion of Lebanon in 1982, and the subsequent crisis in the PLO—led to increasing calls for freedom of political expression. In response, the king disbanded the NCC and in 1984 reconvened parliament (which had been elected in 1967).

Elections were held to fill vacant seats on the East Bank. West Bank vacancies were filled indirectly, with members of the lower house serving as electors. Typical of this parliament's activities was its criticism of the 1988 budget (presented in late 1987) for failing to curb spending and allowing foreign and domestic debt to rise. Parliament also expressed doubt as to whether Jordan would get the $438 million in foreign aid the government seemed to be counting on as a secure resource for the upcoming fiscal year. Despite such accurate criticisms, the budget was approved unanimously. In any case, this parliament was in turn disbanded when Amman broke its links to the West Bank in 1988.

Democratization and the Economic Crisis

Mass dissatisfaction with the country's economic management led the king to dismiss the Rifai government and replace it with a cabinet headed by the chief of the royal court, Sharif Zeid Bin Shaker—a former armed forces commander and cousin of the king with a reputation for toughness. The new government announced that general elections would be held (and they were) on November 8, 1989. It also embarked upon political reform. Detainees who had participated in the April riots were released, and partial amnesty was granted to other prisoners, including some jailed for political offenses. Journalists proscribed under the previous government were reinstated, and the media was allowed more freedom to comment on internal affairs. Censorship was eased, and political parties (although still illegal) gradually surfaced and operated with impunity. Once the official campaign period began, the country was filled with political banners and posters, with myriad public appearances by candidates.

This stage of democratization ended in open elections. More than 640 candidates vied for the lower house's eighty seats. Political parties were banned, so candidates ran as independents. Nevertheless, the regime ignored electoral blocs and political groupings, ranging from Communists to Islamic fundamentalists. Martial law was finally lifted in April 1992, in a major step toward normalization.

The democratic movement was not strong enough prior to the 1989 riots to push its demands successfully. However, the upheaval induced in 1989 by economic strain gave proponents of political liberalization a means to exert pressure. Democracy had been on the agenda of some for a while, but the regime's fear of riots brought the process into the open, as professionals and businessmen used the opportunity presented by "the street" to push for change.

The most effective demands for democratization and government accountability came mainly from intellectuals and professional associations. These educated groups resented their inability to break into the ruling elite on the basis of merit. Top positions were always given to the same faces, families, and clans. Businesspeople shared these resentments: "Sweetheart" deals and commissions were traditionally channeled to friends by insiders in a blatant system of favoritism. During the riots, professional associations hinted that the credibility of the regime would be undermined in the absence of a more stable economy and greater public participation to prepare the masses for austerity measures.[10]

Many in Jordan now insist upon applying democracy on a wider scale, one encompassing the educational system, the universities, and the entire culture while fully embracing freedom of thought, research, association, and debate. Presently, liberalization is limited to parliament, parties, and the press, but it could include socioeconomic rights—including the right to form associations that would organize or further consolidate the interests of women, farmers, students, workers, and others.

But democratization is not social liberalization, and not all who support the former favor the latter. Both Islamists and securalists seek to break the closed clique of regime favorites and open the system. Where they go then depends upon how they view broader questions. Islamist victories within professional organizations illustrate that there is no recognized inherent contradiction between being a professional advocating democracy and also supporting the Muslim Brothers' call for instituting their new morality.

In Jordan there is definitely a movement toward achieving the forms of democracy, but substance is another matter.[11] The economic crisis and aspects of the political culture may make progress difficult.

Communications media in Jordan have traditionally been under direct or indirect state control. Media quality is therefore uneven and runs the gamut from outstanding individuals and organizations to the mediocre and worse. The following illustration of the media's position exemplifies some current problems in a sector that theoretically should spearhead the democratization process.

On September 2, 1991, the Public Liberties Committee of the lower house of parliament shocked the country by issuing a report on the torture of political detainees in Jordanian prisons. The shock did not arise because no one knew of this but rather because the report had been issued by parliament. It referred specifically to the abuse of detainees belonging to Muhammad's Army, an underground Islamist group, who had been arrested on charges of illegal arms possession and plotting attacks against various targets in Jordan. Despite two years of Jordanian glasnost, only *al-Ribat*—the weekly publication of the Muslim Brotherhood—initially printed the full report, although each of the country's three Arabic dailies carried the interior minister's denial of the parliamentary committee's accusations.

This episode illustrates the fragility of the liberalization process in Jordan. Although the government press and publications department approved the article in *al-Ribat,* the important fact is that such a department still exists. *Al-Ribat* is published outside of Jordan and has not yet received official recognition inside the country.

Media liberalization remains a guided experiment. The government still owns large shares of the newspapers, which hesitate to exercise their new freedoms, either because of remaining obstacles or because old-guard publishers and editors are too accustomed to the heavy hand of the government to break out of the habit of self-censorship.

The Economic Implications of Democratization

Regardless of IMF advice, Jordan needs economic restructuring to deal with the all-encompassing problems of growth, private-sector development, and public-sector institutions. The government is committed to freeing the economy from public-sector control. It is to be hoped that such a major step, although not a panacea, will lead to more private-sector activity, competition, efficiency, and growth. The government has accepted the principle of economic disengagement. In practice, however, things may not be so simple. Success in business in Jordan should depend upon what one knows and can do—commercially, technically, and so forth—not upon who one knows in the regime. This must be the essence of economic liberalization in the country. Some believe this goal might be reached with the help of democratization.

A number of particular economic issues are obviously and directly related to the democratization process in Jordan. I have chosen a limited number to illustrate the implications of democratization for the country's political economy, although it is still very much a case of developments in the latter impinging upon the former.

Privatization

Jordan's economic policy should be one that recognizes that easy solutions that address the symptoms or parts of the problem are no solutions. More often than not, such "solutions" worsen things. Only drastic reforms can separate big problems into smaller, more manageable pieces. Privatization, to which Jordan has been committed over the past few years—although without taking any concrete measures—could be such a reform.[12]

Privatization is sometimes associated with economic liberalization, which is the bringing into play of competitive market forces. Are these, then, associated with democratization and social and political liberalization?

The respective roles of the public and private sectors in Jordan are being redefined, and an open, democratic debate can make a contribution here. Although the private sector is, of course, trying to maximize profits, the government is in charge of attaining the economic goals of the country. In order to reach these objectives through the private sector, the government must accept the profit motive as a positive element and harness it in the service of national goals. This is done by encouraging the organized and corporate forms of business activity in which profit is maximized over the unlimited life span of the corporation (thirty to fifty years, in practice). This long-term concept of profits allows for the maximization of investment, of market share (that is, by export), and of spending on productivity increases through technological research and development. When all of this is achieved, the long-run goals of business and the government become compatible, leading to a more cooperative and fruitful relationship between the public and private sectors.[13]

The government's economic role must be to restrict its spending to providing essential services such as education and health, to building and expanding the necessary infrastructure required for growth, to maintaining law and order, and to preserving national security. Beyond that, government must adopt a neutral stance economically. Achieving this impartiality would require that the government privatize many public-sector firms, operations, and activities.

To encourage the growth of private investment and enhance productivity and the quality of output, Jordan could adopt a privatization program that aims at the following:

1. To divest the public sector of all commercial activities (with a few obvious exceptions). This covers both direct ownership and legal and administrative links.
2. To end direct public-sector investment in commercial enterprises.
3. To reduce and codify regulations, making them more transparent and specific and less subject to interpretation, selectivity, and whimsical change. New regulations must be accompanied by institutionalizing effective supervision over the banking system, public shareholding companies, the accounting-auditing profession, and the Amman financial market.
4. To remove all obstacles to free competition, including the practice of giving subsidies, support, and incentives to certain enterprises and investors to the exclusion of others (regardless of the apparent merits of such actions). It must be recognized that such practices actually deter and reduce aggregate investment in the sector in which selective incentives are provided.

Privatization's most important rationale is to achieve a more efficient allocation of resources in the economy, because unlike government, private investors are unlikely to pour money into a bad investment in order to save it. At the same time, private investments are less likely to fail, because private-sector managers are more sensitive to change, demand, costs, and so forth. Moreover, a privatization program that leads to total withdrawal of government from a given sector and succeeds in convincing investors that conditions of free competition will prevail should encourage private investment.

Investment

As it helps to ensure that the Middle East peace process does not falter, Jordan faces the difficult task of keeping internal hardliners at bay. Jordan's economic hopes are riding on the peace process, but opponents of the U.S.-led effort could also discourage external investments.

One of the main problems Jordan may face in trying to assure everyone of its political stability is the presence of a vociferous group of Islamist fundamentalists in parliament. Although it serves as a reminder to the outside world of a credible opposition in an elected legislative authority, some of the positions adopted by the fundamentalist Muslim Brotherhood are hardly attractive to foreign investors. However, the country's strategic location, its basically sound infrastructure, and the relatively high level of education and expertise found among Jordanians, coupled with cheap wages, are elements that could encourage foreign investors.

Bills pending in parliament restrict foreign ownership in certain sectors while permitting total foreign ownership in others. The government has also laid some of the groundwork for foreign investment and reduced some of the bureaucracy to encourage investors. Nonetheless, against the background of the lingering Arab-Israeli conflict, it remains almost impossible to attract investors. But if the peace process flourishes, the government hopes Jordan will assume its rightful economic role. However, the vociferous fundamentalism unleashed by democratization is belligerent and xenophobic—opposed to both peace and foreign investment.

Industrial Relations

Industrial action in general and strikes in particular have traditionally been rare in Jordan. But with democratization, the picture appears to be changing. Groups that have been active recently include the electricity workers and engineers, with the former staging a sit-in in early 1992. Both appear to have obtained satisfaction.

A group currently demanding higher pay and better conditions is the general practitioners and specialists employed by the Health Ministry. Since staging a token strike in the spring of 1992, these physicians continue to complain about work overloads, low basic salaries, and few incentives. The health minister promised to study their grievances, and the issue is still pending. Meanwhile, the matter is being taken up by the press and the official media, so the doctors have received a good deal of publicity.

Consumer Activism

The doctors' plight comes at a time when hints of austerity are abundant and consumers are becoming more vocal. As one small example, the National Society for Consumer Protection (NSCP) demanded that drug prices recently fixed by the Health Ministry be respected by all wholesalers and pharmacies. The call came from the NSCP at a press conference during which the society discussed its role in providing advice to the Jordanian public on matters concerning consumption and self-protection against exploitation.

Such events, although tame by the standards of other countries, are fairly new for Jordan. The NSCP is itself a fledgling organization and is benefiting from the limited but growing media coverage being given to issues affecting consumers.

Business Lobbying

Jordan's businessmen do not lack influence, but they have usually acted very discreetly. This seems to be changing in the more democratic atmosphere now prevailing in the country. For example, in a 1991 controversy over a proposed tax, businessmen worked as a pressure group during several weeks of uproar and intense lobbying. Both businessmen and the government ultimately claimed victory. Businessmen were happy that the proposed measures to collect the tax were expected to be watered down, and the government was glad that the businessmen accepted the tax.

Nonetheless, the government was taken aback by the vehemence of the outcry. Finance Minister Basil Jardaneh, a technocrat charged since 1988 with guiding and supervising Jordan's economy, came under particular attack from the businessmen. Immediately giving assurances of his support for Jordanian industries, he met with the businessmen and managed to squeeze out an agreement. It was a face-saving measure for both sides, but it also contributed to the uneasiness of a government already under pressure.

The cabinet resigned a short time later, because of the failure of parliamentary blocs to agree on the distribution of cabinet seats, political priorities, and the peace process. A contributing factor was the pressure brought to bear upon the cabinet by businessmen over the new tax. The pressure did not cause the government's resignation, but it did help to further the cabinet's demise.

Basil Jardaneh, the man behind Jordan's economic adjustment, survived the government changes—as he did several other cabinet reshuffles and changes. With the tax controversy having abated, businessmen appear confident, given the support they enjoy in parliament, that things will go well. Business lobbying in Jordan is not new, but it has usually been conducted behind the scenes. The public process described here could not have taken place without a fair measure of democratization. How strong this trend will be, and how good it will be for the country as a whole, remains to be seen.

Corruption

Corruption in government helped spark the riots of 1989. The link between public discussion of government corruption and democracy is obvious, but many Jordanians remain reluctant to delve into allegations of wrongdoing in the public sector. Nevertheless, it is becoming acceptable to discuss corruption openly.

An example occurred recently with a court judgment against a contractor who failed to meet his obligations related to the Abu Nseir housing project. Former prime ministers and other public figures testified during the proceedings, and the possibility of corruption in the awarding of contracts was raised.

A report submitted by the attorney general after conducting probes ordered by the lower house of parliament in 1990 into a series of alleged corruption cases found that former ministers were involved. Under Jordanian law, former ministers charged with a crime can only be tried by a special court. The Abu Nseir project was among several that were investigated by the attorney general, whose report stated that there were sufficient grounds to suspect involvement of at least six former ministers in several possible cases of corruption. These included a highway project, a prison construction contract, and Ministry of Supply purchases. Other cases were dropped after the attorney general found no grounds to suspect corruption.

Regardless of the outcome of any legal action (which is, of course, important), the mere discussion of corruption in public is a new phenomenon in Jordan, one tied to the country's rising level of democratization. As in many other countries in both the North and the South, corruption in Jordan is common in the public and private sectors. Democratization has encouraged a few moves to clean up government and society, but this is obviously a long-term process.

Political and Economic Implications of the Gulf Crisis

Jordan's economic future looks bleak. In making the transition from a traditional society with an undemocratic system and an underdeveloped economy, the country may have to go through a difficult phase in order to modernize, liberalize, and develop. The false economic dawn of the late 1970s and early 1980s papered over the hard reality of inefficiency and contributed to a widening and deepening of corruption. The November 1993 elections strengthened the government's position in parliament, although Islamists continued to form the largest single parliamentary bloc. In any case, foreign political and financial support for Jordan will probably ensure the regime's survival.

Meanwhile, Jordan is plagued by nagging problems: the struggle over the nature and bounds of democracy and the role of political parties; the sense that Jordan is an incomplete entity that needs to be reunited with some larger, organic whole; and the question of what political role Jordan should play in the Palestinian conflict. The Islamists, and the Muslim Brothers in particular, are well prepared to handle the new, democratic reforms in Jordan. They are organized and positioned to pursue their policies in the spheres in which they dominate. The posts they have gained and the new freedoms they enjoy have allowed them to propagate their ideas.

The left has not surrendered to the fundamentalists but is struggling to retain its customary place in the Jordanian opposition, with a number of leftist and nationalist groups joining together in 1991 to form a coalition. Even the old elite is fighting for survival, albeit in new, democratic garb. The traditional cliques that received support on the basis of family ties and patronage in the past are also making strides to recoup their losses, even forming conservative parties as they realize that past links with the regime may not assure their future political survival.

Does the liberalization that has occurred add up to democratization? Many feel Jordan is undergoing an experiment in openness but has not yet begun serious restructuring. Certain aspects of Jordanian political life have been liberalized, but others have not.[14]

The liberalization process has proceeded at a moderate pace since mid-1989. In the interval, Jordan has tried to define the basis of pluralistic politics. The process has been peaceful, and the stability of Jordan has been maintained through the integration of diverse political forces into an organized political structure. These political forces and ideologies have seemingly reached a commitment to peaceful coexistence through the National Charter, branding as unconstitutional any attempt to impede democratic pluralism.[15] At the time of this writing, Jordan appears committed to democracy, and it will probably remain so.

Several factors support this view. The government has forbidden the dismissal of employees on the basis of political orientation, reinstated activists in their former government positions, allowed exiles to return to the country, returned confiscated passports, and permitted freedom of travel for blacklisted activists. New parties have held open political debates and congresses, and opposition journals are circulating (although some are still published abroad). The Jordanian Communist Party is no longer underground and even has a representative in parliament. However, the company that publishes the party's newspaper was threatened with closure if it printed anything that had not been approved by the intelligence service. The liberalization process is still in a precarious stage. Other factors that threaten liberalization include popular apathy, growing polarization between fundamentalists and liberals/leftists, conservative opposition, and, finally, popular suspicion about the authenticity of the regime's liberalizing commitment.

Jordan's economic crisis preceded the Gulf War of 1991, but the war severely exacerbated the situation. Economic difficulties pose the threat of social unrest. A deteriorating standard of living has left many Jordanians below the poverty line, including some who cannot afford basic human needs. The economic malaise has supplanted questions of political liberalization with concerns for issues of daily livelihood. There is a general feeling of trauma in the country and little interest in politics among some groups.

Jordan's disengagement from Palestine suffered a setback during the Gulf Crisis when thousands of Palestinians carrying Jordanian passports arrived in the country. This accounts in part for the regime's support for the peace process as a way of keeping the country's mounting economic difficulties from spilling over into Jordanian-Palestinian tensions. The government fears de facto Israeli annexation of the West Bank, to accommodate Commonwealth of Independent States (CIS) Jewish immigration, could make Jordan the dumping ground for millions of Palestinians from all over the world. A resolution of the conflict with Israel would also allow reduction of the country's defense budget (which accounts for more than 30 percent of government spending) and reconciliation with Saudi Arabia and the United States, from whom financial assistance is badly needed.

King Hussein signaled his stake in the peace process in June 1991 by replacing Prime Minister Mudar Badran with Taher Masri, a Palestinian who favors the peace process and enjoys good relations with the PLO. The king also adjourned the extraordinary session of parliament until December, after the Madrid talks. The press has shifted away from the attack mode it initially adopted toward U.S. efforts to revive the peace process. The government banned a rally organized by Islamists against the Madrid conference and seized editions of two Islamic opposition newspapers.

Politically, the Gulf Crisis strengthened the regime. In several television speeches and other direct addresses to the nation during the worst days of the crisis, the king rode a crest of popularity, and the regime recouped the losses of popularity it suffered in the late 1980s.

Economically, however, the picture is quite different. Among the adverse economic effects of the Gulf Crisis on Jordan was the sudden, massive influx of returnees. A survey conducted by the National Center for Educational Research and Development and the Department of Statistics indicates that around three hundred thousand Jordanians and Palestinians have returned, mainly from Kuwait and other Gulf countries, in addition to an estimated twenty thousand people of other nationalities.

Jordanian returnees comprise two categories: Jordanians and Palestinians living in the East Bank and Palestinians holding a Jordanian passport and living in the West Bank. A majority of the Jordanian-Palestinian community in the Gulf states originated in the West Bank, but many in this category are barred from returning to that area by Israeli restrictions. The 300,000 returnees form a total labor force of 70,500, representing 9.5 percent of the population in 1991.[16]

Jordan faces a number of obstacles relating to the absorption of these returnees. Economic problems and shortages have meant that the country is experiencing difficulty in coping with the large number of people now needing homes and jobs and also in dealing with the new structure of society. Such problems further increase the pressure on Jordan's fragile economy. The huge influx of people has forced unemployment and inflation upward, and water and social services are also being used to full capacity. Lacking adequate aid, the government can do little to offer relief or job opportunities to the returnees, large numbers of whom are both professional and skilled.

Nonetheless, various measures have been taken to cope with the returnees' immediate needs and the adverse economic effects created by their presence. Government schools now operate on a double-shift basis, and water rationing has been implemented to guarantee a constant minimal distribution. The government recently announced a long-term repayment plan allowing returnees possessing non-Jordanian vehicles to pay customs duty over a period of four years. In addition, the government has increased its expenditures for public amenities and services. Despite belt tightening in some areas and increased efforts to maximize government revenues, gains made prior to the Gulf Crisis in reducing the government deficit have ceased or even been reversed. Thus, the government has undertaken measures designed to encourage the inflow of capital, both Jordanian and non-Jordanian, from both private and official sources.

According to the latest reports of the UN Economic and Social Commission for West Asia (ESCWA), the total costs of absorbing returnees will reach over $3.1 billion for the period 1992 to 1994. Such a financial burden is clearly beyond Jordan's limited resources.

In addition, despite an initially positive contribution to the balance of payments stemming from capital brought home by returnees, the medium-term impact is negative. ESCWA estimates that between 1992 and 1994, imports will increase by $570 million and remittances will fall by $825 million, due to the return of the expatriate workers. The need for external aid from major donor countries and regional and international organizations is very clear, but amounts already received appear to be less than the country needs.[17]

Conclusion

Jordan's experiment with democracy has left many savoring a taste of political freedom but frustrated by the slow pace of reform. What happened in Jordan is more of a political "openness" than anything else. The country still has much to do before it can call itself a democracy.[18] Citizens of this conservative Arab state say they have yet to reap many of the benefits associated with democratic reform. "Unfortunately, democracy has improved neither our economy nor our living standards" is a familiar lament in Jordan today.

The government—concerned by the example of unrest in Algeria, where 1992 elections were suspended after Muslim fundamentalists nearly won power—has proceeded cautiously with reforms. The king continues to hold constitutional powers, such as the ability to name and dissolve governments, dissolve parliament, and block new laws. Some conservatives in the security forces and among tribal leaders continue to resist changes that might undermine their privileges.

Parties more liberal than the Muslim Brotherhood, including a left weakened by the fall of Soviet power, have not been sufficiently organized to help democracy take root. Torn by personal rivalries and unable to offer practical programs, they lack the expertise and financial resources to become significant forces, at least to this point.

Many expect the Muslim Brotherhood to continue to gain popularity in the future. This may well be the case if the economy does not improve, if Arab-Israeli talks stall, and if other parties fail to grow. Much will depend on whether secular democratic forces develop the skills, programs, and resources required to appeal to the broader public.

Although Jordan's political reforms may seem limited by Western standards, Jordanians correctly judge them to be highly significant in a kingdom that has had thirty-five years of near-absolute rule—and in a region dominated by one-party states. Indeed, some argue that what has happened in Jordan over the past three years could be a model for democracy in the region. Regardless of whether this is true, it is striking that Jordan started the democratization process and is continuing it against a hostile social, economic, and political background. Some observers, however, fear the growing gap between Jordan's rich and poor may spark destructive tensions as the kingdom adheres to a stringent economic reform program.

A major alternative facing Jordan is a continuing effort to liberalize its economy. As indicated early in this chapter, a large body of theoretical literature also claims that the market is the only economic system that can preserve individual freedom. However, this claim is not as easy to evaluate as some would like to think. There is a serious problem in deciding what sort of freedom we are talking about. Different people have different conceptions of freedom.[19]

This is particularly true of Jordan's Islamists. The Brotherhood has been accused of using democracy as a tactic to monopolize power in order to undermine the democratic process. Some have sought to make a comparison with Algeria's fundamentalist phenomenon.[20]

Ultimate political power still rests solidly with the throne, and King

Hussein is willing and able to exert his authority. This has led many to perceive no real change in Jordan's political institutions and internal balance of forces. Some feel Jordan is a decorative and superficial democracy in which the reality of the people's situation has not changed; the power centers that administer and run the country still exist.[21]

Meanwhile, the economic crisis threatens to get worse. Can the regime maintain stability and a minimum standard of living for the country's poorer classes? Without outside help, the answer is no. But such help has always been forthcoming, and there are no signs of a major change in the present phase of the New World Order. Despite the need for drastic reform in the economic system, the situation may limp along in essentially its present form, with the regime performing the political and diplomatic balancing act that has become its trademark. This prospect will not likely be seriously undermined by economic troubles if a peace conference and other tension-reducing arrangements bring about major regional change in the near future. Otherwise, Jordan will suffer from the pressure of its own citizenry and from correspondingly heightened prospects for unfruitful instability.

Notes

1. Geoff Hodgson, *The Democratic Economy* (Harmondsworth: Penguin, 1984), p. 5.

2. Ibid. See also N. Frohlich and J. Oppenheimer, *Modern Political Economy* (New York: Prentice Hall, 1978); and Anthony Downs, *An Economic Theory of Democracy* (New York: Harper Collins, 1965).

3. Hodgson, *Democratic Economy,* p. 5.

4. Ibid.

5. Although see Asaf Bayat, "Free Market and Democracy in the Third World," *Civil Society* (April 1992), pp. 4–6.

6. Milton Friedman, *Capitalism and Freedom* (Chicago: University of Chicago Press, 1962), p. 8.

7. Ibid., p. 9.

8. Ibid., p. 15.

9. As'ad Abdul-Rahman and Riad Al-Khouri, "The Meaning of the Intifada for Jordan," in M. Hudson (ed.), *The Palestinians: New Directions* (Washington, D.C.: Center for Contemporary Arab Studies, 1990).

10. Abla Amawi, "Democracy in Jordan," *Middle East Report* 22 (January/February 1992), pp. 26–27.

11. Ibid., p. 29.

12. Jawad Anani, and Rima Khalaf, "Privatization in Jordan," in Said Naggar (ed.), *Privatization and Structural Adjustment in the Arab Countries* (Washington, D.C.: International Monetary Fund, 1989), pp. 210–225.

13. Interview with Safwan Bataineh, economic adviser to the Jordanian prime minister, in *Economic Perspectives,* April 16, 1992, p. 3. This interview, and similar remarks by government spokesmen, are signs of the government's direction on

this issue—and represent an important departure from the previous low profile adopted by some officials on economic matters.

14. Amawi, "Democracy in Jordan," p. 26.

15. The initiative for this change came from the regime. The king formed a sixty-member Royal Commission in April 1990 to draft a National Charter that would regulate political life, allow for the return of political parties, and be a common denominator among the various parties and ideologies. The king emphasized that only "national" parties would be tolerated. The way in which "national" is interpreted will hold importance for the new parties.

16. Lina Arafat, "Influx of Returnees Leads to Shift in Jordan's Economy," *Star* (Amman), March 31, 1992, p. 3.

17. Ibid.

18. See, for example, Kamel S. Abu Jaber, "The Hashemite Kingdom of Jordan," in Tareq Y. Ismael and Jacqueline S. Ismael (eds.), *Politics and Government in the Middle East and North Africa* (Miami: Florida International University Press, 1991), pp. 247–248. The author states that Jordan's liberal atmosphere "is not based on established rights and can be ended by the regime at will." The fact that this was probably written before the creation of the National Charter (as well as before Dr. Abu Jaber's appointment as foreign minister) does not change things, in my opinion. In any case, I have been unable to reach him for comment.

19. Charles Dyke, *Philosophy of Economics* (New York: Prentice Hall, 1981), p. 117.

20. See, for example, Lamis Adoni, "The Dilemma for Jordan," *Middle East International,* January 24, 1992, pp. 6–7.

21. Amawi, "Democracy in Jordan."

Part 3
Political Issues in
the Arab World

9

The Gulf War: A Defining Event?

ADEED DAWISHA

Before the first bombs fell on Baghdad on January 17, 1991, many people around the world simply did not believe war would occur. In retrospect, we might consider that view to have been merely wishful thinking, but at the time the belief was rooted in recognition (and fear) of the immense human and material losses war would bring. And indeed, when the bombs finally stopped raining down on Iraq, when people could assess the damage, there was little doubt that the Gulf War would be etched in memory as a major historical event.

Beyond its gruesome consequences, so visible in Iraq, the war was widely expected to have political consequences that would transform the political and ideological nature of the Arab world. That the Gulf War was a major historical event is undeniable. But many continue to wonder whether it will go down in Arab historiography as a *defining event,* in the sense of bringing about fundamental change in the region.

Two events in contemporary Arab history can be considered defining events: the Suez Crisis of 1956 and the June 1967 Arab-Israeli War. In this chapter I analyze the profound, sometimes traumatic, political and ideological changes brought about by these two events and how the changes they generated affected not just one or two states but the entire Arab political order. The focus then shifts to the post–Gulf War Arab environment in an effort to discover whether any such consequential changes have occurred, or are likely to occur, as a result of the Gulf Crisis.

The 1956 Suez Victory

Before the Suez Crisis, the Arab world constituted a system of sovereign states that espoused close political and economic ties with the West. The perceived victory of Egypt, under Gamal Abd al-Nasser, over Britain and France at Suez would radically alter the prevailing ideology and political arrangements of the Arab world. This victory ushered in the ideology of pan-Arabism, which contemptuously dismissed state sovereignty as a shameful residue of colonial perfidy, preaching instead the organic unity of all Arabs as the only way to confront the West's political and cultural domination.

Admittedly, it was fairly easy to attack the notion of the "state." After all, the contemporary Arab state did not appear on the global political map until well after World War I. In the 1920s and 1930s, only a handful of sovereign Arab states existed. Other Arab lands became states only after World War II, and some did not acquire sovereignty until well into the 1960s and 1970s.

Nor did these states enjoy the kind of political legitimacy that is born of political consensus. In fact, many Arabs fervently believed these states were carved out of the old possessions of the Ottoman Empire by Britain and France simply to serve the interests of the two colonial powers. In general, then, the Arab state was not only new, but also lacked legitimacy. Thus, the state remained a troubled creation, and people tended to identify far more readily with their clans, villages, and towns.

Yet, wherever they came from and whatever their backgrounds, the vast majority of these people spoke the same language and identified with a larger, more encompassing culture. They knew that whatever else they might be, that whatever sect or clan they might belong to, they were ultimately Arabs—speaking Arabic and sharing a historical experience that can be traced back fourteen centuries to the Arab-Islamic civilization that dominated the entire region after the seventh century.[1]

Nasser's victory at Suez in a sense encapsulated what the peoples of the various Arab countries had subconsciously come to recognize each time they contrasted their own situation with that of the West. When they saw how much they lagged behind, how far they needed to go to catch up, the Arabs concluded that hopes of deliverance should not be entrusted to the state—a weak entity, lacking legitimacy and universally perceived as a Western creation—but rather to their unity as one people and one culture. For their emancipation from Western dominance, they needed to look to their roots, to their history, to the time when the Arabs—under the banner of Islam—overcame tribal rivalries and became a force that created an empire and a civilization that marked the pinnacle of Arab endeavor.

Most Arabs have tended to perceive the 1956 Suez War as the moment when they were finally able to rise against the order that had been imposed by colonial and imperialist Europe. This rebellion, spearheaded by Egypt under the charismatic leadership of Gamal Abd al-Nasser, was conducted not through the mechanisms of the Arab states but rather through revolutionary Arab nationalism—the ideological foundation of pan-Arabism. The victory of Nasser and of revolutionary Arab nationalism at Suez not only led directly to the amalgamation of Syria and Egypt into the United Arab Republic in March 1958 but also, in July of that same year, led to the demise of the strongly pro-Western Iraqi monarchy. Had it not been for U.S. and British interventions, Lebanon and Jordan would also have suffered Iraq's fate. By the late 1950s, the revolutionary pan-Arabist creed seemed to permeate all levels of Arab society, breaking all notions of the sovereignty of states. Egypt and Nasser even devised a "theory" to rationalize and legitimize the constant intrusion of Egypt's revolutionary ideology into the affairs of other, considerably weakened Arab states. The theory of "state and revolution" drew a distinction between political and revolutionary entities; between "Egypt as a state and [as] a revolution. . . . If as a state Egypt recognizes boundaries in its dealings with governments, Egypt as a revolution should never hesitate or halt before these boundaries but should carry its message beyond the borders to the people in order to initiate the revolutionary mission."[2]

It should now be clear that along with weakening the concept of the state, the 1956 Suez War transformed the Arab world's foreign relations from a pro-Western to an anti-Western stand. In the post-1956 period, anti-Westernism became almost synonymous with nationalism and pan-Arabism. The ideological environment was such that many Arabs believed they were destined to be united into one powerful political unit that would confront, and eventually defeat, the West.

The June 1967 Defeat

Pan-Arabism and Nasser, the main purveyor of its revolutionary creed, met their waterloo in the Arab-Israeli War of 1967. After only six days of fighting, the Arabs suffered the most humiliating defeat in their contemporary history.

The result was clear. On the issue of Palestine, the pivotal concern of Arab nationalism, pan-Arabists had failed ignominiously—and with that failure sank the hopes and aspirations of the nationalist generation. After more than a decade of nationalist rhetoric and revolutionary politics, the Arabs were summarily—and seemingly effortlessly—defeated by Israel, the country pan-Arabists had labeled "the illegitimate creation of Western imperialism."

There is little doubt that the June War was a watershed for revolutionary pan-Arabism. In the shocked aftermath, the Arab world was to undergo another ideological transformation. Popular acceptance of the theory of "state and revolution" diminished swiftly and markedly, because the war was a dramatic exhibition of the bankruptcy of the tenets of the Arab revolution proclaimed by Nasser. Many began to argue that a revolution—with all the weight of its ideals, with all the moral and material resources it absorbed—was perhaps too heavy an albatross for a state to carry. Their conclusion was that Egypt and the Arab world might have been better served had Egypt's radically nationalist leaders devoted more resources to the home front and less to the heralded pan-Arabist, anti-Western revolutionary march.

Just as crucial to the change in Arab attitudes was Egypt's sudden adoption of a policy of coexistence with the other Arab states. Due to the disastrous economic impact of the war, Egypt quickly became dependent upon financial assistance from the oil-rich, but conservative and pro-Western, Arab states—the very states against which Nasser's pan-Arabist crusade was primarily directed. It was only natural that once pan-Arabism's high priest was forced to abandon his revolutionary policies, the flock would follow and begin to see the role of the state in a more traditional sense.

The June War ended the notion of the dual roles of "state" and "revolution." Instead, a growing rift developed between states and revolutionary movements, with states exhibiting increasing confidence in their impregnability, their raison d'etre, and their coercive ability to take on revolutionary movements—whether secular or religious. In contrast to the pan-Arabist period brought about by the Suez Crisis, the prevailing ideology of the 1970s and 1980s therefore became statecentric.

The resilience of the state in the post-1967 period was helped by the effect of time. The Arab state of the 1970s and 1980s was no longer a new political phenomenon, as it had been in the 1950s. Some of the more established Arab states—such as Egypt, Iraq, Saudi Arabia, and Oman—had been sovereign since the 1920s and before; others—such as Syria, Jordan, and Lebanon—had been independent since the end of World War II. In most Arab countries, newer generations had known nothing but the state in which they resided—the state that provided them with services, collected taxes, and maintained law and order.

Moreover, the attitudes of these generations had been molded by educational systems that constantly emphasized the centrality of the state, its sovereignty and legitimacy. To put it differently, the imagery and symbolism that were fed into people's minds during their most formative years and that ultimately defined political attitudes were skewed heavily in favor of the state. Furthermore, because of the state's dominance over economic and social issues and its power to offer economic and financial opportunities, the interests of an important and ever-growing segment of the population—the middle class—had been symbiotically tied to the survival of the state.

In short, the disillusionment with revolutionary pan-Arabism generated by the June War was buttressed by natural historical developments. The result was the creation of a prevailing ideology whose central feature upheld the state.

The state itself helped this process. First, state authorities became adept at effectively using internal security mechanisms to combat potentially disruptive forces. Second, state authorities were able to control other aspects of individuals' lives through a variety of means. Thus, the media in Arab countries, and therefore the dissemination of information, was—and continues to be—an easy and frequent target of state manipulation. Even in the less conservative Arab states, the press operates within strictly circumscribed parameters that it transgresses at its peril. Radio and television essentially tend to be government-owned and government-operated. Such pervasive dominance over information and ideas allows the state to interfere vigorously with what people know and to shape political and social aspirations.

Governments also developed other methods to safeguard the state's sovereignty and unity. One was the practice of co-opting potentially destabilizing forces. For instance, in an environment in which Islam permeates people's lives, a number of Arab states endeavored to use religious institutions and symbolism in the interest of state authority. By means of preemptive action, the authorities would assume the role of the authentic guardian of Islam, thereby acquiring an important source of legitimacy and allowing the state greater leverage to combat dissident Islamic groups as well as other subversive forces.

A related method was the absorption of a large segment of the population into the state's administrative structure in order to heighten people's dependence on the state for their livelihood. Thus, the creation of government jobs in Arab countries almost became an objective in its own right.[3]

A further essential aspect of the changing ideological climate of the 1970s and 1980s was a shift in the dominant economic philosophy. This resulted in economic systems that bear little resemblance to the strident socialist ideals that accompanied the pan-Arabist tide of the 1950s and 1960s. Even the socialists of today are socialist more in name than in deed. The change occurred not only because of enthusiastic support from a public frustrated by years of fruitless socialist austerity but also because socialism was a constituent element of the ideology whose bankruptcy was epitomized by the 1967 disaster.

The June War was indeed a defining event. The transformation of the prevailing ideology would have been complete had it not been for one variable of political power that remained obstinately constant: the persistence of centralized political structures. Authoritarian rule, most commonly exercised by a single leader, continued to be the major characteristic of Arab political systems during the 1970s and 1980s, just as it had been in the 1950s and 1960s.

The Gulf War: The Next Defining Event?

For the Gulf War to be characterized as a defining event, it must be shown to have provoked a fundamental transformation of the Arab world's prevailing ideology. Abd al-Nasser and his followers blamed the 1956 Suez War on the conservative, pro-Western ideology of Arab states, and consequently the Suez Crisis ushered in the revolutionary pan-Arabism, which in turn was discredited by the June War of 1967. In the 1970s and 1980s, the state became the focus of the Arab ideological environment: *Al-wataniya* gradually superseded *al-qawmiya.*

Fundamental political and ideological transformations do not occur overnight. Sometimes, only in retrospect—years later—can the analyst detect the kind of change that establishes the existence of a defining event. Great caution must therefore be exercised in making judgments about an event that occurred in the recent past. In examining the effects of the Gulf War, we must recognize that beneath the veneer of political stability may lurk the kind of social turmoil that may lead to future ideological and political transformations. The most that can be done at this stage, therefore, is to look at existing political arrangements and conditions and then endeavor to make probabilistic prognostications about the choices and alternatives that may lie ahead.

Nearly three years after the carnage ended, the Gulf War appears to have brought few substantive changes to the Arab world. Because generic statements tend to have one specific exception, some might argue Iraq stands as such an example. And indeed, few countries in modern history (Germany and Japan come to mind) have undergone the kind of devastation that Iraq suffered at the hands of the U.S.-led international coalition in the winter of 1991. Iraq was left economically in shambles, with its agricultural and industrial infrastructures severely damaged. Its domestic political environment was nearly as bad. A Kurdish insurrection in the north of the country, aided by the United States and its allies, eventually established a virtually autonomous region outside the central government's control. In the south, Shi'ite rebels, supported by Iran, continued to deplete the government's preciously few available resources. Government retaliation, at times brutal and indiscriminate, led to an allied decision to institute a No-Fly Zone over much of southern Iraq. Baghdad was warned that any Iraqi fixed-wing or rotary aircraft flying south of the 32d parallel would be shot down. Thus, by the end of 1992, Baghdad exercised complete sovereignty over only the area south of the 36th parallel and north of the 32d parallel. This was perhaps the starkest and most dramatic illustration of how the international community consistently treated Iraq's sovereignty with the utmost contempt. These were immense economic and political setbacks for a country that before the war had proclaimed itself victorious in its conflict with Iran, had swiftly revived its economy, and had made a bold bid for the leadership of the Arab world.

But the question here is not whether structural change occurred; it is whether this change was accompanied by a perceptible transformation of the country's ideological orientation and its political dynamics. Three years after the war, no such transformation had taken place. Iraq remained as rigidly authoritarian as it had been before the Gulf War, led by a man whose humiliating defeat seemed to have no impact on his political control, which continued to be exercised through coercion and a pliant mobilization party.

It is true that immediately after the war, Saddam Hussein's personality cult appeared to have been severely (some, including the U.S. government, hoped irreparably) damaged. His public appearances decreased markedly in number, and, apparently under pressure from reform-minded members of the political elite, he promised to build a democratic society based on party pluralism. This, he announced, was an "irrevocable and final decision."[4]

He then appointed Saadoun Hamadi, a Shiite and moderate Baathist, as prime minister. Hamadi was to head a cabinet of technocrats whose primary goal was to institute political and economic reform. Hamadi promised early elections and caused a stir when he said that Saddam Hussein's political fate would be determined by the electoral process.

Six months later, however, Hamadi was abruptly dismissed. All talk of elections and of Saddam Hussein's political fate immediately ceased. It was soon announced that political reforms would be postponed indefinitely. As though nothing of note—neither war nor defeat—had occurred, Iraq's political system returned to the procrustean, personalized rigidity of pre–Gulf War days.

On the inter-Arab level, old groupings did give way to new alliances in the wake of the Gulf War. The Arab Cooperation Council—consisting of Egypt, Iraq, Jordan, and Yemen—was touted before the war as a new, moderate alliance to balance the radical Arab camp headed by Syria. Yet, during the Gulf War, Egyptian and Syrian military forces worked together to drive the Iraqis from Kuwait. Indeed, in the immediate aftermath of the war, Syria—which had become a close ally of Egypt—was perceived as moving toward the pro-West camp and in the direction of moderation. Jordan, long favored by the West as a staunch ally, was treated coolly because of its friendly disposition toward Iraq, the new pariah in the Middle East state system.

The problem with these shifting alliances is that they occurred because of political and tactical considerations rather than because of a fundamental change in the prevailing ideology. The intense antipathy between Iraq's Saddam Hussein and Syria's Hafez al-Asad was undoubtedly a pivotal factor in the decision of radical "anti-Western" Syria to join the Western alliance against Iraq. Similarly, the promise of substantial Western help in addressing Egypt's severe economic woes could only have had a major impact on President Mubarak's decision to lead the Arab anti-Iraq front.

The changes in alliances notwithstanding, what has been most striking is the degree of political constancy and ideological continuity in most Arab countries. Two years after the 1956 Suez Crisis, an ideological revolution had already begun. Syria had united with Egypt to form the first United Arab Republic under the leadership of the fiercely nationalist Gamal Abd al-Nasser. Iraq's pro-Western government had fallen to revolutionary Arab nationalism, and only the introduction of British and U.S. forces saved the governments of Lebanon and Jordan from similar fates. Two years after Suez, a major transformation in the Arab world's prevailing ideology was clearly in process.

Similarly, it was apparent by 1969 that the 1967 June War had signaled the end of the Arab revolutionary tide. Because they were able to bankroll the badly damaged economy of Nasser's Egypt, Saudi Arabia and the oil-rich Gulf sheikhdoms—all conservative states virulently opposed to the notion of pan-Arabism—emerged after the June War as the key power brokers of the Arab world. These states led the counteroffensive against pan-Arabism and toward a statecentric ideology. By 1969, even the high priests of revolutionary pan-Arabism were talking less about revolution and more about cooperation among sovereign Arab states. And the only vigorously revolutionary movement of the time was no longer coy about conducting its war of liberation under the banner of Palestinian, rather than Arab, nationalism.

Yet, three years after the Gulf War—one of the most traumatic events in contemporary Arab history—Arab states have remained structurally intact and shown themselves to be ideologically resistant to transnational revolutionary forces, be they secular or Islamic. Consider, for example, the Arab alliances during the Gulf Crisis. It was deemed unthinkable before the war that Egyptian, Syrian, or Saudi soldiers would, as overt Western allies, go into combat against an Iraqi soldier—a "brother Arab." Experts warned Arab leaders that such an event would be deemed blatantly "un-Arab," transgressing a cardinal rule of the inter-Arab system. Many feared the inevitable wrath of the Arab people and predicted that popular explosions would shake the very foundations of the Arab states and of the inter-Arab state system. Yet, in the end, Arab did fight Arab, and an Arab country was devasted by the international coalition's firepower.

The few demonstrations that occurred in some Arab capitals hardly constituted the popular revolutionary onslaught many had foreseen. Three years after the war, the Arab regimes were as eager as ever to preserve the inter-Arab state system.

By then, this determination even extended to attitudes toward Iraq. In the immediate aftermath of the war, many Arab leaders publicly called for Saddam Hussein's forcible removal from power. However, as time passed, and as Saddam Hussein not only remained in office but was clearly gaining power and control in Iraq, the attitudes of the Arab regimes began to shift. They were beginning to weigh their distaste for Hussein and their fear of his irredentism against the probability of widespread chaos that might accompany his elimination from the political scene.

Of utmost concern to the Arab regimes was the possible balkanization of Iraq: the country's division along ethnic and sectarian lines into three new entities. Much publicity was given to the Arab regimes' expressed concern for the well-being of the Iraqi people, but their unspoken concern was over the health of the inter-Arab, statecentric regional system. The Arab regimes could clearly see that the balkanization of Iraq might have serious spillover effects on other states in the area, which—not unlike Iraq—suffered from ethnic and sectarian divisions, socioeconomic disparities, and dormant, yet volatile, political frustrations. Two years after the war, many Arab states had begun to retreat significantly from their earlier strident calls for Saddam's removal. The preservation of the state system was far more important than the removal of the irritating leader of one of its members.

In contrast, then, to the two earlier defining events in contemporary Arab history, three years after the Gulf War the prevailing inter-Arab ideology of state centrality still seemed very much intact. Nor had there been much change in the prevailing ideology *within* Arab states, which remained clearly authoritarian. Indeed, in the aftermath of the war, once the dust had settled it was business as usual in the Arab states. Some regimes might have been considered winners and others labeled losers, but all were back in business, contemptuous of true internal change and dismissive of meaningful domestic reform.

Admittedly, a few Arab states—notably Egypt, Jordan, and probably Yemen and Morocco—have begun to liberalize their political structures, thereby lessening the burdens of authoritarianism borne by their populations.[5] But even in these cases, the state continues to exercise inordinate control over the individuals' political preferences and orientations. In short, since the end of the Gulf War, no perceptible change has occurred in the prevailing ideology at the level of intra-Arab or inter-Arab politics.

The obvious conclusion, therefore, is that the Gulf War cannot be called a defining event, at least not yet. But as noted earlier, such fundamental and far-reaching changes hardly happen overnight. It may be that a shift in the prevailing ideology will only be detected with the passage of time.

Notwithstanding the resilience of the statecentric ideology, it is worthwhile to chart the most likely possible paths fundamental change may take in the future. Present indications suggest that should a basic change in the Arab world's prevailing ideology occur, it would probably follow one of two possible roads: the road to democracy or the road to militant Islam.

There is a true yearning for democracy in the Arab world today. The victory of Abd al-Nasser over the old colonialists at Suez in 1956 did legitimize a political order that emphasized charismatic leadership and mobilizational one-party systems. Proponents of the post-Suez order did argue that the daunting tasks of national development and defense against imperialism rendered unnecessary—and indeed harmful—the endless political debates so characteristic of pluralist societies.

But Arabs were forced to learn painful lessons following the June War, lessons that were significantly sharpened by the Gulf War disaster. It became progressively clear that all the one-party mobilization systems seemed to produce was not the promised unity of spirit that would drive away the imperialists but the spiritual bankruptcy embodied by an institutionalized system of graft, nepotism, and corruption.

Perhaps the most valuable lesson was provided by the Gulf War itself. Even neutral observers had argued in the 1970s and 1980s that Saddam Hussein—despite his heavy-handed authoritarianism—was doing much good for Iraq. In contrast to other oil-producing states in the area, Hussein's government used much of the massive oil returns to finance a socioeconomic policy geared toward bridging the gap between the rich and the poor in Iraq. Numerous economic and social programs—such as social security systems, pension plans, minimum wage levels, and free health and education—were implemented in order to bring the excluded and disenfranchised into the mainstream of Iraqi society.

The Gulf War proved unequivocally that no matter how much authoritarian leaders may accomplish, they are liable eventually to lead their people to catastrophe. Functioning virtually by definition within institutional structures that require people to idolize and lionize their governments as all-knowing, authoritarian leaders become accustomed to listen to little more than their own intuition. Can any other conclusion be drawn from Saddam Hussein's disastrously idiosyncratic conduct of his country's foreign policy between August 1990 and March 1991? The conclusion facing the Arabs is, therefore, that there is no substitute for argument and debate, for the existence of an opposing view.

The yearning for democracy in the aftermath of the Gulf War, especially among the rapidly expanding middle classes, is genuine. However, the path to real democracy continues in most cases to be blocked by rulers who, accustomed as they are to absolute power, have tended to characterize opposition as subversive. Even in Arab states in which a measure of liberalization has been allowed, rulers continue to exercise a disproportionate amount of control over the political process. The consequence is either a complete absence of organized political parties or, where parties do operate, the existence of an ineffectual opposition that is prevented by a pervasive and highly intrusive internal security apparatus from having much impact on the public.

The militant Islamist opposition, however, is the exception. Despite government intimidation and harassment, Islamists are in a better position to organize than are other, mostly secular opposition groups. Their advantage in this respect arises from the ability to spread their message through thousands of mosques and attendant religious and social networks that tend to lie virtually outside of government control.

The Gulf War was a godsend to the Islamists. First, the massive defeat of the secular Saddam Hussein and his Baath Party was used by Islamists as a generic illustration of the sort of disasters that befall ungodly rulers espousing secularism. They were also able to lambaste other Arab leaders for allying themselves with latter-day crusaders in the destruction of an Arab Muslim country. The Gulf War undoubtedly contributed immensely to the prestige of the Islamists and to the potency of their message.

Were the Gulf War's ultimate effect be to open the way for Islamists to dictate a new prevailing ideology in the Arab world, the area would, in a sense, return to a political environment similar to that which existed in the pre-1967 period. That is, the region would again come under the full sway of authoritarian leaderships espousing a universalist ideology, but this time the ideology would be Islam rather than pan-Arabism.

The constant factor here is authoritarianism. We must admit that some Islamist leaders have committed themselves to democracy. However, it is equally true that they tend, as Mustapha El-Sayyid notes, "to use the word democracy to mean something entirely different from what Thomas Jefferson had in mind. . . . Islamists regard an Islamic political order as the ideal, arguing that is unnecessary to borrow institutions or techniques of government from the West."[6]

Regardless of their pronouncements on democracy, most of the present Islamist leaders draw intellectual and doctrinal sustenance from the writing of Sayyid Qutb, a major theoretician of the Muslim Brotherhood who was executed by the Nasser regime in 1966. Qutb strongly objected to the notion of popular sovereignty, condemning it as a form of tyranny because it usurped the sovereignty of God. To Qutb, therefore, the only solution was "to restore the supremacy of divine command."[7] A realistic assessment of today's Islamist groups suggests that this notion of governance, or at least some derivation of it, would be implemented if these groups were to come to power.

Nearly three years after the Gulf War, the Arab world's prevailing ideology has not undergone any observable change. As stated above, we can therefore argue that the Gulf War cannot be characterized as a defining event. But this conclusion must be tempered by noting that widespread socioeconomic disparities, graft and corruption in high places, pervasive political malaise, and the gap between rulers and ruled (which is constantly widened by repressive security machines) are all destabilizing agents lurking under the sometimes thin veneer of stability and normalcy. If the Gulf War has had any potentially long-term impact, it is that it has sharpened the forces of destabilization and made the general malaise more acute.

A change in the prevailing ideology could still occur. It is impossible to predict which path such change might take, but unless secular democrats are allowed to organize, develop coherent socioeconomic programs, and take their message unhindered to the people, the next prevailing ideology in the Arab world will—when and if it arrives—probably belong to militant Islamists.

Notes

1. For a sense of this historical and cultural unity, see Albert Hourani, *A History of the Arab Peoples* (New York: Warner Books, 1991).
2. *Al-Ahram,* December 29, 1962.
3. For more detailed accounts of the methods used by Arab states to bolster their stability and resilience, see Adeed Dawisha and I. William Zartman, eds., *Beyond Coercion: The Durability of the Arab State* (London: Croom Helm, 1988).
4. Quoted in Ahmed Hashim, "Iraq: The Pariah State," *Current History* 91: 561 (January 1992), p. 15.
5. For more on contemporary efforts at political liberalization in the Arab world, see Michael C. Hudson, "After the Gulf War: Prospects for Democratization in the Arab World," *Middle East Journal* 45 (Summer 1991), p. 411.
6. Mustapha K. al-Sayyid, "Slow Thaw in the Arab World," *World Policy Journal* (Fall 1991), pp. 722–723.
7. John L. Esposito and James P. Piscatori, "Democratization and Islam," *Middle East Journal* 45 (Summer 1991), p. 435.

10

Redefining the Arab and Arabism in the Aftermath of the Gulf Crisis

BASSAM TIBI ⸺⸺⸺⸺⸺⸺⸺⸺⸺⸺⸺⸺⸺⸺⸺

With the creation of the Arab state system after the decolonization of Arab lands, the rhetoric of Arab unity became the prevailing pretension within inter-Arab politics. However, Arab politics has consistently been characterized more by divisive coalitions than by true integration.[1]

Prior to the Gulf Crisis, the basic belief underlying pan-Arab rhetoric was that all Arabs share everything on all levels and therefore need to be unified under one, centrally governed nation-state. The fact that Arab unity remained a dream rather than a reality was attributed to external conspiracies. The prominent Baathi politician Saadoun Hamadi offered this typical view: "In the Arab homeland there exists no movement that suffers from the hostility of Western imperialism more than Arabism does. The reason . . . is that the West is aware of the consequences that may result for its presence in the area if a mighty pan-Arab state could be built up."[2]

Although Hamadi and other pan-Arabist spokesmen also blamed Arabs themselves for the absence of this "mighty Arab state," the notion of external *mu'amarah* (conspiracy) remained central. In the text of his declaration annexing Kuwait, Saddam Hussein charged that the West's "major crime" against the Arabs was the division of their lands and claimed that the region was "one entity when it was ruled by Baghdad."[3] Although the confusion of the Ottoman Empire with the Abbaside Caliphate in this statement is striking, the notion of a sinister *mu'amarah* and the perception of threat related to it are the salient features of this example of pan-Arab rhetoric.

For too long, Arab political discourse discouraged serious questioning of the major underlying premises of the idea of a united Arab state. Critical thinking was seen as playing into the hands of foreign conspiracies. The Gulf Crisis, ignited by an invasion of one sovereign Arab state by another, rather than by a foreign power, has changed this. Moreover, efforts to deal with the conflict on a regional level—that is, within the framework of a *hall 'Arabi* (Arab solution)—conclusively established the lack of an Arab institutional framework for conflict resolution. The fact that the Arab state system disposes of a regional organization—the Arab League—only emphasizes the point. That organization lacks the institutions and related mechanisms of collective policymaking needed for regional conflict resolution.[4]

European integration provides a model from which the Arabs could benefit in their obviously needed efforts to redefine Arabism in the aftermath of the Gulf Crisis. My argument is based upon the supposition that had the Arab League been institutionally of the same caliber as the European Community, the conflict between Iraq and Kuwait would not have occurred, let alone the repercussions that sprang from the failure to resolve the conflict on regional grounds.[5]

We must note that the concept of Arabism that prevailed until the Gulf Crisis was related to the ideology and rhetoric of pan-Arab nationalism but not to an existing citizenship pattern nor to a model of integration of regional states. Pan-Arab ideology is directed against the extant institution of the nation-state in the Arab world. In the language of pan-Arab ideology, existing Arab states are not described and accepted as nation-states. They have been downgraded and labeled as *al-dawla al-qitriyya* (the domestic state).[6] The term *Arab nation-state—al-dawla al-qawmiyya*—is reserved for the desired pan-Arab state, whose realization, it is argued, remains frustrated by alleged Western conspiracies.

Thus, pan-Arab ideology, even though it negates the existing Arab nation-states, is imprisoned within the nation-state idea. It aspires to a larger pan-Arab state uniting all Arabs. It is significant that although harmony and brotherhood have been the central themes of pan-Arab ideology, real interstate Arab politics, as with any other politics, has been characterized by conflict.

The difference between Arabs and Europeans, whose experiences are compared later in this chapter, has not been one between harmony and a conflict-ridden group of states. Rather, it has been a difference between European states, equipped with collective mechanisms of conflict resolution and a realistic concept of "Europeness," and an Arab world blinded by ideological formulas such as "brotherhood" and "pan-Arab harmony."

To put it bluntly, one of the lessons of the Gulf Crisis ought to be that "Arabness" should be defined in policy-oriented, rather than ideologically oriented, terms. As already noted, in pan-Arab ideology the existing nation-states were denounced as *al-dawla al-qitriyya,* a form of organization standing in the way of *al-dawla al-qawmiyya,* the pan-Arab state. In fact, with the exception of Egypt and Morocco, all existing Arab states can be described as nominal nation-states. They lack the substance of the nation-state institution first developed in Europe and then, in the course of globalization, adopted by the entire world.[7] Nevertheless, existing Arab nation-states are here to stay. A major lesson of the Gulf Crisis is that any effort to induce boundary changes in the existing Arab state system is virtually certain to spark dangerous conflict.

Before proceeding, I must stress that to question the ideological concept of pan-Arabism and plead for a redefinition of Arabness is not to reject or disparage the Arab aspiration for integration. Were this aspiration to be redefined in policy terms, it could develop into a pragmatic program for effective integration. In redefining Arabness along these lines, I want to explore Europe's experience with integration as a model for the Arab world.

In this context, two propositions are advanced. First, redefining Arabness must be directed at developing a new design for inter-Arab relations, a design that clearly accepts those relations as parts of an interstate structure of sovereign states. The process of integration should not question or violate the national sovereignty of existing Arab states. The second proposition is that it is necessary to redefine the Arab as a citizen of a democratic state, thus divorcing the notion of the Arab from its hitherto-prevailing ethnic connotations. This would permit the Kurds of Syria and Iraq, the Dinka of Sudan, and the Berber of Algeria and Morocco to feel they are Arab citizens rather than marginalized by a quasiracist, ethnic, and exclusive definition of the Arab. Furthermore, redefining the Arab in nonethnic terms should also be secular, because not all Arabs are Muslims. A secular redefinition of the Arab smooths the way for Arab Christians to honor Arabness as a citizenship that puts them on equal footing with their Muslim compatriots.[8]

European Integration as a Model for Redefining Arabness

Common sense dictates that the overall problems of the Arab world cannot be solved solely through the efforts of existing discrete nation-states. Integration seems to promise new avenues for solutions. In this regard, the European Community provides a model from which Arab policymakers could learn a great deal—if they functioned within democratic systems. But because they do not face the threat of being turned out of office by voters, they may not learn these lessons. Yet, if the nascent and tentative signs of interest in democratization in the Arab world ultimately flower into a true process, the ideas advanced here may be useful.

Technically, at least, integration is not a new theme in Arab politics.[9] The problem is that the term has been used consistently by Arab politicians as equivalent to the blurred concept of a unified pan-Arab state. In Arabic there are important differences in nuance among integration (*indimaj*), cooperation (*ta'awun*), and unity (*wihda*). However, all of these terms are defined in the language of Arab politics by the pan-Arab concept of central unity.[10] If Arab leaders are to redefine Arabness in a productive way, they should look seriously at the structure and achievements of the European Community.

In the course of an interview I conducted with the sheikh of al-Azhar, Jadulhaq Ali Jadulhaq, in September 1989, he responded to a question concerning Muslim unity with his own question: "You are coming from Europe. What are the Europeans doing there?" In the Sheikh's mind, the European Community provided a design for Arab or Muslim unity. His reasoning was that pan-Arabist hopes could be achieved through following Europe's example. A closer look at the European Community helps overcome such misconceptions and makes it clear that the realities of European integration "do not fit with the notion of either a 'superstate' or a 'United States of Europe.'"[11] What, then, is European integration, and to what extent can it serve as a model for the goal of Arab integration?

A recent study by the Brookings Institution found that "national governments are prominent actors in the [European] community, integral to its very identity."[12] This observation cannot be welcomed by those who look to the European Community (EC) as a model for pan-Arabist unity. Equally, of course, it must relieve those Arab statesmen who pay lip service to pan-Arab unity but deep in their hearts, as well as in their policies, treat pan-Arabism as a threat.

The European states are—with little noise—pursuing the politics of integration while maintaining and acknowledging the existing state units as the basis of representation within the community. The EC is therefore obviously not like the Arab League. The former promotes substantive integration rather than rhetoric.

The substance of integration in the European model pertains to two issue areas. The first is the creation of an internal market encompassing all member states and including goods, services, capital, and labor. This eliminates all previously existing nontariff barriers among member states. The second area of integration is policymaking. In substance, the political process of integration in Western Europe means nothing more than the building of institutions as a framework for policymaking. This is not unity but is a deep model of integration. A prominent example for such institutions is the European Court of Justice, an important policymaking organ. Another example is the European parliament. The other major institutions are the EC Commission, the Council of Ministers and the European Council.

These institutions present an extraordinarily complex system of policy-making on all levels, which nonetheless does not infringe upon the member states' sovereignty and which is capable of translating "institutional capacity . . . into the effective representation of diverse national interests and needs at the community level."[13] Most important, the system is under-pinned by an intrinsically democratic political culture in which qualified majority decisions are recognized and unanimity is not basically required. Democratic leadership, democratic coalitions, diversity, bargaining, con-vergence, policy differentiation, and national sovereignty are the terms in which the system of European integration can be described. Thus, decision-making in the European community involves interplay among member states and the institutions of the community.[14] In short, European political integration rests on an institutional framework for interaction among sover-eign states. The single internal European market underpins this integration. Were a pragmatic and realistic effort to redefine Arabness undertaken, this model might be promising for the Arab world.

The essence of European integration cannot attract Arabs for whom *al-wihda* (unity) is a substitute for religion, a kind of religion *civile*. However, in the aftermath of the Gulf War, the community believing in this political religion has been diminishing.

Yet, pan-Arabism is by no means dead in Arab political discourse, and it is unfortunate that the Arabic language provides so many stinging epi-thets that are applied to those who do not believe in this political faith: *kha'in* (traitor), *'amil* (agent), and so forth. Any effort to redefine Arabism is certain to provoke much controversy and the ready use of emotion-laden labels against those questioning pan-Arabist pretensions.

Nonetheless, the sad history of pan-Arabist politics demands that the effort be made. Eberhard Kienle's recent study of the relationship between the two varieties of pan-Arabism dominating in Syria and Iraq provides a revealing insight into the dangers of allowing this ideology to prevail in Arab politics.[15] Each of these allegedly pan-Arab regimes has sought to monopolize the secular religion while branding the other as an agent of Zionism and imperialism. However, behind the smokescreen both regimes have jealously protected their national state sovereignty.

This cannot be considered a pattern for promoting Arab integration on any level. Nor, of course, can the invasion of Kuwait by pan-Arabists' long-awaited "Arab Bismarck" be touted as such a model.[16] Ghassan Salame's statement that Arab governments claiming to pursue the utopian goal of a single Arab state have actually pursued "isolationist policies with pan-Arab vocabulary" is true. This discrepancy between rhetoric and realpolitik has been the hallmark of Arab politics since the creation of the Arab state system.

Nowhere is this more clearly visible than in the history of the Arab League. Even in terms of modest integrative goals, such as frameworks of cooperation, the Arab League's record is extremely poor. In an environment in which the political culture required for responsible—that is, accountable, democratic—governance is lacking, the Arab League has provided a forum for rhetorical calls for unanimity rather than a setting for realistic and productive bargaining among sovereign member states. The result is emptiness. Salame points to the four thousand resolutions adopted by the league since its creation: "80 percent of them, though adopted by unanimous votes, were never applied . . . there is no need to establish majority rules, since even when unanimity is possible it remains ineffective."[17] Salame's overall view of the impressively large number of agreements signed under the league's auspices is worth quoting extensively:

Applied, they would have created a very high level of pan-Arab integration. This is obviously not the case. . . . The major obstacle [is] the lack of implementation even of unanimously voted resolutions. It is the discrepancy . . . between the dream of unity and the reality of inter-Arab politics. Arab regimes . . . would be threatened by a higher level of integration in the Arab World. And they clearly, systematically, oppose this integration even when the state religion is Arab nationalism.[18]

Integration is not perceived by Arab regimes as a threat because the incumbents are "traitors," "agents of imperialism and Zionism," and the like. Every undergraduate student of international relations is familiar with the fact that nation-states have national interests. The utopian and illusionary ideology of pan-Arab nationalism aims at abolishing existing boundaries and establishing a central pan-Arab government at the expense of established definitions of particular national interest.[19] No Arab state wants to be submerged in this way.

However, if integration is understood as a politico-institutional framework for policymaking among equal nation-states—as is the case in the European Community—the described threat perception of Arab policymakers would abate. The Arabs can benefit greatly from studying the European process of political and economic integration, particularly because no single Arab state can cope with its problems in the absence of true regional cooperation.

It is not inconceivable that Arab integration could take place while simultaneously acknowledging and maintaining the importance of the participating national governments as sovereign actors. Policymaking within a framework of integration along the lines of the EC would be a democratic process that would avoid violating the national interests of the member states. In this way, "The role of national governments [could] be incorporated into . . . policymaking within the community," as the EC model teaches us.[20]

Why European Integration Matters for Redefining Arabness

In this section I list and briefly discuss issue areas related to the European model of integration that seem pertinent to a new understanding of Arab integration, one going beyond the populist and undemocratic ideology of pan-Arabism coined and practiced by Nasser and the Baath. I believe that any new concept of Arab integration also requires redefining Arabness. Moreover, such a new concept must be compatible with a democratic framework; that is, it should be oriented toward the needs of the populations rather than be merely an ideology obsessed by political utopias.

Given that the European Community is neither a state nor an international organization but rather a state system of policymaking, it becomes clear that in the European model of integration, "the nation-state truly becomes the member state."[21] In this light, the following issue areas become relevant to a new approach to Arab integration:

• The political culture of decisionmaking in the European Community seems appropriate as a model for promoting integration among Arab states—not in the ideological sense of Arabism but rather in creating institutional patterns for regional cooperation.

• In such a political culture, decisions are taken within a framework based on acknowledged and explicit interest-oriented bargaining, not on pretentious notions such as "brotherhood" and the like. If this framework is accepted as a model for the Arab world, then the issue would be the necessity of ideological legitimization of particularistic national interests. Politics must be openly accepted as related to interests, not to primordial values such as *ukhuwwa* (brotherhood).

• In the European Community, a balanced relationship exists between the state and the overall community structure. This involves interplay between national governments and community institutions. This pattern seems worthy of emulation by efforts to promote Arab integration on the basis of interaction among actors seeking stable and tenable common ground.

• The Gulf War forces the conclusion that the Arab League lacks the needed institutional capabilities for regional conflict resolution. It makes no sense to argue that the league failed to foster an Arab solution in the Gulf without referring to the lack of institutions that were capable of pursuing this end. Under these conditions, the *hall al-Arabi* (Arab solution) formula was merely an Iraqi propaganda formula. The result was an over-whelming fragmentation of the Arab state system.[22]

Comparing the Arab situation to the European Community, one finds that the European system of integration has solved a variety of interstate European conflicts on all levels within the existing institutional framework. In contrast, the Arab experience in this regard has been a resounding failure. The Arab state system urgently needs an institution similar to the European Court of Justice, with all of its legal-institutional capabilities for peaceful conflict resolution. Integration is not only a system of brotherhood and harmony. In the first instance, it requires viable institutional structures for conflict resolution and the peaceful settlement of disputes.

• Another area of comparison underlining the Arab system's weakness is credibility. In Arab politics, credibility is either related to ideologies or to primordial norms and values, such as the personal honor of the policy-maker and the like.[23] In the European Community, credibility is, on the contrary, a pragmatic issue associated with costs. If an actor in international relations cannot bear the costs associated with policies, then this actor's credibility is reduced. With regard to Arab integration, no Arab actor has ever seriously pursued this goal on the basis of an explicit linkage among credibility, capacity, and willingness to bear the costs of policies adopted. This is the major source of the loss of credibility in the system of Arab integration. Rhetoric alone cannot sustain credibility. Exhortation and empty insistence on fantasies are limited political tools. This is exactly the case in Arab politics. Unlike the case in the Arab state system, credibility in the European Community is a secular issue that is approached pragmatically by calculating policymakers.

I restrict myself to one last comment in a listing that could go on almost endlessly. Before the Gulf War, and more intensely after it, much talk occurred in Arab political circles about the transfer of funds from rich to poor Arab states.[24] Europeans held similar discourses. Poor EC members, such as the southern European states—in particular, Spain—have also asked for transfers of funds from the rich to the poor. At the Maastricht Summit in December 1991, this issue came up. Instead of payments by rich countries to poor European countries, structural policy was given prominence over unattached transfer of funds, which was fully in keeping with Europe's approach to integration. Straightforward payments by rich states to poor states without a framework for development can serve as simple political bribes. Saudi funds given to other poor Arab countries have often been described in precisely such terms. In contrast is the European system of "structural policy," which places the transfer of funds within a framework of development policy.[25] Formally, development-oriented funds are available in the Arab system. However, most regionally based aid structures suffer from a devastating combination of a lack of capability and a lack of credibility.

Redefining the Arab:
Toward a Secular, Nonethnic Arab Citizenship

In the pan-Arab ideology of Sati al-Husri, who—as a former Ottoman—was not a native speaker of Arabic, Arabness was defined along the lines of Herder's romantic German idea of the nation as a *Kulturgemeinschaf*—a community determined by sharing a common language and history.[26] Basically, al-Husri's concept was secular. Nonetheless, this concept became mingled with Islam and Arab ethnicity in Arab politics. Non-Arab minorities, such as the Kurds, the Dinka, and the Berber, as well as non-Sunni Muslims, such as the Christians and the Shi'a, were virtually outlawed or at least not considered full members of the community. Muammar Qaddafi put it most blatantly in saying that Arab Christians should convert to Islam if they wanted to become true Arabs.

Although it is hypothetically possible to switch from one religion to another through conversion, ethnic identity cannot be escaped. Kurds, Dinka, and Berber could never become ethnic Arabs, even if they were willing to do so. The uprising of the Kurds and the Shi'ites in Iraq after the Gulf War reveals the consequences of defining Arabness in strictly religious, ethnic terms. In light of the Gulf Crisis, a redefinition of the Arab is urgently needed. In my view, a secular, nonethnic concept of citizenship in a civil—that is, democratic—society provides a solution.

Even ethnic Arabs do not share a common identity. Their identities are linked to subethnic, sectarian, and tribal communities.[27] Arab societies are still traditional societies characterized by ethnic strife and tribal identities. As Anthony Giddens tells us:

> The population of traditional states did not know themselves to be "citizens" of those states nor did it matter particularly to the community of power within them. . . . The expansion of state sovereignty means that those subject to it are in some sense . . . aware of their membership in a political community.[28]

Modern citizenship is not based on commonly shared ethnic origins but rather "is anchored psychologically in distinctive features of modern societies. . . . The extension of communication cannot occur without the 'conceptual involvement' of the whole community in a way in which traditional states were not."[29]

In sum, redefining the Arab in the aftermath of the Gulf Crisis needs to take place along these lines of nonethnic and secular features of citizenship. It is regrettable that, at least initially, the outcome of the Gulf Crisis appears to have strengthened Islamic fundamentalism instead of developing an awareness of the need for secular and nonethnic citizenship.[30]

Conclusion

Under the present conditions of globalization, individual Arab states cannot function optimally on their own. Yet the old Arab dream of a single united Arab state has proved fallacious. Between the two extremes—the isolation of some Arab states and the expansionism of others disguised as pan-Arabism—exists the middle way of integration, of which the European Community serves as the most successful example. Arabs can learn a great deal from this model while redefining Arabness and the Arab. The first thing they can learn is the need for a highly institutionalized structure, yet not a superstate.

However, in suggesting Europe as a model, we must note that the institutionalization of the European policymaking system would have been impossible in the absence of one requirement: the process for which Charles Tilly coined the term "the civilianization of governments." Tilly tells us the story: "The state-transforming processes . . . produced . . . civilianization of government."[31] These processes created the substance of the nation-state. Elsewhere I have given evidence that the present nation-states in the Middle East are nominal nation-states, which means they lack this substance.[32]

The task of redefining Arabness and the Arab must start first on this very unit of action, the state. The civilianization of governments and the related institutionalization of the nominal Arab nation-states are the first requirements for establishing a functioning inter-Arab state system and democratic citizenship as indispensable bases for Arab integration.

It follows that a new definition of the Arab League is also needed. The league, established by "politicians more experienced in intrigue than in the debate, mediation and compromise of international relations," has proved most unsuccessful.[33] In addition to its lack of an institutional structure for policymaking, one of the sources of the consistent failures of the Arab League has been "its reluctance to accept its role as a regional organization. The inclination has been to regard the League as a step along the path to Arab unity."[34] However, this inclination never went beyond rhetoric.

Arabs need to free themselves from rhetoric while working for the democratization and civilianization of their governments. Anything else would be wishful thinking, of which there has been enough in the recent past. In the wake of the Gulf Crisis, ideological and rhetorical pan-Arabism should be buried once and for all—not for the sake of a further fragmentation of Arab politics but rather for the sake of establishing a viable process of Arab integration based on a redefined concept of Arabness and a democratic, nonethnic, and secular understanding of the Arab.

Notes

1. See David Fromkin, *A Peace to End All Peace: The Fall of the Ottoman Empire and the Creation of the Modern Middle East* (New York: Avon Books, 1989). On the ideological foundations of the pan-Arab unity theme, see Bassam Tibi, *Arab Nationalism: A Critical Inquiry,* 2d ed. (New York: St. Martin's Press, 1991). See also Malcolm Kerr, *The Arab Cold War,* 3d ed. (New York: Oxford University Press, 1971).

2. Sa'dun Hamadi, *Qadaya al-Thawra al-Arabiyya: Al-Thawara al-'Arabiyyua wa al-Widha,* 2d ed. (Beirut: Dar al-Tali'a, 1970), pp. 166–167.

3. "Hawl 'Lan al-Widha al-Indimajiyya ma'a al-Kuwait," in *al-Muntada* (Amman), 5 (September 1990), pp. 19–20.

4. See the chapter on the Gulf War in Louis Kriesber and Stuart J. Thornson (eds.), *Timing the De-Escalation of International Conflicts* (Syracuse: Syracuse University Press, 1991), pp. 267–273. See also Robert W. Macdonald, *The League of Arab States: A Study in the Dynamic of Regional Organization* (Princeton: Princeton University Press, 1965).

5. See Dan Tschirgi and Bassam Tibi, *Perspectives on the Gulf Crisis, Cairo Papers in Social Science,* Vol. 14, Monograph 1 (Cairo: American University in Cairo Press, 1991).

6. George Tarabishi, *al-Dawla al qitriyya wa al-Nazariyya al Qawmiyya* (Beirut: Dar al-Tali'a, 1982).

7. For more detail, see Anthony Giddens, *The Nation-State and Violence* (Berkeley: University of California Press, 1987), Ch. 10.

8. See the secular position of the Christian Lebanese Joseph Mughaizel, *al-'Uruba wa al-Ilmaniyya* (Beirut: Dar al-Nahar, 1980) and the contrasting position of the Egyptian fundamentalist Muhammad 'Imara, *al-Islam was al-'uruba wa al-'Ilmaniyya* (Beirut: Dar al-Wahda, 1981).

9. See the contributions in Giacomo Luciani and Ghassan Salame (eds.), *The Politics of Arab Integration* (London: Croom Helm, 1988).

10. For a critical analysis of this concept, see Tibi, *Arab Nationalism.*

11. Alberta Sbargia, ed., *Euro-Politics: Institutions and Policymaking in the "New" European Community* (Washington, D.C.: Brookings Institution, 1992), p. 2.

12. Ibid., p. 12.

13. Ibid., p. 3.

14. Ibid., pp. 2–3.

15. Eberhard Kienle, *Ba'th Versus Ba'th* (New York: St. Martin's Press, 1990).

16. In the declaration of the annexation of Kuwait, both terms—*wihda* (unity) and *indimaj* (integration)—were united into one term as the text's title, *Wihda Indimajiyya.* The Arabic text can be found in the special issue of *al-Muntada* (September 1990), published by the Arab Thought Forum, Amman. The idea of an Arab Bismarck stems from the work of Sati' al-Husri. See Tibi, *Arab Nationalism.*

17. Ghassan Salame, "Integration in the Arab World: The Institutional Framework," in Luciani and Salame, *The Politics of Arab Integration*, p. 276.

18. Ibid., p. 278.

19. See Tibi, *Arab Nationalism*, "Arab Nationalism Revisited," pp. 1–26.

20. Sbargia, *Euro-Politics*, p. 12.

21. Alberta Sbargia, "Thinking About the European Future," in ibid., p. 258.

22. Bassam Tibi, "The Gulf Crisis and the Fragmentation of the Arab World," in Tschirgi and Tibi, *Perspectives on the Gulf Crisis*, pp. 73–107.

23. See Michael Hudson, *Arab Politics: The Search for Legitimacy* (New Haven: Yale University Press, 1977), pp. 1–30.

24. See the early debate in the contributions in Malcolm Kerr and Sayid Yassin (eds.), *Rich and Poor States in the Middle East* (Boulder: Westview Press, 1982).

25. Gary Marks, "Structural Policy in the European Community," in Sbargia, *Euro-Politics*.

26. Tibi, *Arab Nationalism*.

27. See my contribution to the volume edited by Philip Khoury and Joseph Kostiner, *Tribes and State Formation in the Middle East* (Berkeley: University of California Press, 1990), pp. 127ff.

28. Giddens, *Nation-State*, p. 218.

29. Ibid., p. 219.

30. See James Piscatori (ed.), *Islamic Fundamentalism and the Gulf Crisis* (Chicago: American Academy of Arts and Sciences, 1991).

31. Charles Tilly, *Coercion, Capital and the European States* (Cambridge: Basil Blackwell, 1990), p. 122.

32. Tibi, in Khoury and Kostiner, *Tribes and States Formation*.

33. Macdonald, *The League of Arab States*, p. 281.

34. Ibid., p. 300.

11

The Future of Regional and Subregional Organization in the Arab World

IBRAHIM AWAD ⎯⎯⎯⎯⎯⎯⎯⎯⎯⎯⎯⎯⎯⎯⎯⎯⎯⎯⎯⎯⎯

The study of regional and subregional organization in the Arab world cannot be divorced from an analysis of the system that is supposed to be regulated.[1] The Gulf Crisis dealt a devastating blow to the organization of the regional system, highlighting its profound deficiencies. The contempt in which the Arab Cooperation Council (ACC) was held, the inability of the Gulf Cooperation Council (GCC) to ensure the security of its members, and the paralysis of the paramount regional institution, the League of Arab States (LAS), offer eloquent proof of the failure of the system and its organization. Taking notice of this poor performance, regional actors have already begun to forge new links among themselves and with external actors. The most pressing question regarding the organization of today's Arab world is, therefore, future-oriented: What characteristics are likely to mark the area's future organization at the regional and subregional levels?

An exploration of this issue requires taking into account developments that began to unfold in the months following the end of the Gulf War. Particular reference is made here to the rejuvenated Middle East peace process, launched in the fall of 1991. Bilateral negotiations are now taking place between Israel and the Arab countries whose territories it occupies, and multilateral talks on topics of concern for the region are also being held. Parties to these talks include countries from outside the region.

These new interactions will probably contribute to the shaping of novel structures. New actors have forced their way into the Arab system or have been asked to join it. The future organization of the system at the regional and subregional levels will largely be the product of issues raised in the new interactions and of demands formulated by regional and extraregional actors.

In contemplating the possible future regional and subregional organization of the Arab world, I proceed in two stages. First, I deal with the two challenges that shaped the Arab world's current dynamics—the Gulf Crisis and the Middle East peace process. I then turn to the issues and demands faced by the system. Prospective actors are identified, and the performance of present Arab institutions is assessed. I assume that functions the latter cannot perform will have to be handled by new structures. It is hoped that this approach will allow the probable new face of the Arab system at the regional and subregional levels to be roughly outlined.

Challenges to the Arab System

The Gulf Crisis

Whether the eruption of the Gulf Crisis in the summer of 1990 resulted from deficiencies in the Arab system or from a choice made by the Iraqi leadership and imposed upon the entire Arab world is debatable. Signs of improvements in relations among Arab countries prior to the crisis can be cited. Among these are the control of open conflicts, the mitigation of inter-Arab divergences and rivalries, and the formulation of a growing Arab consensus on the Iraq-Iran War and the Arab-Israeli conflict.

However, justifications for considering the crisis a product of the deficiencies of the system also exist. Several scheduled Arab summits failed to convene. Inter-Arab military conflicts had not been fully solved. The Syrian-Iraqi rift still resisted all efforts at mediation and had found extension in a war by proxy in Lebanon.

In any case, the May 1990 Baghdad Summit had been the scene of a heated confrontation between moderates and hardliners. In the end, the former gave in and agreed to formulate decisions in language borrowed from the Iraqi president's discourse. They had preferred to yield on the different questions under discussion rather than escalate inter-Arab tensions. By contrast, Iraq's posture heralded its preference for confrontation. When it invaded Kuwait on August 2 of that year, Baghdad acted on this proclivity.

The Gulf Crisis split the Arab system into two almost equal parts. A collective approach was briefly sought. On August 3, the Council of the League of Arab States held an emergency meeting at the ministerial level. At the same time, foreign ministers of the Gulf Cooperation Council (GCC) met on their own.[2] A minisummit was to be convened in Riyadh the following day, but it never materialized. Several other bilateral and multilateral meetings took place until a summit conference was held in Cairo on August 9 and 10, but nothing availed. Indeed, in the time between the meetings of

August 3 and August 10, the number of countries supporting decisions condemning the Iraqi invasion of Kuwait and calling for the withdrawal of Iraqi troops decreased from fourteen to twelve. Objections, abstentions, and reservations had increased. The Arab summit not only failed to find a solution to the crisis but also consummated the polarization within the Arab system.[3]

Prior to August 2, few realized the extent to which Baghdad was willing to press its quarrel with Kuwait. No clear effort was therefore made to warn Iraq not to undertake military action against Kuwait. Following the invasion and the emergency summit, the Arab system was paralyzed by the rift within its ranks. Exploiting procedural weaknesses and contradictions, many Arab actors failed to honor the substance of their obligations under the Charter of the League of Arab States. Failure to observe rules and implement decisions was not new, but this time the issue was one many Arab countries considered intimately related to their existence as independent states. The political and legal foundations of the Arab system as laid down in the LAS Charter and other constitutional documents were being sapped. In the face of the weakness of regional organizations, and given the strategic importance of the Gulf subregion, the international system took over management of the crisis.

Iraq's invasion of Kuwait portended a total revolution within the Arab system, one aimed at effecting a basic change in its membership. It is only natural that the attempted revolution's military defeat would create new political realities that would have been difficult to assimilate within old institutional frameworks. These realities are now giving rise to new local debates and demands among Arab political actors.

The Middle East Peace Process

Since its development after World War II, the modern Arab system has been structured around the Arab-Israeli conflict and its primordial manifestation, the Palestinian question. This conflict has been the driving force shaping the system and its political discourse. It has dominated the Arab world's political agenda and constituted a foundation for its structure.

The consequences of a settlement of the Arab-Israeli conflict for the future of the Arab system were already well understood by the end of the 1970s. Declarations by spokesmen for the Palestine Liberation Organization (PLO) that accepted the existence of Israel and statements to the same effect by Egyptian President Anwar al-Sadat, before he eventually made peace with the Zionist state, were considered fundamental changes in the system's values and were seen as indicating a transformation of the system and of the challenges it faced. Egypt's conclusion of peace with Israel in 1979 was a major blow to the Arab system.[4]

By the end of the 1980s, most of the Arab world had—albeit reluctantly—come to view Israel as a reality that would have to be dealt with rather than removed. In the wake of the Gulf War, this view rapidly crystallized into practical political steps, as Arab states met with Israel to discuss not only the Palestinians' future but also that of the entire region.[5] In the eyes of Israel's Arab interlocutors, a relatively stable settlement of the Palestinian question was a necessary step toward the creation of a new, more productive and reliable Arab system.

The U.S.-sponsored peace process is, therefore, a confirmation of new attitudes in the region. More important, it establishes the Arabs' formal acceptance of regional political realities they had long sought to deny. To be sure, the Arabs did not start from an advantageous position. They have had to accept most of Israel's conditions in order for the process to get under way. In this altered context, the nature of Arab regional organization will likely be profoundly affected.

The Arab-Israeli conflict has structured the Arab system since the 1940s; thus, it is only normal that the conflict has also been the primary concern of the system's central institution, the League of Arab States. The safeguarding of Palestinian interests and rights was the mission set by the league and its member states. Resolutions of the league's organs in this respect are innumerable. In March 1946, an Arab summit declared the question of Palestine to be inseparable from other Arab causes, branded Zionism as a danger to all Arab countries, and called for a halt to Jewish immigration into Palestine.[6] At its fifth session, in December 1946, the LAS council rejected all schemes for partitioning Palestine. When partition was recommended by the UN General Assembly, the league rejected the resolution and called on Arab governments to stand by the Palestinians until they gained independence and sovereignty. In 1950, the council adopted a resolution forbidding member states to negotiate political, economic, or military agreements or to conclude peace with Israel. When Tunisian President Habib Bourguiba publicly talked of peace with Israel in 1965, the council categorically rejected his proposals. The 1967 Khartoum Summit's triple rejection of Israel (no peace, no recognition, no negotiation) is well-known. Finally, when the largest Arab country concluded peace with Israel, it was excluded from the institutions of the Arab system. Regardless of its performance, the league has certainly been a defender of the purity of the cause.

The first sign of evolution was the 1982 Fez Summit's adoption of the Fahd Plan and the implicit recognition of Israel that this entailed. In subsequent years, there was a progressive softening in the LAS attitudes. Yet, it is difficult to envisage that the institution, which has lived by and for the Arab-Israeli conflict, can (at least in its present form) survive the conflict's resolution. It is doubtful that the league as it stands will be able to meet the demands of its members, who are immersed in a new regional environment.

Regional Issues in the Aftermath of the Gulf Crisis

The Gulf Crisis and the Middle East peace process have provoked or consummated changes in moods and attitudes. However, they have not solved the major issues faced by regional actors, and new problems have also emerged. Regional issues are not only those perceived by the Arab countries. The interests of regional non-Arab actors and of extraregional actors must also be considered to be factors linked to regional issues. Whether such interests are legitimate is irrelevant for the purposes of analysis; the fact is that they exist, and they must be dealt with by Arab actors.

The array of interests and issues determines the constitutive units of the contemporary Arab system. Of course, one can object that interests alone do not necessarily qualify those advancing them to be considered participants in a system. But this can only be true when a system is not as open as is the case with the Arab system at present—a period marked by the willingness and ability of extraregional and non-Arab actors to advance their interests by direct intervention.

The purpose of regional and subregional organization is to establish institutions and procedures for mediating issues of common concern. It is therefore worthwhile to examine briefly the major issues that are being raised in the Arab world. Possible divergences of interests marking the various actors in the Arab system will not be scrutinized because my objective is only to delineate issue areas that might lead to future regional or subregional organization. Issues are grouped in three categories: security and military issues; economic, social, and environmental issues; and identitive issues.

Security and Military Issues

The Occupied Arab Territories: I have already argued that the ideological content of the Arab-Israeli conflict has undergone a major transformation. Nevertheless, physical problems have not diminished in force. Territories of three Arab countries are still occupied by Israel. Arab land in the West Bank is still being confiscated, and Jewish immigrants from Russia are being settled there.

It is to be hoped that in the ongoing peace negotiations, these problems will be dealt with bilaterally between Israel on the one hand and Syria, Lebanon, and Jordan-Palestine on the other. Given past attitudes and the Egyptian-Israeli precedent, Israel can be expected to insist upon keeping relations and even the management of eventual settlements on a bilateral level. The United States, possibly accompanied by Russia, may act as a guarantor. Agreed patterns of interaction will not, in this case, enter the mold of formal institutions.

Security in the Gulf: The importance of oil to the industrial world protected the Gulf subregion until the eruption of the 1990 crisis. Even at the height of the Iraq-Iran War, and in spite of Iranian acts of destabilization, the security of the Gulf countries was not seriously threatened.

The situation changed totally with the invasion of Kuwait. Suddenly, the absence of credible defensive capabilities in these rich, small states became dazzlingly clear. Not only the West but relatively distant Arab countries, such as Egypt and Syria, awoke to the security concerns in the Gulf. Iran, a coastal state, has continually displayed clear attitudes toward the issue.

Western and regional actors—the latter including the Arabs and Iran—pursue different interests and therefore promote different security schemes for the area. Some potentially viable structures have emerged, at least in principle—for example, the agreements between Kuwait and Western countries and the Damascus Declaration. The idea of a joint declaration of the GCC countries and Iran that would lay down the bases for their relationship is being discussed. Thus, the trend is toward a complicated organization of security arrangements and understandings, with the role of central actor reserved for the United States.

However, the GCC has entrusted a working group, chaired by Oman's Sultan Qabus, with studying ways of furthering the joint military capability of its member countries. The group has developed the idea of mobilizing a joint army of two hundred thousand troops. However, no definitive stand has yet been taken on this issue. Even if some viable form of cooperative defense arrangement is ultimately erected by the GCC, its effectiveness will necessarily be limited by the modest populations of member countries.

The "Misfits" Security Question: Ten years after triggering hostilities with Iran, the large, well-equipped Iraqi army again underlined the security problems of the Gulf subregion. Supported by a sophisticated research and development program, Iraq's armed forces had become a source of instability. Yet, the systematic implementation of UN Security Council Resolution 687 should also raise serious concern. It seems likely to result in a security void at a time when the Iraqi-Iranian conflict has not yet been fully settled and northern Iraq is destabilized by the Kurdish conflict, as well as by Turkish raids against bases of the Kurdish Workers Party.

Iraq's situation is at present directly affected by the UN. But Iraq is an essential element in balances of power in the Gulf, in the Fertile Crescent, and in respect to Turkey and Iran. Because of its implications for other countries in the region, the situation in Iraq needs to be managed—at least partly—at the regional level. A mechanism for restoring to Iraq sovereign parity with its neighbors and reintegrating the country into regional politics will be necessary over the medium term.

Closely related to Iraq's situation, and indicative of the importance of the "misfits" to the region, is the Libyan case. The implementation of UN Security Council Resolution 748 and the possible subsequent escalation of sanctions against Libya are bound to produce serious economic and psychological consequences in neighboring countries. The regional system must come into play as its members at least seek to protect their own narrow interests.

We can envisage a role for regional institutions in respect to the misfits. The LAS might be expected to act as an agent for their socialization, for securing their observance of the international system's political rules.[7] The mediation attempted by the league in the Libyan crisis is a clear indication of this possibility. Yet, the political culture inherent in the system will probably make this role difficult to realize.

Inter-Arab Disputes: A number of territorial and political disputes exist among Arab countries. They are presently dealt with either multilaterally at the international, regional, and subregional levels or bilaterally. These levels may change, but they demonstrate the necessity of collective structures to mediate such disputes or to defuse the threat they represent to regional security and stability. Without elaborating, examples of such problems include the Lebanese question and Syria's presence in Lebanon, the Bahraini-Qatari dispute, the Western Sahara question, and the Egyptian-Sudanese dispute over Halayeb.[8] This is the most natural area in which the league can meet the demands of its members. Its success in this respect is vital for the integrity of the system. Yet, we must note that the league met with success in only six of seventy-seven conflictual situations it attempted to settle between 1945 and 1981.

Arms Control and Disarmament: Prominent on the agenda of multilateral peace negotiations in the Middle East is the question of arms control and disarmament. Iraq is the first country to pay for this relatively new concern by having its military power reduced under the direct supervision of the United Nations. Shipments of armaments to Syria have also been monitored and controlled, but this has been done through channels other than those of the United Nations. A settlement of the Arab-Israeli conflict will have to include provisions on arms control and disarmament, which should cover conventional, chemical, bacteriological, and nuclear weapons. Achieving a consensus on the fairness of such provisions will be problematical. However, in the context of a peace settlement, some forms of arms control and possibly disarmament provisions are bound to appear. In view of the coordination required and the technical complexity of the endeavor, institutional capabilities will have to be developed. Such arrangements will obviously have to include countries of the region, permanent members of the UN Security Council, and armaments suppliers. This is an area that falls outside the scope of present regional institutions.

Economic, Social, and Environmental Issues

Multilateral negotiations under the sponsorship of the United States and Russia make use of a working group chaired by the European Community (EC) that focuses on questions of economic cooperation. These also include social and environmental issues.

Economic Cooperation: A number of Israeli scholars have been concerned for some years with issues related to economic cooperation in the Middle East.[9] But now the question is also openly addressed on the Arab side. Some believe that if peace were achieved, countries of the region would reap gains through greater economies of scale, specialization, and competition. This would be brought about through more effective regional harmonization of economic relations supporting, rather than substituting for, greater integration with the international economy. The ideas raised by scholars and floated around during the peace negotiations point to possible future interactions and the structures that could develop to regulate them. They can be classified into the following:

• *Trade:* It has been suggested that a free trade area in the Middle East be established, at least for industrial products. Such a project would probably begin with Israel, Jordan, and Palestine. The idea rests on the reasonable assumption that an expanded market will promote development in the region. However, even setting aside political considerations, this would not guarantee success. The record of Arab experiments with free trade areas and common markets is more than sufficient cause for skepticism.[10]

• *Basic infrastructure:* Ideas are raised in the fields of land transportation to connect the Maghreb to the Mashrek countries and the Gulf through Egypt, Palestine, and Israel; rail transportation, specifically the rehabilitation of the Egypt-Gaza-Palestine line and its extension; solar energy generation, storage, and use by setting up a project at the juncture of the borders of Palestine, Israel, and Egypt; electric power generation and distribution by implementing existing plans for connecting grids in Egypt, Jordan, Syria, and Turkey and by including Israel in the prospective network.

At present, there are no institutions by which such ideas might be comprehensively reviewed, and perhaps acted upon, by countries of the region. The UN Economic and Social Commission for Western Asia (ESCWA) could be adapted to serve in this respect.[11]

Development of Water Resources: Cooperation between Arab and non-

Arab countries in the field of water resources is frequently mentioned as a development that will mark the Middle East's future. Ideas range from proposals for various sorts of bilateral cooperation to multilateral projects. Examples of the latter are the adoption of a "water charter" that would cover water sharing, the use and management of rivers and transnational aquifers, and the development of a regional water authority.[12] Concepts with a wider geographical scope are building "peace pipelines" (originating in Turkey) and increasing regional rainfall by sea mixing in the eastern Mediterranean. Parties to such arrangements would be Arab and non-Arab. The institutions required for realizing such projects might be bilateral or multilateral, subregional or regional; but the implication is that they would not be exclusively Arab.

The Environment: Proposals for the protection of the environment span the Mediterranean, the Gulf of Aqaba, and countries in between. Regarding the Mediterranean, plans contained in the Mediterranean Action Programme are considered adequate, but the establishment of an Eastern Mediterranean regional center for marine pollution involving Turkey, Syria, Lebanon, Cyprus, Israel, Egypt, and Libya is also proposed. Moreover, proposals have been made for the Gulf of Aqaba; these include a regional environmental authority and a regional natural reserve authority comprising the coastal states. In each case, by definition, the suggested institutions would not be purely Arab. On the bilateral level, proposals are made for setting up Israeli-Egyptian and Israeli-Jordanian institutions to conduct research and development on arid zones and to work out plans for the protection of the Dead Sea region.

Human Resources: There have long been calls for rules to govern the exchange of manpower and to provide protection to migrant labor in the Arab world. Current proposals are meant to cover all migrant workers in the region, including Palestinians working in Israel. Setting up regional centers for vocational training has been suggested. In this field, too, effective institutions could not be exclusively Arab.

Financial Institutions: Ideas for the creation of a Regional Development Fund and a Middle East Bank for Reconstruction and Development (MEBRD) have also been advanced. Such a bank would channel investment funds from one country to another in order to promote the economic development of all of the parties involved. The Organization for Economic Cooperation and Development (OECD) countries are mentioned as sources of the bank's capital. In justifying the undertaking, it is argued that the Middle East is currently the only developing region without a multilateral development bank for mobilizing substantial resources and channeling them to productive use through project and program lending. Arab sources admit that the Arab Fund for Economic and Social Development is the nearest approximation of this concept. But, they add, there are a number of important differences, including limited membership and the fact that this institution does not act as a financial intermediary between international capital markets and productive investment opportunities in the region. They feel a new institution functioning as an intermediary would facilitate the mobilization of private capital in support of development.

The establishment of a MEBRD is admittedly seen as a protracted process that will have to await, inter alia, tangible progress on military and security issues. Yet, the proposed interim mechanism includes extra-regional parties. Thus, there is a clear tendency toward the institutionalization of foreign financial aid within the region.[13] It seems generally accepted that the region's development requires its opening up to extraregional actors.

"Identitive" Issues

The existence of the Arab system has been explained by the particular patterns of interaction among states sharing a common cultural identity. The Arab system has been described as not only regional but also national and characterized by a high degree of linguistic, cultural, and social cohesiveness. These features may have existed in other regional systems but not to the extent reached in the Arab world.[14]

Cultural factors were the origin of the Arab system. In their absence, the system would not have existed. However, in an enlarged regional system, the situation is different.

Closely related to cultural issues are ideological ones. Both types of issues are elusive; hence, apprehending them is more difficult than identifying security and economic processes and actors. In fact, they are "identitive issues"; that is, they imprint the behavior of actors. In the newly emerging Middle East environment, ideological and cultural issues can be expected to exert an impact on Arab reactions to various other issues.

Ideological Issues

The emergent Middle East/Arab system will largely be influenced by the interplay of ideologies characterizing its members. Three issues seem likely to form key focal points of ideological convergence and tension: the secular-confessional issue; the issue of democracy; and the issue of socialization to norms of interaction.

• *Secularism Versus Confessionalism:* The issue of whether the state is to be organized along secular or confessional lines is one that affects all countries of the region, even avowedly secular political systems such as

Turkey. Israel is a particular case, because religion was the basis for the state's creation. In the other countries, the extent of confessionalism differs greatly, with Saudi Arabia and Iran on one end of a continuum and Turkey—followed by Lebanon, Egypt, and Syria—on the other. Such countries as Turkey and Egypt may be brought close together as a result of their proximate locations on the continuum, but others may not. Saudi Arabia and Iran are separated by sectarian considerations and intensive rifts over other ideological issues. The secular-confessional divide has been a recurrent issue during the lifetime of the Arab system. It will now be projected on a wider regional scope. As it did with the old system, it will probably undermine the cohesiveness of the newly expanded one.

• *Democracy:* For purposes of this analysis, the term *democracy* covers concepts of pluralism and competitive elections. To borrow an expression used elsewhere, it may be said that a clear "democratic deficit" exists in all countries of the region. Yet here, too, differences exist. Restrictions on pluralism are less stifling in Turkey, Egypt, and Jordan and most severe in Saudi Arabia, Oman, and Qatar. Competitive elections are held in Iran, Turkey, and Israel and are unknown in Syria and countries of the Arabian Peninsula.

These different domestic structures and processes will necessarily affect interactions related to military, security, economic, and environmental issues. Regarding pluralism, the different outlooks toward democracy should be expected to undermine the cohesiveness of any new regional system.

• *Socialization to Norms of Interaction:* The difficulty of forecasting how actors will be positioned on this issue is matched only by the importance of socialization as a function of all political systems. The positioning will be determined by the final arrangements affecting territorial and other substantive issues. As of now, we can say that Iran, excluded from talks over the future of the region, is likely to resist the new norms. It is in the nature of arrangements to reward actors differently. Therefore, the behavior of Arab countries will be proportionate to the interests that, in their respective perceptions, the new norms will achieve for them. The difficulty will be compounded further if the fairness of such norms is perceived differently within each country.

Common ideological orientation reinforces the integration of any political system. The heterogeneity of attitudes toward secularism and democracy within the Arab world is obvious. To overcome the clear disintegrative potential, divergences must be minimized. This can only be achieved if events that are still unfolding—such as the peace process—lead a majority of the actors to believe the new Middle East system meets their demands and promotes their interests.

Cultural Issues

These include the question of cultural identity and the production of cultural goods. Arabs gave their name to the regional system as it has existed since World War II. This was resented—without effect—by cultural and national minorities living within the confines of the system. In an expanded system, minorities will probably favor dilution of the system's Arab identity. Working in the same direction will be the Turkish, Iranian, and Israeli elements of the Middle East system. The presence of extraregional actors in the system will further undermine the Middle East's Arab character.

Yet, given their numbers and their linguistic and historical links, the Arabs can imprint the system with their culture. Inter-Arab links can be the bases of a distinct Arab subsystem that can affect the behavior of its constitutive units in relation to security, economic, environmental, and other issues. Interactions among Turkish, Iranian, and Arab cultures can enrich all participants and further develop their common elements. This is closely related to the way ideological issues are dealt with and to the production of cultural goods.

The preservation of a distinct Arab identity will be affected by the capacity to produce cultural goods. Competition is intense in cultural areas of all regional systems. Regional actors face the huge productive capacities of central actors in the international system. Yet, there is a specific demand for Arab goods.

Conclusion

Incapable of performing the functions required by its members, the post–World War II Arab system has further lost much of its cohesiveness as a result of the two challenges it faced in the early 1990s. The first challenge, the Iraqi invasion of Kuwait, left the system wide open to the presence of extraregional actors. The second challenge, that of the Middle East peace process, spectacularly confirmed the extroversion of the system.

The relationship between a system and its institutions is dialectical. The existence of a regional system provides the rationale for the creation of regional institutions that reinforce the system itself. If such institutions fail to perform the functions expected of them, the system cannot hold for long: It either undergoes an implosion, or extraregional actors penetrate its structure. Both outcomes have been the fate of the Arab system, and a process of transformation is therefore under way. The Arab world is progressively being immersed in a broader regional system. If this new system finally crystallizes, it will require either the creation of new institutions or the adaptation of old ones. Thus, new forms of organization will almost certainly emerge in the region.

The cohesiveness of the Arab world is most likely to survive in one area. Culture clearly distinguishes Arabs from non-Arabs; hence, it provides a basis for an Arab cultural subsystem that can affect the behavior of other members of the system. Furthermore, the elements of a common cultural heritage that Arabs share with Turkey and Iran provide the former with the possibility of enlarging the area of their cultural radiation.

In a new regional organization, Arabs may initially lament the loss of seclusion their old institutions failed to preserve. Yet, this new organization can offer them the chance to imprint the entire region with their common cultural identity. Nothing is determined in advance. Mastery of resources and their efficient use will be the real determinants of the region's future.

Notes

1. The term *system* is used to refer to the regional subsystem when no mention is made of the international system.
2. The Gulf Cooperation Council was formed in 1981. Its members include Bahrain, Kuwait, Oman, Qatar, Saudi Arabia, and the United Arab Emirates.
3. For a review of the reactions of the Arab system to the invasion of Kuwait, see *Arab Strategic Report 1990* (Cairo: Al-Ahram Centre for Political and Strategic Studies, 1991), pp. 266–290 (in Arabic).
4. See Gamil Matar and Aley-el-Dine Hillal, *The Arab Regional System: A Study in Arab Political Relations,* 4th ed. (Beirut and Cairo: Center for Arab Unity Studies and Dar Almostaqbal Al'arabi, 1983), pp. 195–196, 204 (in Arabic).
5. Gamil Matar, "The Future of the Arab Regional System," *Al Mustaqbal Al Arabi,* no. 158 (April 1992), p. 14.
6. See Ahmed Fares 'Abdelmon'em, *The League of Arab States 1945–1985: A Historico-Political Study* (Beirut: Center for Arab Unity Studies, 1986), pp. 44–59 (in Arabic).
7. On roles and functions of international organizations, see Clive Archer, *International Organizations* (London: George Allen and Unwin, 1983), pp. 126–169.
8. On inter-Arab disputes and approaches to the settlement of disputes, see Ahmed Youssef Ahmed, *Inter-Arab Conflicts (1945–1981)* (Beirut: Center for Arab Unity Studies, 1988) (in Arabic); and Hassan Nafaa, "The Settlement of Arab Conflicts," paper presented to the workshop "New Perspectives for Arab Regional Cooperation in the 1990s," jointly organized by ESCWA, the Forum for Arab Thought, and the Al-Ahram Center for Political and Strategic Studies, Cairo, September 7–9, 1991 (in Arabic).
9. Examples are R. Arad, S. Hirsch, and A. Tovias, *The Economics of Peacemaking: Focus on the Egyptian-Israeli Situation* (London: Macmillan, 1983); H. Ben-Shahar, G. Fichelson, and S. Hirsch, *Economic Cooperation and Middle East Peace* (London: Weidenfeld and Nicolson, 1989); D. Fichelson (ed.), *Economic Cooperation in the Middle East* (Boulder: Westview Press, 1989); and V. Lavy and E. Sheffer, *Foreign Aid and Economic Development in the Middle East* (New York: Praeger, 1991).
10. On the experience of Arab economic unity and the Arab common market, see Ibrahim Awad, "Theorie de l'integration politique et application au Monde

arabe. L'etude deux processus dans une perspective neo-fonctionnelle," in *Etudes politiques du Monde arabe: Approches globales et approches specifiques* (Le Caire: Centre d'Etudes et de Documentation Economique, Juridique et Social, 1991) (Dossiers du CEDEJ, 1991).

11. On activities of UN economic commissions within subordinate international systems, see Lynn H. Miller, "Regional Organizations and Subordinate Systems," in Louis J. Cantori and Steven L. Spiegel (eds.), *The International Politics of Regions: A Comparative Approach* (Englewood Cliffs: Prentice-Hall, 1970), p. 359.

12. Among the Arab scholars raising the idea of cooperation in water resources management are Heba Handoussa and Nemat Shafik. See their "The Economics of Peace: The Egyptian Case," paper delivered at the conference "The Economics of Middle East Peace," organized by the Institute for Social and Economic Policy in the Middle East, John F. Kennedy School of Government, Harvard University, November 14–16, 1991, p. 27.

13. Multilateral financing for development in the Middle East had already been dealt with by Israeli scholars. See, for example, Arnon Gafny, "The Middle East Development Fund" and Joyce Starr, "A Marshall Plan for the Middle East," both in Fichelson, *Economic Cooperation.*

14. Matar and Hillal, *The Arab Regional System,* p. 53.

12

National Security in the Arab World: The Persistence of Dualism

BAHGAT KORANY

The analysis of national security has been basic to the study of domestic politics and international relations. Consequently, different schools of political science—Realist and Classical, Behavioralist and Contemporary—have something to say about the concept of national security. Indeed, most of these schools find the raison d'être of international relations as a discipline that is distinct from political science to be the need to study in its own right the state's (in)security dilemma. According to this dominant mainstream paradigm, developed by such different thinkers as Raymond Aron, Kenneth Waltz, Kal Holsti, and James Rosenau, the crux of the argument is that the international system—in contrast to domestic political systems—does not possess a centralized government or political authority.[1] Thus, it is a system in a "state of nature," one fundamentally manifesting Hobbes's war of all against all.

In this chapter I address the way in which the concept of national security applies to the Arab world after the 1990–1991 Gulf Crisis—that is, how national security is defined and how its concerns have, or have not, changed in the wake of the Gulf War. Certainly, the Gulf War—as any other war—constituted a breakdown in the normal pattern of diplomatic life, something, as Roger Owen says, akin to an earthquake in the daily life of people. Wars and earthquakes both generate appalling effects in a very short time. They are consequential.

The Gulf War was a major event by any standard. For instance, thirty-seven countries participated in the international coalition that challenged

Iraq's occupation of Kuwait, and they acted in the name of the entire international community. The levels of military technology employed during the hostilities ranged from Smart Bombs to Stealth warplanes, with many weapons being used in combat for the first time. The war's financial cost was exceptional—provisionally estimated at around $61 billion. The intensity of military action was no less impressive: During the forty-three days of hostilities, coalition forces conducted 109,876 air strikes against Iraqi targets and dropped between 120,000 and 130,000 tons of explosives.

I first briefly examine fundamental elements of the concept of national security, seeking to relate theoretical generalizations to concrete conditions in the Arab world. I then directly confront the main question at issue: whether the Gulf War has finally laid to rest long-established skepticism over the applicability of statecentric orthodox views of national security in the Arab context. In the concluding parts of this chapter I deal with this question by drawing attention to the persistence of societal and transstate issues at the root of Arab security concerns.

National Security: The Dominant Paradigm Questioned

Among professional students of politics, mainstream approaches to the study of national security are solidly rooted in the traditional power paradigm, whose "core . . . and . . . subject matter are the struggle for power among sovereign nations."[2] The power paradigm synthesized with disarming clarity the most visible aspects of international politics. By doing so, it captured the imagination of laypersons, provided an easy theoretical guide for practicing political leaders, and conditioned the outlooks of generations of students of global politics. Almost forty years after its initial publication, Hans Morgenthau's *Politics Among Nations* is still described as "the most influential textbook of the early post-war period . . . thought by many, if not by most, to have redirected those working in the field from idealist advocacy to realist analysis."[3] Indeed, the book captured in one volume the ideas of an entire generation of international relations scholars—from E. H. Carr and Harold Nicholson to Raymond Aron and George Kennan. Moreover, it influenced succeeding generations, outselling all other textbooks in the 1950s and still ranking in the late 1970s as the field's most utilized textbook.[4] I should also note that the power paradigm has been presented to the Third World as *the* framework for understanding international politics. *Politics Among Nations* has been translated into various languages, including Arabic, Chinese, Turkish, and Swahili.

In short, the power paradigm laid the groundwork for widespread consensus on the definition of national security. Examples abound: "A nation is secure to the extent to which it is not in danger of having to sacrifice core values, if it wishes to avoid war, and is able, if challenged, to maintain them by . . . victory in such a war."[5] And national security necessarily implies "that security rises and falls with the ability of a nation to deter an attack, or defeat it. This is in accord with the common usage of the term."[6]

Simple, direct, and logically consistent, the power paradigm nonetheless distorts the complex nature of international politics. In terms of national security, four such distortions are especially important.

First, the power paradigm envisages the state as the sole international actor. International organizations and multinational companies are either ignored or implicitly considered inconsequential. For example, Raymond Aron defined international relations as interstate relations and limited international action to the diplomat and the soldier—the two representatives par excellence of state activity. The analysis presented in his *opus classicus,* however, is dominated by the action of the soldier, even in the absence of war. Thus, such conflicts as those arising from nationalizations of multinational companies or internationally relevant massive social unrest arising from International Monetary Fund (IMF) or World Bank dictates is neglected.

A further distortion of contemporary international reality stems from the fact that the power paradigm not only conceptualizes the international system within the limited framework of purely interstate relations but also focuses overwhelmingly on the strongest of state actors—the powers of the "center," those who count in a military-industrial sense. Joseph Stalin expressed this outlook in extreme form when, upon being urged to take the Vatican into consideration, he brushed the pope aside by retorting, "How many battalions does he possess?"

A third, related, distorting tendency of the power paradigm lies precisely in its automatic assignment of states of the periphery to the role of junior partners in the global power game. The only alternative role available to peripheral states within this paradigm is that of countersystemic upsetters thriving on "nuisance power" and therefore liable to the techniques of counterinsurgency.

Finally, the power paradigm suffers from an inherent bias that focuses its application on what are automatically defined as "interesting" issues: "high" as opposed to "low" politics. Thus, questions of interstate conflict and national security are high on the analytical agenda for understanding international relations, whereas issues of culture, economy, and society are very low—almost falling beyond the paradigm's ken.

The basis of these distortions is not only the primacy assigned by the power paradigm to the state as *the* international actor but also that the state itself is viewed in terms of a very specific model: the European state of the eighteenth and nineteenth centuries. From this flow two related results: the ethnocentrism of mainstream national security studies and the growing irrelevance of such studies to Third World state formation and survival.

An Arab Specificity?

Applying the power paradigm narrowly to the regional context that interests us here would produce a distorted political picture, a rendering of the Arab world as a mere group of sovereign states that are no more interconnected than a group of billiard balls. Actually, there is an "Arab specificity": the collective feeling of constituting a distinct community across state frontiers. Thus, the majority of Arabs—elites and masses alike—have been torn between overlapping and sometimes competing allegiances.

First, there is raison d'état—political identification with the territorial state, or *al-dawla al-qitriyya*. Political identification with the particular Arab state—Morocco, Tunisia, Yemen, Egypt, and so forth—is no myth. Yet, there is also *raison de la nation*—a sense of transstate community. This pan-Arab identification underlies a set of general security concerns— Arab versus non-Arab—that cannot be accounted for by the orthodox power paradigm. Moreover, these particularly Arab security issues are distinct from, and at times in conflict with, security concerns related strictly to the territorial state.[7] Indeed, at the root of the Arabs' different alignments during the Gulf War were differing perceptions of security requirements— and these, in turn, were determined by whether Arab actors thought of security primarily in terms of the individual territorial state (*Amn Qutri*) or in terms of the broader collectivity: Arabs versus non-Arabs.

I should stress that these differences in perception did not simply divide Arab governments. Divisions also existed within Arab states, highlighting differences between regimes and the societies they govern. Thus, Morocco—a member of the pro-Kuwait coalition that sent troops to Saudi Arabia—witnessed massive demonstrations protesting the use of "foreign" troops against Iraq. The miscalculations of Iraq's decisionmakers can be partly explained by the dualistic nature of Arab security concerns. For instance, Baghdad appears to have grossly overestimated the extent to which Saudi Arabia's government would hesitate (either by choice or because of societal pressure) before inviting non-Arab troops to shield the Saudi state and liberate Kuwait.

In itself, this underlines the fact that an important consequence of the Gulf War has been the consolidation of territorial state sovereignty in the Arab world. What has been furthered is the "routinization"—in Max Weber's sense of the term—of the Arab territorial state; that is, the Arab state has gained increasing acceptance as normal, or standard.

A Paradigm Rehabilitated:
The Rise of the Arab Territorial State

State security concerns—or *Qutri* security issues—have never been absent from inter-Arab politics. We can go even further and argue that the raison d'état aspect of inter-Arab relations was codified in the 1945 Charter of the League of Arab States (LAS). My content analysis of the Charter shows that the term *state* appears forty-eight times in the Charter's twenty-two articles. Moreover, the Charter affirmed that the LAS was to be based upon "respect for the independence and sovereignty of each state" and that decisions taken by the LAS council would not be binding if differences between member states involved "a state's independence, sovereignty, or territorial integrity." We can, therefore, argue that the Charter is a state-oriented document.[8]

By dramatically reinforcing the territorial state dimension of Arab security concerns, Iraq's invasion of Kuwait was a watershed.[9] More to the point, we can argue that Iraq's adventure reinforced Arab concerns for state security *at the expense* of the collective Arab orientation. Indeed, the intensity with which Saddam Hussein embraced the pan-Arabist ideal to justify his assault on Kuwait was something akin to a fatal bear hug.

Shortly before Kuwait was invaded, Iraqi Foreign Minister Tareq Aziz declared that his government considered the Arabs

> over and above national boundaries to be one nation, that what belongs to [any] should belong to all and benefit all. . . . Despite its division into states, the Arab World nevertheless remains one country, every inch of which must be considered in accordance with a nationalistic vision . . . and the demands of common Arab security.[10]

It is not surprising that Baghdad sought to muster support during the Gulf Crisis by harping on collective issues that have mass appeal. Thus, for example, Iraq endeavored to depict its struggle to retain Kuwait as a jihad against non-Muslims and their stooges, who were contaminating the holy places in Saudi Arabia. Baghdad also justified its invasion of Kuwait as part of a political process to attain a variety of collective goals, including the liberation of Israeli Occupied Territories and the redistribution of Arab oil wealth.

Although these appeals had some degree of success—as demonstrated by pro-Iraqi demonstrations during the crisis in various parts of the Arab world—they were generally met with skepticism and lingering mistrust. This was hardly surprising. After all, Saddam and the Baath had long waged war against Iran's Islamic revolution in the name of secular nationalism. Then too, Iraq—an oil power second only to Saudi Arabia and enjoying a gross national product (GNP) per capita that was nine times that of Somalia, five times that of the Sudan, and just less than four times that of Egypt—had not pursued any plan for redistributing wealth on a regional basis prior to its invasion of Kuwait.

Such factors generated a widespread perception of Baghad's arguments in support of its takeover of Kuwait as constituting merely a crude effort to harness the pan-Arab ideal to the service of state-oriented realpolitik—and this only downgraded the ideal itself. As a result, a generalized feeling emerged within Gulf countries that threats to their survival would come increasingly from within the Arab family. Abdallah Bishara, secretary-general of the Gulf Cooperation Council, went so far as to declare that the basic threat to the Gulf states is not Israel but is some Arab states.[11] Baghdad's failure to present a convincing case for its invasion of Kuwait enhanced the view that Iraq had simply engaged in a conventional move of territorial aggrandizement. To many in the Arab world, the invasion seemed to be merely an interstate holdup—with the loot amounting to around $150–$200 billion of Kuwait's financial reserves and the possibility of controlling about half of the world's oil production and two-thirds of its known reserves.

All of this provides extensive grounds for cynicism in considering the collective dimension of Arab security concerns. Indeed, we must admit that the effect of the Gulf Crisis may prove fatal to the collective dimension of Arab security concerns. Several factors, including the following, could render this possibility a reality in the future.

1. The development of a contagion syndrome, with the various Arab states explicitly emphasizing particularistic interests above and beyond all else, is one such factor. Indeed, the possibility exists that narrow definitions of state security could become explicitly identified with regime security.

2. A focus on state security and territorial survival (or aggrandizement) would necessarily subordinate Arab core issues and undermine prospects for functional cooperative regional projects. Should this occur, Arab state security policies will become increasingly pragmatic and be based on shifting alliances—including alliances with non-Arabs against other Arab actors. Inter-Arab relations might well come to reflect the traditional balance-of-power model—which in all probability would soon evolve into a regional system characterized by a balance of weakness.

3. The collective dimension of Arab security concerns will probably further weaken in direct proportion to the willingness of individual Arab states to devote increased resources to defense and to seek bilateral defense pacts with non-Arabs. In the three years since the invasion of Kuwait, Saudi Arabia has spent around $10 billion on new arms. According to

Saudi General Khaled Ben Sultan, there are plans to triple the size of the Saudi Arabian army to two hundred thousand men, predicated upon close coordination with U.S. forces.[12]

Multidimensional Bases of National Security

Is this, then, the definitive end of the dualistic nature of national security concerns in the Arab world? Have the Arab states become like any other, lacking the specificity that in the past underlay the dualistic nature of their security concerns? Has their national security now become definitively monistic and centered exclusively on the territorial state? Do we now see the final victory of the traditional power paradigm as the most appropriate conceptual lens for understanding the Arab world?

Issuing a speedy death certificate for the collective dimension of Arab security concerns would be ahistorical and would negate the long-standing specificity of the Arab world. It would lead to unduly state-oriented analyses of the Arab world, a distorted approach that would neglect the societal (that is, transstate) dimension of Arab reality.[13]

For some analysts of international relations, the Arab world remains an exotic mixture—a mosaic of religious fundamentalists, natural resources, raw military power, and myriad political and social tensions. But even if the region is a mosaic, it still has an Arab core—a center characterized by the intensity and multiplicity of linkages (material, political, and, particularly, societal) among its various parts. Linguistic and cultural homogeneity sustains a sense of kinship and larger Arab identity that continues to transcend individual nationalities. As Paul Noble put it, this Arab core resembles a vast sound chamber in which currents of thought and information circulate widely and enjoy considerable resonance across state frontiers. For instance, cross-frontier alliances or associations between the government of one Arab state and individuals or groups in others are common. Another striking example is the frequency with which we find Arab scientists specializing in national security sectors such as nuclear research working in the service of an Arab state other than their own country. Such things underlie Noble's contention that the Arab core has "resembled less the traditional group of states as billiard balls that come in contact only at their hard outer shell, and resembled more a large scale domestic system divided into compartments of varying degrees of permeability."[14]

In short, because of high degrees of interconnections and permeability among Arab countries, state frontiers have been less important as barriers in the collective psychology than has the distinction between Arab and non-Arab. This distinction will become even more pronounced if a political and military imbalance develops further in favor of non-Arabs. Indeed, this is precisely what appears to be happening in the post–Gulf War period, as can be seen by briefly reviewing the current roles of Iran, Israel, and Turkey in the region.

During the 1980s, Iran threatened the Arab status quo not only by virtue of its physical size and strength but also because of its revolutionary Islamic ideology. The support extended by Arab Gulf states and other Arab regimes to Iraq during its eight-year war against Iran stemmed especially from the hope of undermining the credibility of revolutionary Islam. During the 1990–1991 Gulf Crisis, Iraq found it necessary to rebuild bridges to its erstwhile enemy. In a desperate bid to minimize the destruction of its military machine, Iraq sent part of its air force—23 planes according to Iran, 135 according to Baghdad—to the safety of Iranian airfields. Tehran's Islamic Republic—after long being considered a pariah state—seemed to be rehabilitated in the wake of the Gulf Crisis at Iraq's expense. With Iraq still in disarray, the potential for future regional muscle flexing by Iran must be seen as high.

The Gulf Crisis further consolidated Israel's military predominance in the region. Conventional indicators establishing Israel's military superiority over the Arab world are too well-known and numerous to be repeated here. It suffices to point out that Iraq's defeat obviously tilted the balance even more in Israel's favor. More important, however, is the degree to which the Gulf Crisis furthered Israel's political integration within the region. Three years ago, few would have imagined the convening of multilateral Arab-Israeli talks. Visions of Omani delegates speaking publicly with Israeli counterparts in Moscow corridors would have seemed fantastic, as would suggestions that Saudi Arabia's Prince Bandar might coordinate moves with U.S. Jewish leaders or that his country would host visiting Jewish delegates.[15] These events have now occurred, and the ongoing Middle East peace talks have moved from discussions of military and political matters to technical and cultural issues. The fact that all of this has transpired with no radical transformation of Israel's approach to basic conflict issues—withdrawal from the Occupied Territories, the application of the principle of self-determination to the Palestinian people, and the status of Jerusalem—starkly shows how far the balance of power has moved against the Arabs.

Turkey was one of the greatest winners of the 1991 Gulf War. After the end of the Cold War, Turkey was in danger of losing its strategic importance between the East and West. The Gulf War gave Turkey a new strategic role at the expense of its Arab neighbors. Again, the military gap is too clear to be labored, but Turkey is now capitalizing on a much more important strategic asset: water resources.

In a region of overuse and undersupply, as is the case of the Arab world, water is literally a factor in survival and is at the basis of any program of food security. It is, therefore, notable that 67 percent of the Digla's sources and 88 percent of the Euphrates's sources originate in Turkey. With the decline of Iraq's military power, Turkey is in an even stronger position to exercise substantial pressures for political concessions on both Iraq and Syria. Turkey's blockage of the Euphrates's water flow for a month in early 1990 not only affected agriculture in Syria and Iraq but also led to frequent electricity cuts in both countries. At present, there are serious concerns over the effects of Turkey's planned $20 billion water control project, a massive undertaking that envisages the construction of twenty-one dams and seventeen power stations. If Turkish hopes of extending water pipelines to Jordan, Palestine, Iraq, and the Gulf are eventually realized, Ankara will be in a good position to barter water for oil and, more important, to dominate daily life in much of the Arab world.

Characteristics of the Arab State
and a Societal Basis for Security

By limiting considerations of Arab security to the traditional focus on the state, the power paradigm would yield an incomplete analysis. As indicated earlier, this stems from the paradigm's inherent tendency to utilize the European state as its model and to neglect the specific contexts and characteristics of state formation in Third World areas. The fact is that the typical Third World state is characterized by conditional legitimacy and is based on a praetorian society.[16]

Primarily because of the imposition of foreign rules and institutions and the telescoping of historical phases of state formation, the typical Third World state's survival is threatened not so much from the outside as it is by internal dissent and lack of sociopolitical identification.[17] As Mohammed Ayoob put it when referring to a particular case of the South Asian context of the early 1970s:

> Any perceptive observer of the South-Asian scene . . . would have realized that the Indian "threat" to Pakistan was very secondary to that posed by East Bengali nationalists; also that the Indo-Pakistani war of 1971 would either not have been fought, or, if fought, would have had a very different outcome if the bulk of the East Bengali population had not been disenchanted with the existing structure of the Pakistani state.[18]

In this respect, we are reminded that the fundamental causes of the Iraq-Iran War went far beyond questions of border demarcation. Iraq came to fear for its survival as the Shi'a-dominated Islamic Revolution began encouraging Iraq's Shi'a majority to topple the Sunni-dominated regime in

Baghdad. This was merely one example of the Third World tendency to exploit intrastate conflicts in interstate relations. Such seminal domestic tensions tend to arise from racial heterogeneity, religious animosities, linguistic diversity, tribal divisions, regional differences, and other societal factors.[19] Thus, the "made-in-Europe" model of the nation-state failed to relate adequately to territorial, ethnic, religious, geographic, and cultural traditions in Third World areas.

The colonial experience was the vehicle through which the orthodox intellectual model led to the construction of concrete political structures in the Third World. The upshot in the Middle East, as one student notes, was the following:

> What this means in practice . . . is that the division of the community of Moslems and Arabs into numerous nation-states since World War I has not only to a large extent ignored the traditional ethnic and religious groupings but has also resulted in the governments of the various national entities starting to lodge claims which are almost bound to lead to conflict with other countries.[20]

The basic contradiction between the European state model and historical Third World reality constitutes a structural handicap that manifests itself in a very characteristic way: lack of consensus on the rules of the game, on fundamental issues of political, social, and economic organization. In consequence, political contests become matters of life and death, vertical and horizontal divisions are exacerbated, and internal threats to the state escalate. The political context becomes what Samuel Huntington popularized as "praetorian society."[21]

Praetorian society is essentially "out of joint" because of the gap between relatively high levels of participation and relatively low levels of institutionalization capable of channeling popular demands in orderly ways. Thus,

> social forces confront each other nakedly, no political institutions, no corps of professional political leaders are recognized or accepted as the legitimate intermediaries to moderate group conflict. Equally important, no agreement exists among the groups as to the legitimate and authoritative methods for resolving conflicts.[22]

This leads to the prevalence of self-help as a standard orientation among competing groups—groups that perceive themselves as acting in zero-sum contexts, where the gain of one is automatically the loss of the other: "The wealthy bribe; students riot; workers strike; mobs demonstrate; and the military coup."[23]

Because of the widespread nature of these characteristics of Third World states and societies, some conflict patterns are identifiable. Two examples can be singled out: the development deficit and the rise of religio-politics and other culturally rooted demands.[24]

The Development Deficit

All Third World countries have immediate necessities: increasing per capita income, providing for a fairer distribution of wealth, and caring for such basic human needs as education, health, and food. The problem is that generating balanced economic growth is a long-term process. However, Third World populations feel they have waited too long for the benefits of development. The result is the well-known widening gap between mass demands and the capacity of political systems to cope with those demands. A traffic control tower faced with too many messages from aircraft during a certain time interval cannot cope within the prevailing operating rules. The outcome of such a situation would be the breakdown of the traffic system. By analogy, the consequence of the gap between expectations and satisfaction in the Third World is social frustration.

Even Third World states that can do well in the enterprise of economic development are not guaranteed escape from the spectre of political instability and insecurity. For although accelerated growth may increase the capacity of political authorities to meet a growing number of demands, studies in political economy still emphasize the thesis of "rapid growth as a destabilizing force."[25] Put succinctly, the reasons for this are as follows:

1. Additional sources of social tension and unrest arise as a result of the widening gap between the rich and those whose standard of living declines in relative, if not absolute, terms.
2. Newly wealthy groups tend to demand increased political power and social status apace with their novel economic empowerment.
3. Increased literacy, education, and exposure to mass media lead to rising expectations that cannot be satisfied in the short term.
4. The attraction of violent political protest grows as a consequence of increasing alienation produced by geographical mobility and the weakening of social ties.
5. Popular discontent is produced by restrictions on consumption designed to promote investment.
6. Controversies over the distribution of economic benefits exacerbate ethnic and regional tensions.
7. The increasing disruption of traditional social groupings (family, caste, tribe) leads to a growing number of people who are ripe for recruitment into revolutionary organizations.
8. Organized groups press their demands at a time when state authorities are not yet able to cope with them.

This last category deserves attention, particularly because the satisfaction of demands generated by competing groups in praetorian societies frequently requires the fragmentation of the state itself. However, even more frequently, praetorian demands require substantial alterations in the state's organization, because they often tend to be rooted in calls for cultural authenticity and religio-politics.

Cultural Demands and Religio-Politics

The foregoing list of destabilizing side effects of rapid economic growth is perhaps applicable to all developmental contexts. Whatever the case, in rapidly developing states, recent years have witnessed the rise of cultural-religious demands and their mobilizing capacity through catchwords such as retribalization, re-Islamicization, and retraditionalization. The most notable recent example is the Ayatollah Khomeini's Islamic Revolution, which in a matter of weeks brought down Iran's Pahlavi regime. The essence of that event is captured by Udo Steinbach, who argues that the

> survival of cultural traditions in a rapid process of modernization and the manner in which the masses are mobilized differ from revolutionary processes with a purely social or economic background. Western-style economic rationality, the cultural foundation of the Western course of development and Western civilization, are all rejected. Instead, the aim is to revitalize the native culture and to adapt it to the needs of the modern state. This conflict of cultures is expressed within a country itself in the confrontation between native chauvinism on the one hand and Westernized elites on the other.[26]

This is why the possible contagion effect of the Iranian Revolution frightened established elites throughout the region. However, the international dimensions of such mass cultural manifestations can be much more direct. The crisis created by the holding of U.S. hostages in Tehran showed how domestic demands for cultural authenticity can be internationalized in striking ways.

An influential school of social science research focuses only on intrastate conflict, not only because it reflects the everyday political order but also because internal tensions can give rise to, or be exploited by, interstate confrontation.[27] The point, as Jusuf Wanandi argues, is that "the greater the threats to security which originate domestically, the greater are the external threats faced by the country."[28] For our purposes, the significance of such insights is that the military means favored by the established power paradigm in strategic studies cannot be seen as a panacea for national security. In the Third World, and in the Arab world in particular, the primary sources of insecurity are political, economic, social, cultural, and ideological—and, above all, domestically rooted. The majority of conflicts are primarily protracted social conflicts.[29]

Conclusion

I began this chapter by showing how dominant paradigms of international relations have equated the essence of their subject matter with the study of national security. From seventeenth-century historians and builders of international law to Raymond Aron and Kenneth Waltz in contemporary Europe and North America, scholars' efforts to analyze and understand the international system have emphasized the plurality of *sovereign* states— that is, the absence of a legitimate suprastate authority. According to the logic of this approach, the salient feature of international relations is the (in)security dilemma: A state's basic survival is threatened by the mere existence of other states in the anarchic international environment of all against all.

Pan-Arabists have rejected the applicability to their region of this Hobbesian militaristic view.[30] The implication is that the Arab homeland is not a mere conglomeration of hard-shelled, billiard ball, sovereign states. Thus, the analysis of security issues in the Arab world should not be limited only, or even primarily, to the raison d'état of the territorial state.[31] Instead, pan-Arabists draw attention to *raison de la nation*—the Arab nation and its multistate civil society. In this perspective, the existence of this suprastate entity—Arab civil society—is the rationale for Arab cohesion on suprastate issues, such as Palestine and the eight-year Iran-Iraq War. Arabic strategic studies literature is littered with discussions of *'Amn qawmi,* or national security, as distinct from *Amn Qutri,* or state security.[32]

However, if the doctrine of a collective dimension of Arab security has been straightforward and emphatic, Arab states' practices have been otherwise. Not only an Arab Cold War but also hot conflicts have placed Arab states at each others throats in both the Mashrek and the Maghreb.[33] Recent studies show that between 1945 and 1991, interstate Arab conflicts (in conjunction with the problem of minorities) resulted in twenty thousand victims, caused about one million people to become homeless, and cost approximately $50 billion.[34]

In fact, disputes over borders are prevalent within the Arab nation. There are at least twelve such potential conflicts in the Gulf region alone. Thus, it is obvious that the *qutri,* or territorial, dimension of Arab security cannot be dismissed. It not only contradicts in theory the postulates of (pan)-national security but also in practice is capable of leading to intra-Arab miniwars. The world's historical record is in keeping with this conclusion.

The relations between modern states reach their most critical stage in the form of problems relating to territory. Boundary disputes, conflicting claims to newly discovered lands and invasions by expanding nations of the territory of their weaker neighbours have been conspicuous among the causes of war.[35]

But the conflict between Iraq and Kuwait was much more than a border issue. Six days after the declaration of Kuwait's political independence on June 19, 1961, Iraqi ruler General Abd al-Karim Kassim denied Kuwait's existence and claimed Iraqi sovereignty over the sheikhdom. British and Saudi forces were immediately brought in to thwart any possible troop movements by Baghdad. The issue was debated by the UN Security Council and the Arab League. The latter replaced British and Saudi troops with Arab forces under its own mandate, admitted Kuwait as a full member (against Iraq's opposition), and decided to regard any attack against Kuwait as aggression against the league's members, to be repelled by force if necessary.

The 1990–1991 Gulf War once more brought to the fore the contradiction between opposition to artificial and colonial borders and ministate survival. This aggravated the more basic contradiction inherent in the contemporary Arab context: that between "say" and "do," between the *doctrine* of (pan)-national security and the *practice* of territorial state security. The Arab dilemma in this context is very real, and it cannot be simplistically explained away by looking for a scapegoat—such as the ambitions of an individual leader. The dilemma reveals contradictory interpretations of the security issue as evidenced by the painful divisions and hesitant alignments that characterize Arab actors—all of whom claim to defend Arab security.

A Moroccan example is pertinent. The government of Morocco sided with the anti-Saddam international coalition and even sent troops to Saudi Arabia. Yet, Morocco witnessed the biggest street demonstration in its history during the Gulf War—a protest against the war and foreign intervention in intra-Arab affairs. Equally important is the fact that the demonstrators were allowed to carry out their protest without being harmed by security forces, despite the latter's history of relying on heavy-handed measures when faced with much less apparent provocation.

Visits to other Arab countries showed me that Morocco was not the only Arab country deeply divided by the Gulf Crisis. Moreover, intra-Arab tensions were not merely the traditional ones of ruler versus ruled. They also manifested intraelite and intramass frictions. The Gulf Crisis left both masses and elites in the Arab world traumatized. This, fundamentally, is why it was indeed a political earthquake, a defining event separating the "before" from the "after." For apart from its immediate effects at the political and military levels, it underscored the basic Arab dilemma between raison d'état and *raison de la nation,* what I have dubbed elsewhere the painful cross-pressures of role conflict.[36]

If the crisis and the war concretized this Arab dilemma in its most acute form, how does the Arab world fare in the wake of the hostilities? The seriously bruised state of inter-Arab relations, as well as the paralysis of the Arab League and its inability to assume a leadership role, seem to decide the issue in favor of the exclusiveness of territorial state security as propounded by the traditional paradigm. Dualism, with its inherent ambiguity, might be taken to have been decisively toppled. Early prophets who forecast the end of pan-Arabism appear to be finally vindicated. Inter-Arab relations now seem routinized—in the Weberian sense—and have become "normal" interstate relations, similar to those in other regions of the world.

However, the analysis presented above casts doubt on these conclusions. I have sought to attract attention to the *structural*—the more permanent—aspects of Arab security issues. I foresee the ongoing presence of the collective-societal security dimension in the Arab world. That dimension's potential return to prominence in the not-too-distant future appears assured, because major regional problems highlighted by the crisis have not been solved.

The invasion of Kuwait did arouse widespread skepticism over the pan-Arabist ethos in view of its abuse by one leader. But disillusionment and even—should it occur—a generalized veering away from pan-Arabist national identification on the part of the masses will not necessarily redound ideologically to the benefit of the national state. Indeed, the outcome could strengthen alternative pan-ideologies, particularly Islamic fundamentalism.

The collective dimension of Arab security will therefore continue to exist alongside that of the narrower concept of state security. Even though the Islamic dimension of security concerns remains to be studied in depth, its mere presence attests to the many faces of security that persist in the post–Gulf Crisis Arab context.[37] Thus, apart from issues revolving around the new international order, the painful debate between *'Amn qawmi* and *'Amn qutri,* between state security and national security, will continue to haunt decisionmakers and challenge analysts.

Notes

This chapter builds on the author's ideas in B. Korany, Paul Noble, and Rex Brynen (eds.), *The Many Faces of National Security in the Arab World* (London: Macmillan; New York: St. Martin's, 1993), esp. pp. 2–19.

1. Raymond Aron, *Paix et Guerre entre les Nations* (Paris: C. Levy, 1962). See also "Qu'est-ce qu'une théorie des relations internationales," *Revue française de science politique* 17 (1967), pp. 309–318. Kenneth Waltz, *Theory of*

International Politics (Reading: Addison-Wesley, 1979); Kal Holsti, *Peace & War: Armed Conflicts and International Order, 1649–1989* (Cambridge: Cambridge University Press, 1991); James Rosenau, *Turbulence in World Politics: A Theory of Change and Continuity* (Princeton: Princeton University Press, 1990).

2. Hans Morgenthau (edited and revised by Kenneth Thompson), *Politics Among Nations: The Struggle for Power and Peace,* 6th ed. (New York: Alfred Knopf, 1985), pp. 4–6.

3. Olson, *The Theory and Practice of International Relations,* 8th ed. (Englewood Cliffs: Prentice Hall, 1991), pp. 217–224. See also William Olson and Nicholas Onuf, "The Growth of a Discipline," in Steve Smith (ed.), *International Relations: British and American Perspectives* (Oxford: Blackwell, in association with the British International Studies Association, 1985), pp. 1–28.

4. James Rosenau, Edwin P. McLain, Dona Stinziano, Richard Stoddard, and Dean Swanson, "Of Syllabi, Texts, Students: Scholarship in International Relations," *World Politics* 29, no. 2 (January 1977), pp. 263–341.

5. Walter Lippmann, *U.S. Foreign Policy: Shield of the Republic* (Boston: Little, Brown, 1943), p. 51, as cited in Mohammed Ayoob, "Security in the Third World," *International Affairs* 60, no. 1 (Winter 1983–1984), pp. 41–51.

6. Arnold Wolfers, *Discord and Collaboration: Essays on International Politics* (Baltimore: Johns Hopkins, 1962), p. 150.

7. Tawfic E. Farah (ed.), *Pan-Arabism and Arab Nationalism: The Continuing Debate* (Boulder: Westview Press, 1987); Rashid Khalidi, Lisa Anderson, Muhammad Muslih, and Reeva S. Simmon (eds.), *The Origins of Arab Nationalism* (New York: Columbia University Press, 1991); Bassam Tibi, *Arab Nationalism: A Critical Enquiry,* 2d ed. (translated from German) (London: Macmillan, 1990).

8. Bahgat Korany, "Alien and Besieged Yet Here to Stay: The Contradictions of the Arab Territorial State," in Ghassan Salame (ed.), *The Foundations of the Arab State* (London: Croom Helm, for the Institut Affairi Internazionali, 1987), pp. 47–75.

9. Rex Brynen and Paul Noble, "The Gulf Crisis and the Arab State System: A New Regional Order?" *Arab Studies Quarterly* 13, nos. 1–2 (Winter-Spring 1991).

10. "Gulf War Anniversary," *Middle East Magazine* 209, March 1992, p. 6.

11. Mohammed H. Heikal, *The Gulf Crisis: Illusions of Power and Victory* (Cairo: Al-Ahram Publications, 1992), p. 592 (in Arabic).

12. "King Hussein Takes Helm," *Middle East Magazine* 208, February 1992, pp. 5–8.

13. For details see Bahgat Korany, Paul Noble, and Rex Brynen (eds.), *The Many Faces of National Security in the Arab World* (London: Macmillan and St. Martin's, 1993).

14. Paul Noble, "The Arab System: Pressures, Constraints and Opportunities," in Bahgat Korany, Ali El Hillal Dessouki, et al., *The Foreign Policies of Arab States: The Challenge of Change* 2d ed. (Boulder: Westview Press, 1991), pp. 49–57.

15. Heikal, *The Gulf Crisis,* p. 475.

16. Bahgat Korany, "The Dialectics of Inter-Arab Relations, 1967–1987," in Y. Lukacs and A. M. Battah (eds.), *The Arab-Israeli Conflict: Two Decades of Change* (Boulder: Westview Press, 1988), pp. 147–163, Bahgat Korany, "Vers une redéfinition des études stratégiques," in Charles P. David (ed.), *Les Etudes Strategiques: Approches et Concepts* (Quebec: Centre Quebecois de Relations

Internationales et Fondation pour les Etudes de Defense Nationale, 1989), pp. 27–49.

17. Korany, "Alien and Besieged."

18. Ayoob, "Security in the Third World," pp. 41–51.

19. Bahgat Korany, *Social Change, Charisma and International Behaviour: Toward a Theory of Foreign Policy in the Third World* (Geneva: Sijthoff, 1976), pp. 123–125.

20. Udo Steinbach, "Sources of Third World Conflict," *Adelphi Papers*, no. 166 (Summer 1981), pp. 20–28.

21. Samuel Huntington, *Political Order in Changing Societies* (New Haven: Yale University Press, 1968), pp. 192–264.

22. Ibid., p. 196.

23. Ibid.

24. Steinbach, "Sources of Third World Conflict"; Jerrold Green, "Islam, Religio-Politics and Social Change," *Comparative Studies in Society and History* 27, no. 2 (April 1985), pp. 312–322.

25. Korany, *Social Change*, pp. 121–123.

26. Steinbach, "Sources of Third World Conflict," pp. 20–28.

27. Ekkart Zimmerman, *Political Violence, Crises and Revolution* (Cambridge: Schenkman, 1983); Michael Haas, *International Conflict* (Indianapolis: Bobbs-Merrill, 1974); Jonathan Wilkenfeld (ed.), *Conflict Behavior and Linkage Politics* (New York: McKay, 1973).

28. Jusuf Wanandi, "The International Implication of Third World Conflict: A Third World Perspective," *Adelphi Papers*, no. 166 (Summer 1981), pp. 14–20.

29. Edward Azar and Chung-In Moon (eds.), *National Security and the Third World: The Management of Internal and External Threats* (London: Edward Edgar, 1988).

30. Gamil Mattar and Ali E. Hillal, *The Arab Regional System,* 3d ed. (Beirut: Center for Arab Unity Studies, 1983) (in Arabic); Kheir E. Hasseed, S. E. Ibrahim, A. Nassar, I. Saad El-Din, and Ali E. Hillal, *The Future of the Arab Nation: Challenges and Choices* (Beirut: Center for Arab Unity Studies, 1987) (in Arabic). This is the final report of a multivolume project bringing together about two hundred scholars researching the future of the Arab homeland. An English translation, edited by Roger Owen, was published by Routledge (London) in 1991.

31. A good recent sample of Arab thinking on this subject is *Civil Society in the Arab Homeland* (Beirut: Center for Arab Unity Studies, 1992) (in Arabic). See also *Middle East Journal* (March 1993), which is devoted to Arab civil society, and Mustafa K. El-Sayyid, "The Civil Society Concept and the Arab World," paper presented to the International Conference on Political Liberalization and Democratization in the Arab World, convened by the Inter-University Consortium of Arab Studies, Montreal, May 7–8, 1993.

32. To gauge the significance of this literature, it is sufficient to glance through conference papers and other works of the Center for Arab United Studies (Beirut), especially its monthly *El Moustakbal El-Arabi,* as well as those of the Arab Thought Forum (Amman) and those of the Al-Ahram Center for Political and Strategic Studies (Cairo). The center's *Arab Strategic Yearbook,* edited by Sayed Yasseen, has dealt in depth with Arab security issues and concepts since it first appeared in 1986. Other relevant works include those by Amin Huwaidi, a soldier-turned-scholar and ex–defense minister of Egypt. See, for instance, his *Militarization and Security in the Middle East* (Cairo: Dar El-Shuruq, 1991) (in Arabic). See also Gihad Auda, "Arab National Security," *El Moustakbal El-Arabi*

(1986) (in Arabic); Ali E. Hillal, "Arab National Security: A Study of Fundamentals," *Arab Affairs* (Tunis and Cairo), Vol. 35 (January 1984), pp. 8–21 (in Arabic). In English, see A. Al-Mashat, *National Security in the Third World* (Boulder: Westview Press, 1985).

33. The standard work on this subject in English is still Malcolm Kerr, *The Arab Cold War* (New York: Oxford University Press, 1970).

34. Ahmed Youssef Ahmed provides very useful tables in his *Arab-Arab Conflicts* (Beirut: Center for Arab Unity Studies, 1988) (in Arabic). Evette Fayez, "Worries of Minorities," *Civil Society and Democratic Transformation in the Arab World* 2, no. 4 (April 1993), pp. 31–33.

35. N. L. Hill, *Claims to Territory in International Law and Relations* (Westport: Greenwood Press, 1976), p. 3.

36. Bahgat Korany, "Egyptian Policy and the Intifada," in R. Brynen (ed.), *Echoes of the Intifada: Regional Repercussions of the Palestinian-Israeli Conflict* (Boulder: Westview Press, 1991), pp. 195–214.

37. Korany, Noble, and Brynen, *The Many Faces of National Security*. See also James Piscatori, *Islam in a World of Nation States* (Cambridge: Cambridge University Press, 1986); and Mustafa M. Mangood, "Political Dimensions of Security in Islam," unpublished Ph.D. diss., Cairo University, 1990 (in Arabic).

13

The Third Wave of Democratization in the Arab World

MUSTAPHA K. EL SAYYID ⸻⸻⸻⸻⸻⸻⸻

The transition from authoritarian regimes that has occurred in countries of Southern Europe, South and Southeast Asia, Latin America, and Eastern Europe at different times since the mid-1970s is described by Samuel Huntington as democracy's "third wave."[1] Using the long-wave theory of economic change, he suggests that the contemporary world has seen three periods characterized in the first instance by pressures for democratization and subsequently marked by antidemocratic trends. Huntington feels the first wave started in Europe in the 1820s and was reversed a century later with the rise of fascist regimes. The second wave gathered momentum at the end of World War II and lost steam three decades later. The third wave, according to this view, started in Southern Europe—with the overthrow of authoritarian regimes in Greece, Portugal, and Spain—moved later to Latin America and South and Southeast Asia, and, finally, shook the foundations of Communist regimes in Eastern Europe.

The political history of the Arab world reveals parallel trends, although not with the same intensity or breadth. I am tempted to call such trends waves of political liberalization, the first of which was manifested in Egypt between 1866 and 1882, when the country experienced its first elected national assemblies under the Khedives Ismail and Tewfik. This first move toward constitutional government, although initiated by the ruler of the country, continued to be given momentum by the nationalist movement. It was halted by the British occupation in 1882.[2]

The second wave corresponded to the establishment of parliamentary regimes in many Arab countries in the Mashrek, the Nile Valley, and the

Maghreb following their independence. Tendencies toward democratization stretched over several decades in some countries (Egypt 1924–1953, Iraq 1936–1958, Lebanon 1946–1975), whereas in others such tendencies were limited to a few years (Syria 1946–1949, 1955–1958; Tunisia 1956–1962). This second wave affected few countries of the Arabian Peninsula and ended in most other Arab states in the 1950s and 1960s. During those decades, democratic tendencies wilted, because the model of the dominant party system or the single mass organization was adopted by radical regimes that arose in several Arab countries after 1952. The Arab defeat in the 1967 June War dealt a serious blow to those radical Arab regimes, shaking credence in their capacities to pursue the struggle for national independence and economic development.[3]

Groundwork for the third wave was laid in the aftermath of this war, with the loss of prestige suffered by military establishments in countries ruled by army officers. Prestige was not entirely restored by Arab successes in the early days of the 1973 October War. Thus, concrete manifestations of a third wave of political liberalization were not seen until the second half of the 1970s, with the reconciliation in Morocco between opposition political parties and King Hassan in 1975 and Egypt's return to multiparty politics in 1976. The third wave followed a tumultuous course. Gathering momentum in the late 1980s, it produced transitions to a multiparty system, on a de facto or de jure basis, in a considerable number of countries—particularly Tunisia, Algeria, Yemen, Jordan, Somalia, and Mauritania.

In the aftermath of the Gulf War, the third wave was echoed in the Gulf countries. The emir of Kuwait promised to hold legislative elections in October 1992, a *Shura* Council was elected in Oman in 1991, and a similar council was promised by the Saudi Arabian regime. Some gestures of limited liberalization were also made by the few remaining radical regimes in the Arab world: Syria, Iraq, and Libya.

Features of the Third Wave—
Liberalization but No Democratization

A comparison of manifestations of democracy's three waves in Arab countries and in other regions of the world reveals substantive differences in both scope and intensity. If comparison is limited to the third wave, the range of political change that took place in the Arab world, although substantial, is still fairly modest compared to change in other parts of the world. The third wave has been a powerful force in other areas—undermining the foundations of many authoritarian regimes in the Third World, as well as in Eastern Europe, and replacing ruling groups of military juntas and Communist leaders with new groups who came to power through popular consent expressed in free general elections. What occurred in these countries was a democratizing process that often flowed in the wake of massive popular mobilization in the name of participatory politics. In contrast, what took place in the Arab world was at best a process of political liberalization, limited by its dependence upon the agreement of ruling groups to extend certain civil and political rights that had hitherto been denied. Concessions mostly involved freedom of speech and of professional and political organization.

Even this modest dose of liberalization did not take place in many Arab countries. Instead, rulers codified decades-old practices of government, including consultation with traditional dignitaries, while maintaining political infrastructures that do not allow political parties or trade unions. In all cases of this type, the process was controlled by the state, which set the pace of change and determined boundaries that could not be exceeded.

Consequently, whereas democratization in other parts of the world led to fundamental sociopolitical changes, changes in Arab countries were very limited. Briefly stated, what occurred in Arab countries during this third wave was mostly political liberalization initiated and controlled from above.[4]

In undertaking such changes, ruling groups were rarely under specific, concrete pressure to "democratize" their ways of governing. Popular dissatisfaction was linked more to the results of government performance than to any fundamental questioning of political processes.

Thus, in most cases Arab governments faced severe domestic crises that cast powerful doubts on their legitimacy. Confrontations with Islamist militants and public protests caused by harsh economic measures were the triggering events that led governments in Egypt (1981), Tunisia (1987), Algeria (1988), and Jordan (1989) to take steps toward political liberalization.

To be sure, in other cases demands by sections of the elite for political participation or for the right to be consulted, together with friendly advice from a major foreign ally, pushed governments—particularly in the Gulf region—to go some way toward meeting the requirements of a modern political system. The examples of both Kuwait and Saudi Arabia are instructive. In other instances, the demonstration effect of changes in Eastern Europe and in other Arab countries pushed the more authoritarian political regimes in the region—particularly those of Syria, Iraq, Libya, Somalia, and Mauritania—to make efforts to show that they too would respond to the new international discourse on democracy.

However, the degree of real transition has been uneven in the Arab world. Change has been only cosmetic in some Arab countries in which freedom of expression and association remain severely curtailed. This has been particularly true in countries ruled by the area's few remaining radical regimes.[5]

Moreover, no matter how far the transition from the old ways of governing has gone, respect for civil and political rights remains problematic in all Arab countries. Serious violations of human dignity in nearly all Arab states are reported by the most credible international and regional human rights organizations. The February 1992 issue of the *News Bulletin* of the Arab Organization of Human Rights cited cases of torture in Egypt and Tunisia, restrictions on trade unions and political participation in Sudan, violations of academic and civil freedoms in Bahrain and Saudi Arabia, unfair elections in Mauritania, and a setback to democratic processes in Algeria.[6] An examination of the most recent annual reports of Amnesty International and the Arab Organization of Human Rights only heightens this bleak picture. Specific types of human rights violations do vary from one regime to another, because some rights—namely, freedom of speech and freedom of association—are more respected in certain countries than in others. However, the pattern of selective respect for human rights is common to all Arab states.

The course of political liberalization is not yet a solid new departure in the Arab world. Instead, it seems to be more of an expedient method of managing the current crisis faced by Arab states, a charade that will be abandoned once ruling groups recognize the risk of losing power to other forces released by the very hopes for democratization that are being raised. Thus, the process of political liberalization may stagnate. Moreover, the entire trend may be reversed, with authoritarian structures being restored, as was the case in Sudan in June 1989 and in Algeria in early 1992.

Prospects for Further Political Liberalization

Better insight into the political realities of today's Arab world is gained by thinking of liberalization as a dynamic process, with the measures taken by different governments to date seen as opening gambits in an evolving game. In this light, players—each acting to further its particular interests— would include incumbent governments, entrepreneurial groups, intellectuals, the so-called popular sectors, and major foreign actors. How might this game evolve in the near future?

Ruling Groups in Arab Countries

Ruling groups that currently hold the reins of government are probably the most influential actors shaping the outcome of the liberalization process.

They are not likely to undertake any initiative that would obviously jeopardize their hold on power. The Egyptian and Tunisian governments are unlikely to grant Islamist movements the right to establish political parties. Nor is the Algerian regime likely to permit the Islamic Salvation Front (FIS) to resume functioning as a political party. Indeed, assuming a basically rational calculation of interest, neither radical nor conservative Arab regimes are likely to permit full freedom for the establishment of political parties.

In Arab countries in which governments claim to be based on popular consent expressed through competitive elections, ruling groups not only determine who may participate in the political process but also define the rules of competition. Thus, ruling groups generally have exclusive control of electronic media and administrative agencies charged with supervising elections.

Moreover, the concept of democracy adhered to by Arab rulers leaves no room for the peaceful transfer of power to opposition groups. An examination of speeches and statements of some Arab heads of state in those countries that permit a measure of political pluralism reveals that for them, democracy is merely allowing others with different views to express themselves without the threat of punishment. For such leaders, the distance between respecting freedom of speech and allowing the popular will to determine who governs seems to be a dangerous leap into the unknown. Being cautious, they are unlikely to make that move.

Entrepreneurial Groups

In the historical experiences of England, France, and the United States, the bourgeoisie championed the struggle against absolutist rulers and despotic governments. The role of bourgeois groups in the transition from authoritarianism in some Third World countries has also been notable.[7] Might entrepreneurial groups perform a similar role in the process of political liberalization in Arab countries?

My own effort to deal with the question suggests that private entrepreneurial groups in Arab countries are more dependent on the state for capital accumulation than are their counterparts in other Third World countries. The share of gross domestic product controlled by the state in Arab countries tends to be higher than in other developing states with similar levels of per capita income.[8]

Political liberalization has been accompanied in nearly all Arab countries by an extensive dose of economic liberalization. Demands of private entrepreneurial groups were at least partly met by lifting restrictions on private initiative and by selling public enterprises to private groups. In the long run—if and when trade barriers are generally eliminated—full liberalization programs will adversely affect some entrepreneurial sectors. However, so far, Arab businessmen have generally been swayed by the short-term attraction of economic restructuring. Because economic liberalization is not usually emphasized by the nationalist, Islamist, and Marxist groups that comprise the main opposition groups in the Arab world, incumbent regimes have benefited.

In short, despite ethnic and ideological cleavages among themselves, prominent businessmen tend to be powerful allies of governing parties. This seems to be the case in Egypt, Jordan, Tunisia, and Morocco. Major entrepreneurial groups in Algeria expressed concern for the country's economic future in the aftermath of the first round of Algerian legislative elections in December 1991. The founders of the National Committee to Save Algeria—constituted after this election was won overwhelmingly by the Islamic Salvation Front—included (in addition to the General Federation of Labor) various entrepreneurial groups, such as the National Union of Public Contractors, the General Confederation of Economic Agents, the Society of Heads of Enterprises, and the Society of Cadres of Public Administration. Some of these groups were formed by public-sector officials; however, as is true in many Third World states, the line between public-sector and private-sector entrepreneurial groups tends to be fairly fluid in Algeria.[9]

Arab governments do not hesitate to rely on the power of the purse to attract important business groups and divide opposition ranks. This was demonstrated by the Kuwaiti government's offer to buy private Kuwait business debts amounting to around $25 billion. The proposal caused a split in the Kuwaiti opposition. Some major opposition figures suspected Machiavellian machinations behind the move, which came only a few months before scheduled legislative elections. This view was not shared by senior members of the country's Chamber of Commerce, who were also prominent opposition leaders.[10]

Of course, nothing guarantees that businessmen will continue to support Arab governments in the long run. Eventual dismay over the heavy burden that must be borne by businessmen in some countries as the necessary price for limited economic liberalization policies, and possible virtual collapses of some national economies in the Arab world, might cause large numbers of businessmen to defect to any other party that promises an easier or healthier economic environment.

Arab Intellectuals

Despite innumerable pronouncements by Arab intellectuals proclaiming democracy the sine qua non for resolving the problems of Arab society, the transition to pluralist political arrangements in parts of the Arab world has subjected Arab thinkers to difficult tests. As the Islamist movement came gradually to occupy a prominent place among opposition forces, Arab intellectuals divided into two opposing camps, with supporters of an Islamist political and social platform on the one side and supporters of secularist, liberal, Marxist, or nationalist alternatives on the other. The contrast has been most clearly manifested in Algeria and Egypt, but the division is felt throughout the Arab world.

Supporters of an Islamist platform in Egypt endorsed judicial and administrative measures to censor novels, books, and films deemed incompatible with Islamic values. The slogans of Algeria's Islamic Salvation Front and statements of its leaders, who are members of the Algerian intelligentsia, called for abolishing the constitution and outlawing political parties. Secularist Algerian and Egyptian intellectuals were dismayed by the FIS victory at the polls, although the outcome reflected the position of the majority of Algerians who cast ballots on December 26, 1991. Egyptian intellectuals warned President Hosni Mubarak against any hasty transition to democracy, expressing alarm at the prospect of an "Algerian scenario."

If large numbers of Arab intellectuals are so strongly divided by their conceptions of democracy, how can they be expected to mobilize others in the struggle for a more democratic political order? The absence of widespread mobilization on behalf of democracy in the Arab world is due largely to the Arab intelligentsia's ambivalence toward the value of democracy itself.

The Popular Sectors

The attitude of Arab masses, or the so-called popular sectors, toward democracy is one of the major unknowns in Arab social science. The few existing studies of Arab public opinion have relied mainly on interviews with members of the middle class. No recent study has attempted to explore the attitudes of manual workers, illiterate peasants, and the urban lumpen proletariat toward governments, political parties, or elections. In this realm, we can only make informed guesses.

Typically, the popular sector's political significance takes two forms in the Arab world. Members of the lumpen proletariat and manual workers have frequently conducted protests against economic deprivation and political corruption. Cairo, Tunis, Casablanca, Algiers, and Amman have all witnessed such protests. However, recent elections in some Arab countries, particularly in Egypt and Algeria, were marked by a considerable degree of voter absenteeism. Most absentees probably belonged to the popular sectors, although low turnout rates were also observed among members of the educated middle class. In any event, the Arab masses have been largely absent from movements urging greater political participation. Perhaps these masses yearn for a political order that guarantees decent living conditions and a measure of respect for their dignity and national values, be it democratic or authoritarian.

Foreign Powers

The role of foreign powers in stimulating a transition from old-fashioned authoritarian political structures has been important in several instances, although it was felt indirectly in most cases. Arab governments embarking upon economic liberalization have been particularly concerned about their images in the Western media. Certain Western governments began to tie aid levels to performance in the areas of civil and political rights, which helped encourage Arab governments to sustain—as much as possible—liberalizing facades and to resort to repressive measures only against those who threatened the degree of public order required for a good investment climate.

However, the resolve of Arab radical regimes to maintain political structures dominated by a leader, a party, or a single mass organization was shaken by the collapse of socialist systems in Eastern Europe. Some cosmetic gestures toward political liberalization were made in South Yemen in 1989, in Iraq and Syria in 1990, and in Libya in 1991.[11]

Finally, during the Gulf Crisis U.S. officials called for a new regional order in the Middle East that would be based partly on increased political participation. The U.S. position perhaps induced Kuwaiti and Saudi rulers to take cautious liberalizing steps—in one case to call for the election of a new national assembly and in the second to endow the country with basic statutes, a rudimentary consultative council, and a modern local administration.[12]

However, the position of Western governments was, to say the least, ambiguous when political liberalization seemed to promise power to political groups not to their liking. This was particularly visible in early 1991, when democratic processes were on the verge of bringing Algeria's FIS to power. The absence of strong Western condemnation of the cancellation of the second round of Algerian elections and the installment in power of a military-backed government was sharp proof of Western ambivalence toward democracy in the Arab world.

The bottom line seems obvious: In all cases of a conflict between an ideological commitment to liberal democracy and concern for strategic interests, Western governments will give priority to the latter.

Conclusion

If the above analysis of positions held by major actors is accepted, the inescapable conclusion must be that the cause of democracy will advance little in Arab countries in the near future. The uneven pace of liberalization will continue to characterize political structures in the Arab world, with the highest degree of political liberalization being attained in countries that already have pluralist regimes—Lebanon, Morocco, and Egypt—followed by Jordon, Yemen, Mauritania, and Tunisia. Radical regimes and the Gulf countries, excepting Kuwait, can be expected to show the fewest liberalizing tendencies.

Several explanations have been suggested for the Arab world's relative political stagnation during a period in which a considerable degree of democratization has occurred in other regions of the world.[13] Political culture, level of economic development, and the role of political leadership are often mentioned by social scientists as possible key variables. Serious students of politics tend to argue over whether one or another of these best explains the Arabs' lag in democratizing.

Samuel Huntington finds the most powerful determinant of democratic potential to be levels of development; he points out that all economically advanced countries also have democratic political systems. On the basis of this analysis, he suggests that wealthy Arab countries, those forming the Gulf Cooperation Council (GCC), are the best candidates for transition to democracy in the near future.

This argument overlooks the difference between two types of economies and societies. In the one, economic growth results from the expansion of productive capacity and collective action on the part of working and middle classes. This is not true of the second type of society, which is known as the rentier state. Here, economic well-being results from an accident of nature or history that has provided the society with some natural income-generating resource. Mediated through the state, this resource benefits the local population. This arrangement, an economically comfortable one for rulers and ruled alike, does not seem to be conducive to the growth of political participation. Apart from Kuwait, there are no signs at present that economic well-being has prepared grounds for the diffusion of democratic values within GCC countries.

Gulf societies are definitely not stagnant. Certain sectors of their populations have manifested discontent with the prevailing political systems. However, the little information available on such manifestations indicates that members of the clergy are the prime actors and that their protests are largely conservative in nature.[14] Whether such conservative activism might pave the way for genuine respect of civil and political rights of men and women in these countries is an open question. The evidence from neighboring Iran, Yemen, and Jordan encourages little optimism in this respect.

In the medium and long terms, political leadership may prove to be the most decisive determinant of democracy's future in the Arab world. This may be particularly true of Arab countries that are economically deprived at present but that have already embarked on the path of political liberalization. Continued economic strain may eventually lead regimes in such countries to conclude that the transition to democratic politics is the most effective way to elicit the sacrifices required for "structural adjustment with a human face."

This line of evolution may be even more attractive because the alternative—simply reversing the process of liberalization and employing increased repression—would be costly indeed. Although Algeria's recent experience provides an example of an aborted democratization process, the experiment could be tried again in other countries. The lessons of Algeria might induce restraint on the part of leaders of both ruling parties and the opposition. Debates about enlarging the power of the legislature in Morocco and preparations for local elections in Egypt on the basis of a new electoral law that offers better chances for opposition candidates are tentative signals pointing to a possible gradual shift from mere liberalization to a true process of democratization in these countries.

The Gulf War does not seem to have had a major impact on political change in the Arab world. With the exception of Algeria, the political structures that existed in the region before the war are still in place. The same political leaders who led their countries during the crisis remain in power. The relative power of the major political actors in each country is the same as it was before the crisis. The only section of the Arab world in which some new structures have been instituted is the Gulf region, with the election of a *Shura* Council in Oman, the election of a national assembly in Kuwait in late 1992, and the appointment of a consultative council in Saudi Arabia in 1993.

Perhaps the greatest long-range consequence of the Gulf Crisis is that it underscored the inability of Arab regimes to protect the security and integrity of their territories and to safeguard pan-Arab national security. In that regard, the legitimacy of all regimes has shrunk. However, this in itself has not been enough to lay the foundation for a more democratic Arab order.

Notes

The author thanks Nevine Tewfiq for the valuable assistance she provided in collecting research materials for this chapter.
1. Samuel P. Huntington, "Democracy's Third Wave," *Journal of Democracy* 2, no. 2, (Spring 1991), pp. 12–34.
2. Jacob Landau, *Parliament and Parties in Egypt* (Tel Aviv: Israel Publishing House, 1953).
3. See Fouad Ajami, *The Arab Predicament: Arab Political Thought and Practice Since 1967* (Cambridge: Cambridge University Press, 1981); and Michael

C. Hudson, *Arab Politics: The Search for Legitimacy* (New Haven: Yale University Press, 1977).

4. Louis J. Cantori (ed.), "Democratization in the Middle East," *American-Arab Affairs* (Spring 1991), pp. 1–30. See also Muhammad Muslih and Augustus Richard Norton, "The Need for Arab Democracy," *Foreign Policy* 83 (Summer 1991), pp. 3–19.

5. Arab Organization for Human Rights (AOHR), *Human Rights in the Arab Motherland* (Cairo: AOHR, 1991).

6. *AOHR News Bulletin,* February 1992.

7. Guillermo O'Donnel and Philippe C. Schmitter, *Transitions from Authoritarianism* (Baltimore: Johns Hopkins University Press, 1986).

8. Mustapha K. El-Sayyid, "Slow Thaw in the Arab World," *World Policy Journal* (Fall 1991), pp. 711–738.

9. *Al-Hayat,* January 5, 1992.

10. *Al-Hayat,* December 12, 1991.

11. Robert Burrowes, "Unity of the Two Yemens," paper presented to the Seventeenth Conference of the Center of Contemporary Arab Studies, Georgetown University, Washington, D.C., 1992.

12. Robert L. Rothstein, "The Middle East After the War: Change and Continuity," *Washington Quarterly,* no. 105, pp. 138–160.

13. El-Sayyid, "Slow Thaw," pp. 715–726; Huntington, "Democracy's Third Wave," pp. 21–34.

14. *International Herald Tribune,* December 31, 1991, p. 1.

A Palestinian View on the Implications of the Gulf Crisis

AHMAD SIDKI AL-DAJANI

In the years since Israel's establishment in Palestine—a calamity that befell the Muslim, Jewish, and Christian Arab peoples of Palestine in 1948—the Palestinian issue never gained as much attention as it did during the Gulf Crisis and in its aftermath. The reason for this is simple: the five and a half–month crisis, and the six-week war that followed it, established beyond doubt the centrality of the Palestine issue to the political dynamics of the Middle East.

In trying to understand the implications of the Gulf Crisis for the Palestine problem, we must keep in mind that that issue is multitiered. Both in the Middle East and abroad, it has serious domestic ramifications for major actors. At the same time, it is a major element in the Middle East's regional political environment, and it also has major importance at the global level.

The Palestine issue has from its inception been part of an Arab-Zionist struggle that is connected to Western designs on the Arab world. The Zionist party to this struggle includes Israel and the international Zionist movement. Originally formed in Europe, and then shifting its search for support to the United States on the eve of World War II, political Zionism traditionally sought alliances with Western imperialist powers. The Arab party to the conflict includes the Arab people of Palestine and the entire Arab nation, both of which are part of the Islamic-Arab civilization. For the Arabs, then, the Palestine issue involves the defense of a homeland, a people, and a civilization.

Since the end of the 1967 Arab-Israeli War, the Palestine issue has included four concrete subissues. The first is that of the territories occupied by Israel during the conflict—including the Palestinian lands of the West Bank and Gaza. The second is the question of Jerusalem, which Israel annexed shortly after the 1967 war. The third issue is the problem of Palestinians who were driven from their homeland in 1948, and later. The final problem is that of those Palestinians who remained in their homeland after 1948 only to be forced to become naturalized Israelis without enjoying full rights of citizenship. Taken together, these issues form the Palestine problem that must be solved justly if hopes for peace and stability in the Middle East are to be realized.

I seek here to assess the implications of the Gulf Crisis for such hopes by first examining the main features of the Palestine problem on the eve of the crisis, paying particular attention to the positions and attitudes of the main protagonists—Israel, the Palestinians, and the United States. I then turn to developments during the Gulf Crisis and the ensuing war between Iraq and the international coalition. Finally, I consider salient aspects of the Palestine issue in the aftermath of the war, including the new relationship that developed between the PLO and Israel in the fall of 1993.

Palestine on the Eve of the Gulf Crisis

By 1990 the Israeli government and the World Zionist Organization were pushing forward with a major campaign to "encourage" Soviet Jews to emigrate from their homeland to Palestine.[1] Zionist spokesmen talked of achieving the immigration of around 2 million Soviet Jews during the 1990s. Israeli Prime Minister Yitzhak Shamir was even more optimistic, declaring that up to 1 million Soviet Jews would arrive in 1990 alone. The implications of his hopes were made explicit when he declared on January 14, 1990, "We will need a lot of room to absorb everyone and every immigrant will go where he wants . . . for a big immigration we will need a big and strong state."[2]

At the same time, with the rising visibility of explicitly expansionist and hardline currents within the Israeli establishment, official and unofficial acts of terrorism against the Palestinians under occupation increased. The deaths of Palestinians who protested the settlement of Soviet Jews in the Occupied Territories, the assassination of eight Palestinians and the wounding of ten more by a uniformed Israeli, and revelations that the Israeli government had secretly funded the Jewish settlers' fraudulent purchase of property belonging to the Greek Orthodox church heightened Palestinians' insecurity and determination to resist Zionist encroachments. "By May," correctly notes Paul Cossali, "a dangerously explosive situation existed in the Occupied Territories."[3] Increasingly frequent calls by Israeli public figures for the expulsion of Palestinians from the occupied lands and the recognition of Jordan as "the Palestinian state" contributed to spiraling tensions.

The U.S. government's attitude and position during the period that led to the Gulf Crisis further fueled the deteriorating state of affairs. Washington lent strong support to the Zionist campaign to encourage Jewish emigration from Russia. It escalated pressure on the Soviet Union and Eastern Europe not only to allow emigration but also to cooperate in the success of that large-scale endeavor. Providing financial support for the transportation, assimilation, and settlement of Soviet immigrants in Israel and Israeli-controlled Arab lands, the United States in 1990 also reduced the number of visas it made available to Soviet Jews, thus ensuring a greater influx into Palestine. The tenor of a U.S. State Department note submitted to the Arab Summit Conference in Baghdad at the end of May of that year made plain Washington's belief that the Arab world should accept the massive flow of Soviet Jews as a fait accompli.

In the meantime, the United States remained inflexibly committed to its long-standing determination to ensure Israel's military superiority over all of the Arab states combined. This, together with Washington's ongoing subsidization of Israel's economic infrastructure, effectively provided practical and indispensable support for Israel's consolidation of its hold over Jerusalem and control of the city's Islamic and Christian holy places. Finally, in the summer of 1990, the United States broke off its dialogue with the Palestine Liberation Organization (PLO).

By 1990, Palestinians were entering the third year of the intifada—the massive, unarmed revolt that since 1987 had pitted the inhabitants of the West Bank and Gaza against the might of Israel's occupation forces. With U.S. efforts to promote a peace process continuing to drag on fruitlessly, and with Washington evidently determined to support not only Israel's escalating repression in the occupied lands but also the Zionist campaign for massive immigration from the Soviet Union, Palestinians saw no option but to pursue the intifada ever more vigorously. "No retreat, the uprising must triumph" became the battle cry of the day.

This Palestinian outlook reinforced the atmosphere that prevailed in the Arab world during the first seven months of 1990. It was an atmosphere dominated by alarm over Israel's increasingly flagrant inflexibility and repression and by despair over the lack of U.S. commitment to promote a just settlement. Indeed, the conviction grew that U.S. policy was firmly set against vital Arab interests. The intifada was seen as the primary resource available to combat these threats. All of this was manifested in many fora, including the meeting of the Arab Cooperation Council in Amman in the spring of 1990, the Baghdad Summit, and official and popular Islamic reactions to the U.S. Congress's support of the recognition of Jerusalem as Israel's capital.

The Gulf War and "Linkage"

The onset of the Gulf Crisis quickly caused the world to give renewed attention to the Palestine issue and the Arab-Zionist struggle. This outcome was significantly furthered by U.S. efforts to focus UN attention on the invasion of Kuwait. Led by the United States, the UN Security Council passed Resolution 660 on August 6, four days after the fall of Kuwait. The measure provided for economic sanctions against Iraq if it continued its refusal to withdraw from Kuwait. Iraq promptly countered by proposing that "all issues" in the Middle East resulting from occupation be resolved according to the same Security Council principles. The suggestion was clear: If Iraq was being told to withdraw unconditionally from Kuwait or face the consequences, the same conditions should apply to Israel's occupation of Arab territories in Palestine, Syria, and Lebanon.

Baghdad's initiative immediately raised the issue of "linkage," the essential connection between the values at stake in the problem created by Iraq's invasion and occupation of Kuwait and other problems in the region—particularly that created by Israel's occupation of Arab lands and its long history of failure to comply with UN resolutions. Although Washington immediately rejected the concept of linkage in principle, the force of evidence and logic could not be ignored. Although denying a connection between the Gulf Crisis and the Palestine issue, the United States nonetheless visibly showed signs of recognizing that parallels between the two issues required some modification of its approach to the Middle East. Thus, the joint U.S.-Soviet communiqué issued after the September 1990 Helsinki Summit rejected linkage on grounds that any other course would reward aggression, but it also promised that both powers would work conscientiously to resolve all remaining conflicts in the region once the Gulf Crisis ended.

The Gulf Crisis began as a local conflict between Iraq and Kuwait but quickly became a generalized Arab issue, as well as a major international problem. At the regional level, it revolved not only around the question of Iraqi-Kuwaiti relations but also around the full range of political ties and alignments within the Arab world. At the international level, the issues raised were, if anything, even more complex. Internationalization of the crisis generated serious concern in Arab-Islamic circles over the West's approach, alarm over the prospect of a devastating war in the Arab world, and dismay over a U.S.-dominated international order that seemed determined to apply double standards when dealing with the Middle East.

Under the circumstances, the Gulf Crisis caused many Arabs to reflect upon the historical roots of the region's problems. This revived memories of the West's unilateral establishment of the post-1945 world order—a process in which most of the Third World played no role—British and French complicity with Israel in launching the 1956 Suez War against Egypt, and Israel's U.S.-backed strike against Egypt in 1967. Even deeper historical memories also surfaced: the European powers division of the Islamic world among themselves after World War I; the British mandate over Palestine, which implemented the 1917 Balfour Declaration's promise to establish a Jewish "national home" there despite Palestinian resistance; and, finally, the way in which the West drew state boundaries throughout the Arab world in a manner that compromised the interests of the region's peoples.

This historical record reinforces the fundamental connection between the West's creation of a Jewish national home in Palestine and its ambitions to control the Arab-Islamic region. Western aims were to control the region's constituent states and thereby to exploit its strategic and economic resources. The Gulf Crisis underscored the fact that the historical link between the Palestine problem and external challenges faced by the region as a whole is still vital. The Palestine issue remains at the heart of the region's struggle.

Despite U.S. insistence that no linkage existed between the Gulf Crisis and the Palestine problem, the international community—including Washington—could not evade the issue. On several occasions during the crisis, the UN Security Council discussed the dismal conditions of Palestinians in the Occupied Territories and repressive Israeli practices in those areas. This was especially true after the massacre of unarmed Palestinians by Israeli forces at Jerusalem's al-Aqsa Mosque on October 8, 1990.

Yet, there was a marked difference between the UN Security Council's reaction to Israel's refusal to comply with Resolutions 672, 673, and 681—all of which were related to the conduct of Israel's forces in Jerusalem and the Occupied Territories—and its reaction to Iraqi noncompliance with UN resolutions related to Kuwait. The double standard was evident.

However, it soon became apparent that many UN members were uncomfortable with the U.S. double standard and feared it could jeopardize the UN's credibility. The path charted by the U.S.-Soviet Helsinki communiqué was soon followed by various actors. The president of France spoke out in late September 1990, calling for efforts to be made after the Gulf Crisis to resolve other disputes in the Middle East, including the problem of

Lebanon and the Palestine conflict. Days later, France's prime minister publicly regretted that the international community had not shown the same diligence in seeking implementation of UN Security Council resolutions on Palestine as it had in the case of Iraq. Soon, all permanent members of the Security Council were on record urging postcrisis international efforts to solve the Palestine problem. In late October, the International Parliamentary Union issued a resolution that expressed the hope that a general international conference would soon be convened to settle all major Middle East political problems and uphold the Palestinian people's right to self-determination, as well as Israel's right to have secure and recognized boundaries.

In short, it all amounted to an international promise to the Palestinians, to the Arab world, and to the world in general that upon termination of the Gulf Crisis a major effort would be made to deal with other outstanding issues in the Middle East—especially the Palestine problem—in ways consistent with the principles and actions that shaped the world's response to Iraq's invasion of Kuwait. Credit for reminding the international community of its long-neglected responsibility must largely be given to the Palestinians, who persisted in the costly and painful intifada and by doing so gave clear evidence of the undiminished strength of the same Palestinian commitment that had opposed Zionist incursions since the days of the Balfour Declaration.

Israel and the Crisis

In the months leading to the outbreak of the Gulf Crisis, Israel continued to pursue policies that reflected its longtime role as an imperialist colonialist outpost in the Arab world. Thus, Israel lost no opportunity to promote the strain between Iraq and the West, and its supporters in the West eagerly promoted war as the only option in the face of Iraq's takeover of Kuwait.[4] This was reminiscent of the road that led to the 1956 Suez War, when Egypt, rather than Iraq, was Israel's target. It was also in keeping with what modern history tells us is the tendency of settler states to promote hard-line (or fascist) racist reactions to their Third World opponents. The connection between Marshall Petain and French settlers in Algeria and that between Mussolini and Italian settlers in Libya during World War II is relevant in this respect.

However, if Israel was initially elated by the confrontation that developed between Iraq and the West, it was soon dismayed to discover that its traditional role as an imperialist base seemed to have changed. Long used to being considered a regional "strategic asset" by the United States, Israel now found that in the post–Cold War era, Washington regarded its utility very differently. The fact, of course, is that from the start, Israel's effectiveness had been judged by the West in light of the West's own overall ambition to dominate the Middle East. In the post–Cold War era, the same Western ambition dictated that Israel's role, although perhaps potentially useful, had to be different from what it had been at the time of the Suez Crisis.

According to some reports, as soon as Israeli strategists mentioned "Israel's deterrent capability . . . and the significance of its alliance with the United States," they learned that "Washington had no desire to collaborate with Israel in the Gulf crisis."[5] Writing in the *Washington Times* shortly after the invasion of Kuwait, James Dorsey noted that Israel was "willing to fight while the United States warns it against opportunism."[6] Washington's sudden coolness toward its Israeli connection was also manifested by the postponement of a previously scheduled visit by Israel's foreign minister once the crisis developed.

From the start, Israeli leaders sought to separate the Gulf Crisis from the Palestine issue. Six days after the fall of Kuwait, Prime Minister Shamir declared that "the Gulf crisis puts aside all the region's problems, including our conflict with the Palestinians." Thus, Israel was appalled by the Helsinki communiqué's backhanded de facto acceptance of linkage. The fact that general international opinion steadily coalesced in support of the promise to focus world attention on the Palestine issue after the Gulf Crisis thoroughly disturbed Israel.

Sidelined by the requirements of Western strategy, Israel became increasingly uneasy as the Gulf Crisis gained momentum. Israelis took seriously the possibility that the outbreak of war might lead to chemical weapons being used against them. Additionally, the intifada, which continued unabated during the crisis, increased Israelis' feeling that they were being enveloped by a situation beyond their control.

In this gloomy atmosphere, Israel's leaders had to rely upon the West. Israeli Foreign Minister David Levy was finally received in Washington more than a month after the onset of the crisis. Reports indicated that his talks with U.S. officials centered on enhanced U.S. military and financial aid and on Israel's request to have its debt to the United States cancelled. In circumstances that nullified Israel's traditional role as a "strategic asset," the Jewish state had clearly become a heavy burden on its principal international patron.

Nothwithstanding the Gulf Crisis, Israel's policies remained unchanged in two key areas. The campaign to encourage the immigration of Soviet Jews was retained, with Israel's government even stepping up efforts to settle newcomers in the Occupied Territories. Second, Israel's hard-line reaction to the intifada became even tougher, particularly in the wake of the October massacre of unarmed Palestinians protesting Zionist calls for building a temple on the site of al Aqsa Mosque.

For the Israeli public, the most significant feature of the Gulf War was Saddam Hussein's launching of around forty Scud missiles against the Jewish state in retaliation for the international coalition's attacks on Iraq. The United States quickly supplied Israel with Patriot antimissile batteries and U.S. crews to operate them. However, these did not provide full protection against Iraqi Scuds, which continued to fall on Israel. The reality of Arab military force striking deep within Israel was a new and terrifying experience for Israelis. The *Jerusalem Post* termed Iraq's Scuds "a terrifying weapon that undermined the people's morale."[7]

From its inception to its culmination, the Gulf Crisis underscored two important strategic truths about Israel's ability to protect Western interests in the Arab world. First, Israel's value in safeguarding Western oil interests was nonexistent, despite a long-standing tradition in Zionist and U.S. strategic studies alleging the contrary. Second, the much-touted value of U.S.-Israeli strategic coordination and cooperation amounted merely to Washington's dedicated effort to prevent Israel from disrupting U.S. management of the crisis.

Perceptive Israelis, such as Dan Narglit, noted these developments, linked them to Israel's financial demands on the United States, and concluded that Israel had constituted a heavy burden on the United States and would therefore probably have to redefine its regional role in the postcrisis order.[8]

The war also highlighted two additional facts about Israel. The first was Israel's vulnerability to painful in-depth attacks. The fact that Israel was safe from such strikes for over four decades and that the damage inflicted this time by Iraqi Scuds was limited does not imply security for the Jewish state in the future if it continues hostile policies toward the Arabs. On the contrary, the Arab ability to launch in-depth strikes against Israel is constantly being enhanced.

Second, the conflict also revealed that Israel's assessment of its own power is exaggerated. Events during the war gave clear indications of weaknesses in the constituent elements of Israeli power. Israelis themselves pointed to four areas in which their resources fell short of expectations: the domestic front, intelligence, relations with the United States, and military doctrine. The domestic front showed a lack of resolve once under in-depth attack. According to one poll, fully 44 percent of Tel Aviv's inhabitants wanted to abandon the city during the war. Israel's intelligence capabilities were criticized for having failed to assess correctly the Iraqi threat and Israeli options. This drawback was seen as having left Israel tied to U.S.

strategic planning, which in turn underscored Israel's failure to anticipate its being assigned a passive role by Washington. And that, in turn, emphasized the limits of Israel's political-military doctrine, which relied almost exclusively on heavy-handed preemptive and retaliatory action.[9]

The bottom line is that the war demonstrated weaknesses not only in Israel's concept of its own power but also in its real capabilities. The Israeli military machine, like any other, cannot count on invulnerability.

The question now, nearly three years after the end of the Gulf Crisis, is whether dominant Israeli policies and attitudes have changed. Despite a change in the ruling party, the answer must be no. Israel still lays claim to the Palestinian and Arab lands it occupies, including Jerusalem; Palestinians are still subjected to official and unofficial Israeli terrorism; and Israel still controls parts of Lebanon.

None of this is really surprising. Israel's orientations and practices are true reflections of the essential nature of all imperialist colonizing outposts.[10] This nature is one that can conceive of nothing but violence and aggression in dealing with "natives" and that is therefore unable to face facts rationally. Instead, it faces them with brute force and counts on the imperialist patron for ultimate protection. All historical cases of colonizing imperialism indicate that the end of the colonial experiment came only when colonial outposts were driven to change by force once they were abandoned by the imperialist patron. For indeed, breaks can occur between an imperial power and its colonial outpost. This occurred, for example, between de Gaulle's France and French settlers in Algeria. It is a lesson to be kept in mind.

The Arabs and the Gulf Crisis

The Gulf Crisis split the Arab world, causing both material and moral wounds. In itself, the dispute that pitted Iraq against Kuwait and led to the use of force, in violation of existing Arab pacts and traditions, divided Arab actors. But the flow of events that sprang from the conflict exacerbated and complicated these initial divisions. The stark violation of human rights in occupied Kuwait following the invasion, the devastation wrought in Iraq and Kuwait during the six-week war, and the postwar strife in Iraq, as well as the parallel "settling of accounts" in Kuwait after the war, inflicted both deep wounds on the Arab psyche and gross material loss to the Arab world.[11]

Initial efforts by the Arab world to cope with the onset of the Gulf Crisis soon failed. The Arab order lapsed into a state of paralysis, leaving the problem to the international order represented by the United Nations and, particularly, the Security Council. The West appeared satisfied with this turn of events. All efforts to produce an Arab solution to the crisis failed.

Under these circumstances, official relations among Arab states deteriorated, as the Arab world split into opposed camps. To a degree, official Arab stances were reflected at the popular level, where regime-directed propaganda tended to emphasize the divisive regional dimensions of the crisis. On the whole, however, the majority of Arabs attached greater significance to the international dimension of the crisis—seeing it as a further addition to the history of Western imperialist efforts to dominate the Middle East.

The breach within the Arab world imposed even greater suffering on the Palestinian people. The Palestine Liberation Organization's (PLO's) support of Iraq during the crisis led to anti-Palestinian measures being taken by many Arab regimes that rallied to the support of Kuwait. Kuwait's Palestinian community was largely uprooted, and the Gulf states—together with some other Arab countries—imposed restrictions on the movement of Palestinians in the aftermath of the crisis. In the meantime, Palestinians under Israeli occupation went through a particularly difficult period, being forced to endure an extended curfew during the war.

An oppressively gloomy atmosphere hung over the Arab world by the end of the Gulf War. Arab governments felt weak and unable to take initiatives to resolve the region's problems. The PLO, its relations with previously supportive regimes—particularly among the Gulf states—in tatters, found its financial resources severely reduced at the very time a redoubling of its efforts on behalf of Palestinians was most needed. Nonetheless, the ceaseless continuation of the intifada by Palestinians under occupation kept aloft the banner of a common Arab interest that—despite contrary positions sometimes asserted by Arab regimes—united the people of the Arab world.

Conclusion: Prospects

The Arab world turned its attention to the United States following the Gulf War in anticipation of promised U.S. action to work toward a resolution of the Palestine problem. Speaking to a joint session of Congress shortly after the war, George Bush upheld the well-known U.S. position in favor of an Arab-Israeli settlement that would exchange "land for peace" and be based on Security Council Resolutions 242 and 338. He added that any settlement should guarantee Israel's security and satisfy "the legitimate political rights of the Palestinian people." Apparently keeping in mind Iraq's recent Scud attacks on Israel, the president noted that "security does not just depend upon geographical considerations."

Such tentative signs of a new U.S. approach to the Palestine issue were soon called into question. Only days after addressing Congress, Bush discussed the Middle East with four Arab journalists. It was clear from his remarks that Washington had no intention of applying to Israel the same standards it had used to judge Iraq. Regarding the U.S. view of UN resolutions, Bush reportedly said:

> The interpretation of United Nations resolutions is entangled with many problems, and [it] seems to me that the security of the Gulf, including Iraq and Iran, is more amenable to resolution than the Lebanese and Palestinian issues as both of them are connected with Israel. We are quite flexible in our approach to the problem.

Bush added that the role of the PLO in the search for Middle East peace had "shrunk," at least for the time being. He was also frank in stating that the United States "did not encourage the establishment of a Palestinian state."

All in all, these early indications of U.S. policy in the wake of the Gulf Crisis showed—as I discuss later—that Washington still clung to its old approach; an approach rooted in a post–World War II concept of global security that is inadequate in today's post–Cold War world. This became steadily more evident as the United States launched a renewed Arab-Israeli peace process.

Utilizing the climate that prevailed after the Gulf War to bring the sides to the negotiating table, Washington midwifed the Madrid Conference that opened at the end of October 1991. The "peace process" was not launched under UN auspices but rather under a U.S. umbrella. It therefore remained somewhat distanced from the international community's recently revived demands that UN resolutions be respected. Thus, it afforded more play for Washington's selective approach to international legitimacy. The prelude to the conference, and the conference itself (bowing to Israel's refusal to meet with spokesmen for the Palestine Liberation Organization), danced around the question of Palestinian representation. Peace talks eventually commenced, but only with Palestinian negotiators operating under a number of a priori constraints.

Until late 1993, the peace process produced little more than frustration in the Arab world. Then, in September of that year, the PLO and Israel—under the auspices of the United States—announced their mutual recognition and the beginning of direct negotiations looking toward an eventual final settlement. To what can be attributed the long delay before any sign of possible real movement in the peace process? And why are many Palestinians and others suspicious that these new developments may not lead to peace? Various factors enter into the equation, but the principal element is undoubtedly found in the underlying bases of Washington's post–Gulf Crisis approach to the role of peacemaker.

This has long been—and perhaps remains—an approach linked to an anachronistic vision of "Global Security," a paradigm of the Cold War era. It is a vision that implicitly and necessarily subjugates on-the-ground reality to the high strategy of so-called global security. Thus, it downplays— indeed, ignores—regional realities in favor of abstract postulates that are taken as valid guidelines for international policy. Among these, of course, is the precept that a Palestinian state cannot, must not, come into existence.

One asks why. And no answer is to be found other than in some murky and yet unexplained fear of the consequences. Both the fear and the murkiness are traceable to a Cold War mentality—a mentality linked to circumstances that no longer exist.

American critics of U.S. policy toward the Middle East have not failed to emphasize this. A perceptive commentator, Charles William Maynes, editor of the prestigious U.S. journal *Foreign Policy,* reviewed four reasons the United States was driven into the Gulf War: "oil, order, security and Israel."[12] He concludes that U.S. interests could have been protected without resort to war.

Along the way to forming this judgment, Maynes's analysis touches upon several issues that have major implications for the future of the Palestine problem and U.S. policy. Among these is Maynes's contention that "the world should begin thinking of collective security more in regional than in global terms."[13] The United States has neither the will nor the capacity to undertake a sustained role as global policeman. Global security, in other words, should be sought by enhancing regional security. However, as Maynes correctly points out, Washington's ability to pursue such an approach in the Middle East is undermined by the Palestine conflict. On the one hand, U.S. ability "to help the Gulf states to defend themselves" is limited by Washington's fear that strengthening Arab states, even if this is done to achieve a stable regional balance of power, may adversely affect Israel's security and thereby ultimately prove to be a destabilizing factor. On the other hand, as Maynes notes, the obstacle to reducing the destabilizing effect of fears for Israel's security by extending a formal U.S. defense commitment to the Jewish state is "Israel's unwillingness to respond to the many difficult questions that would have to be answered if it did accept such a U.S. guarantee." Among these:

> Which Israeli borders would the United States be obligated to defend? Would Israel agree to honor the terms of UN Security Council Resolution 242 with its formula of land for peace? Would Israel accept the obligation not to take actions, such as settlements in the Occupied Territories, that

most governments believe violate international law and that are detrimental to the interests of the state offering it protection?[14]

A further point stressed by Maynes rounds out this sketch of the problem the United States will not be able to avoid in the future:

> In [the Gulf Crisis] America has been transformed from Israel's financier to Israel's protector. For the first time in its history Israel finds that the army of a friend is doing the bloody work of subduing and disarming the army of a great enemy. Whatever is said at the level of public relations and however grateful [for Israeli restraint] the United States may be for a few months . . . the US-Israeli relationship will never be the same.[15]

In a Middle East that can only become increasingly dangerous if regional problems are not resolved, the United States will secure its interests only if political stability is nurtured. This cannot be imposed by U.S. force, much less by the use of Israel as a heavy-handed "guardian" of Western interests. The alternative remains working politically to resolve the region's most inflammatory problems, of which the Palestine issue is the most pressing. History will reveal whether the mutual recognition of the PLO and Israel will become an opportunity that is seized to work toward this end.

History also forces recognition of one of the great outcomes of experiments in imperialist colonialism: the arrival of points at which divergences of interest develop between colonial-imperialist outposts and the powers that established and supported them. Such moments provide suitable climates for pressuring colonial states into facing facts they have consistently evaded. Such realism opens the way for the abandonment of dangerous policies predicated on sheer force. A rational search for international peace and security then becomes possible. In this way, Israel may yet come to recognize and accept the rights of Palestinians and, by doing so, accept the logic of liberation.

Notes

1. I have chosen my words carefully here. The objective of the Israeli government and the World Zionist Organization in promoting emigration from the former Soviet Union was to enhance the number of Jewish settlers in the occupied Arab territories rather than within the boundaries of the Israeli state. As noted by Paul Cossali, "Increased immigration helped counter the demographic argument used by those Israelis who favoured a withdrawal from the Occupied Territories and fortified the position of those who favoured increased 'colonization' of the West Bank and Gaza." Paul Cossali, "The Arab-Israeli Confrontation 1967–90," in *The*

Middle East and North Africa 1991, 37th ed. (London: Europa Publications, 1990), p. 49.

At the same time, Zionist "encouragement" of immigration by Soviet Jews into Israel has taken the form of policies that are in effect designed to *force* Jews to go to Israel by *dis*couraging the availability of other destinations. I have discussed this point in detail in an earlier work. See Ahmad Sidki Al-Dajani, *The Palestinian Intifada and the Management of Conflict* (Cairo: Dar al Mustaqbal al Arabi, 1990) (in Arabic).

2. Cossali, "Arab-Israeli Confrontation," p. 57.

3. Ibid., p. 50.

4. Charles William Maynes, "Dateline Washington: A Necessary War?" *Foreign Policy* (Spring 1991), pp. 159–177.

5. James Dorsey, *Washington Times,* August 7, 1990.

6. Ibid.

7. *Jerusalem Post,* January 23, 1991.

8. *Haaritz,* January 27, 1991.

9. *Jerusalem Post,* February 12, 1991.

10.. See Ahmed Sidki Al-Dajani, *What After the Ramadan War?* (Beirut: Al Sharika al Mutahhida, 1974) (in Arabic).

11. See Ahmad Sidki Al-Dajani, *The Palestine Uprising and the Gulf Upheaval* (Cairo: Dar al Mustaqbal al Arabi, 1991) (in Arabic).

12. Maynes, "Dateline Washington," p. 159.

13. Ibid., p. 164.

14. Ibid., p. 171.

15. Ibid., p. 176.

Islamists and the
Gulf Crisis

FRANÇOIS BURGAT

Three years after the events occasioned by Saddam Hussein's invasion of
Kuwait, it seems possible to outline broad answers to important questions
regarding the impact of the Gulf Crisis on Islamist movements in the Arab
world.[1] I focus on two such questions: First, in what ways did the crisis
affect the internal dynamics of the Islamic movement, especially the balance of power among its different components? Second, how did the crisis
affect Islamic political discourse as a whole with respect to other systems
of reference, especially with respect to secular Arab nationalism? The
hypothesis developed here is that the Gulf Crisis has probably contributed
to *emphasizing* and at the same time *strengthening* the nationalist component of the Islamist tendency, enhancing the power of groups that exploit
this combined system of references.

The Internal Impact of the Crisis

Even before the outbreak of the Gulf Crisis, careful examinations of the
nature of Islamic mobilization already tended to indicate that rather than
being based on an alleged "religious revival" or merely expressing economic and democratic frustrations, the Islamist discourse functioned mainly as a channel for nationalist mobilization.[2] Faced with the Gulf Crisis and
its aftermath, however, the Islamic camp has not been totally united.
Differences have marked the reactions of Islamist leaders, and splits have
paralyzed some of the popular efforts to mobilize. Why has this been the
case?

A first step toward answering this question requires consideration of subregional, or local, factors. The attitude of Islamic currents in the Arab world has never been totally unaffected by the national environments in which they developed. The different reactions to the Gulf Crisis of the Jordanian and Egyptian Muslim Brotherhoods provide a telling example. Despite their ideological affinity, each group was strongly influenced by its local environment. In Egypt, no political calculus could totally ignore the fact that Egypt, as a national entity, had everything to lose in the event of a successful Iraqi seizure of Kuwait. This did not apply within the context of the national interests of the small Jordanian satellite of Iraq.[3]

However, the import of such divisions in the Islamist camp must be measured with caution. During the Gulf Crisis itself, this requirement was frequently overlooked. In general, official Arab press analyses—which tended to be picked up enthusiastically by the Western media—argued that the reemergence of secular nationalism as the basis of political discourse offered an "unhoped for" opportunity to undermine the relationship between Islamist activists and their popular bases of support. At times such wishful thinking led to distortions of fact and, more important, to the almost equally wishful thesis that Islamists sought above all to preserve their Saudi sources of finance.

Although some evidence indicates cases to which this thesis appears to apply, it can by no means be taken as a framework for understanding Islamists' reaction to the Gulf Crisis. Indeed, the so-called trap of the Gulf Crisis, into which the entire Islamic current was often alleged to have fallen, is a concept that resulted more in damage to the credibility of its inventors than in illumination of the Arab political scene.[4]

The true complexity of the situation that faced Islamist movements as a result of the invasion of Kuwait was rooted in the dual nature of the ensuing crisis. The first issue involved the annexation of Kuwait by the (big) Iraqi brother—the victim, in addition, being supported by Saudi Arabia—a "good" Islamic regime—and the aggressor being a secular Baathist-atheist regime.

The second issue arose from the method used to solve the problem—the introduction of foreign, non-Arab–non-Islamic forces into the region. The legal justification for Western intervention—the upholding of international law—did not long hide the fact that the intervention also proceeded in line with Western political interests. Although this was perfectly acceptable to the Western strategist, it was far less palatable to Arab public opinion. For many Islamists who sought to define their reaction to the crisis in terms compatible with an "Arab perspective," the eventual political consequences of Western intervention were, in general, negative. These included the destruction of the only Arab actor capable of altering the military imbalance between Israel and the Arab world, the creation of a bitter split within the Arab world that would long postpone all prospects of Arab integration, and the perpetuation of intra-Arab divisions that would enhance the West's bargaining power in obtaining Arab petroleum.

These two issues involved in the Gulf Crisis offered Islamists two ways of perceiving, and reacting to, the event. The upshot underscored a preexisting cleavage in the Islamist camp, but it also has probably reinforced a process of Islamist reintegration.

Although I am conscious of the limitations of "labeling" the range of attitudes fostered by the two aspects of the Gulf Crisis, I will nonetheless lapse into this practice as a means of discussing the Islamist reaction. One major Islamist perspective, that which based its reaction to the crisis primarily on the issue of the invasion of Kuwait, might be termed literalist, or traditionalist. In the Gulf Crisis, this perspective led to support of the anti-Iraq international coalition. Even if its adherents are far from constituting a majority of the Islamist current in the Arab world, their perspective often defines the image of Islamism.

The second Islamist perspective might be termed nationalist, and it derived its reaction to the Gulf Crisis more from the second issue raised by the event. It can be described as more political, more modern, and less conservative than its counterpart. On the whole, of the two perspectives, it is the more representative of the Islamist phenomenon in the contemporary Arab world. It is also probably more capable of establishing a link between activist Islamist core groups and possible electoral majorities. This perspective led to anti-international coalition postures, if not pro-Iraq stands, during the Gulf Crisis. Nationalist Islamism can essentially be identified with such spokesmen as the Tunisian Rashed Ghannouchi, the Egyptian Adel Hussein, the Sudanese Hassan Tourabi, and, in Jordan, Leith Chbeilat.

Cleavages exist not only between the nationalist and traditionalist Islamist camps but also within each. In Egypt, the Muslim Brothers were long unable to agree on how to react to the Gulf Crisis; they did not call for the withdrawal of Egyptian troops from the Gulf until late January 1991. In Tunisia, the crisis and its aftermath led to a similarly disordered reaction on the part of Islamists.[5] As Tunisian activists have put it:

> It is true that . . . in our newspaper we have not immediately given the crisis the place it deserved. Why? Maybe because we were in a phase where we didn't look for an increase in tension—either with the Government or the West. . . . We were, rather, looking for internal and external support and a break in the repression [we suffered].[6]

In fact, however, neither internal divisions nor opportunism prevented Islamists from becoming more cohesive as the implications of Western intervention in the Gulf Crisis became more evident. A massive tendency developed to unite in opposition to official Arab support for the international coalition and to act against the threat of Iraq's total destruction.

Whatever reservations Islamists retained regarding Saddam Hussein as an individual, whatever sincerity marked their support of Kuwait's existence and their condemnation of Iraq's occupation of that country, and, finally, whatever the nature of their financial and ideological ties to Saudi Arabia, the vast majority of Islamists came to perceive the Gulf Crisis as an East-West confrontation. In this context the relevance of the nationalist component of the Arabic Islamist orientation was heightened.

In the end, the Gulf Crisis increasingly required Islamist leaders to clarify their priorities, to choose between two apparently antagonistic rationales, the traditionalist and the nationalist. What resulted progressively was a merging of the two, but one in which nationalist values emerged dominant. Without necessarily destroying pro-Kuwaiti readings of the conflict, the international coalition's air and ground assaults, especially the extreme damage inflicted on Iraq during the hostilities (damage that did not seem necessitated by the requirements of merely liberating Kuwaiti territory), strongly reinforced the appeal of the nationalist tendency in the Islamist perspective.[7]

My argument is that the traditionalist element in the Arab world's Islamist political current was weakened by the Gulf Crisis and its aftermath. This seems particularly true in light of the fact that the limited traditionalist perspective on the crisis has been unable to address political implications that have become more pronounced in the region since Iraq's defeat. Conversely, precisely because of its greater attention to political considerations, the nationalist Islamist perspective was strengthened by the crisis.

The External Impact of the Crisis

Internal dynamics of political Islamism, which, as indicated above, were from the start bifurcated by traditionalist and nationalist orientations, form only part of the story of the latter perspective's ascendancy. The objective nature of the Gulf Crisis fueled the volume of resources available to nationalistic Islamism, making more evident its ability to compete with purely secular nationalism (such as Nasserism and Baathism) and to mobilize popular support.

The aftermath of the Gulf Crisis has seen no reduction in the flow of resources to this nationalist-Islamist current. Although the supremacy of U.S. weaponry has no doubt deeply impressed Islamists, their response to the Gulf Crisis has been even more deeply colored by reaction against the system of Western values as a whole that, in their eyes, produced the destruction of Iraq.

Various factors help account for this, but perhaps the two most important are the approach of the Western media to the Gulf Crisis and the obvious double standard applied by the United States to the Middle East as it set about reviving the Arab-Israeli peace process. The extreme partiality of the Western (particularly the French) media covering the Gulf Crisis was patent. Under the cover of denouncing the Iraqi enemy, "instinctive hate" was frequently aimed at the entire symbolic system of Arabism. This type of journalism amplified the confrontation's deep ideological dimension.[8] The revived U.S. interest in an Arab-Israeli peace process in the wake of the Gulf Crisis graphically reinforced general recognition of differences within Washington's commitment to castigate offenders of UN resolutions. The U.S. treatment of Iraq contrasted sharply with Washington's approach to Israel. The Madrid Conference became an amplified echo of Western anti-Arabism during the Gulf Crisis. The result tended to weaken, in many Arab eyes, the position of regimes that had linked themselves to the United States during the Gulf Crisis. Finally, the West's support of the 1992 coup that deprived the Islamist camp of a legal electoral victory in Algeria strongly reinforced political skepticism within Islamist circles over ties with Western allies.

The course of Arab political discourse unleashed by the Gulf Crisis has also redounded to the benefit of Islamist nationalism. Saddam Hussein's Baathist regime committed the equivalent of ideological hara-kiri by dramatically renouncing the vocabulary of secular Arab nationalism in favor of religious symbolism during the crisis. This recognition by one of the most determined erstwhile opponents of the political power of Islamic discourse must be seen as a major landmark in the strengthening of Islamist orientations in the contemporary Arab world.[9]

In the wake of the Gulf Crisis, secular Arab nationalists have begun to reconnect their discourse to the symbolic system of Islamic culture, which reinforces the increasing appeal of Islamism. Theoreticians of this trend have increasingly moved toward such a reconciliation by tempering their traditional rejection of Arab nationalistic premises.[10]

The distance between the traditional and nationalistic schools of Islamism, therefore, will likely progressively diminish. This, in turn, probably offers a profile of forces that, under the banner of "political Islam," will likely produce the next parliamentary majorities in most states of the South Mediterranean.

However, neither the West nor most existing Arab elites seem ready to accept this unavoidable cohabitation of Islamist trends. In both cases, the image of political Islam remains crudely linked to that of the assassins of

Anwar al-Sadat. What is overlooked is that the social setting of political Islam has long since moved beyond small groups of literalist and totalitarian followers of a strictly religious discourse.

In 1992, Algerian voting booths revealed the widespread popularity of the Islamist alternative. The Algerian phenomenon alone ruins the thesis that the Islamic movement is localized in tiny radical groups who fear being marginalized by democracy and are therefore determined to seize power by force.

In short, Islamism is a force in the Arab world, one that has not only been strengthened by the Gulf Crisis but that also appears likely to be a major player in the Middle East's future. However, any attempt to assess the meaning of Islamist forces only makes sense if it avoids giving the label *Islamist* a limited and narrow definition linked to a precise social base, a precise ideology, and a specific political program. What is actually indicated by the burgeoning Islamist alternative in the Arab world is a heterogeneous, but profound, process of reconnecting with the region's precolonial symbolic universe. Multifaceted and complex, it should not be treated as a monolithic phenomenon. But it is one that, in all its multiplicity, will progressively exert an impact on the entire region.

Notes

1. Material for this chapter is derived from research conducted at the Centre d'Etudes et de Documentation Economique, Jurique et Sociale in Cairo. A more elaborate presentation of research findings will be published by *La Decouverte*, in Paris, as a continuation of *L'Islamisem au Maghreb, la Voix du Sud* (Paris: Karthala, 1988), an updated version of which is available in Arabic in *Al-Islam Al-Siyassi, Sawt Al-Janoub* (Dar al-Alam al-Thalith: Cairo, 1992), as well as in English in François Burgat and William Dowell, *The Islamic Movement in North Africa* (Austin: University of Texas Press, forthcoming).

On the attitudes of Islamists during the Gulf Crisis, I have previously discussed frameworks for analysis in "Le Faux Dilemme des Islamistes," *Jeune Afrique*, no. 1556, October 24, 1990, p. 40; "L'Islam Aujourd'hui," *Quilet Encyclopedia*, Paris, 1991. See also "Les Islamistes et la Crise du Golfe," *El Maghreb y la Crisis del Golfo: Trasformaciónes Políticas y Orden Internacional* (Grandada: Agencia Española de Cooperación Internacional, November 28–30, 1991).

2. See *L'Islamisem au Maghreb*.

3. This may explain to a certain extent why the pro-American posture of the Egyptian government did not create a higher level of domestic protest. See Alain Roussillon, "L'Opposition Egyptienne et la Crise du Golfe," *Maghreb-Machreq, Monde Arabe* 130 (December 1989), pp. 79–98.

4. See, among others, Mohammed al-Ahnaf, "L'Opposition Maghrebine Face à la Crise du Golfe," *Maghreb-Machreq, Monde Arabe* 130 (December 1989), pp. 99–114.

5. In the Egyptian case, financial considerations undoubtedly explain some of the Muslim Brotherhood's reluctance to condemn the U.S. intervention.

6. Interview with Habib Mokni, Salah Karkar, and Abderaouf Boulaabi, representatives of the Tunisian *Hizb en-Nahda,* who live in exile. Paris, July 1991.

7. The best expression of the Kuwaiti reading of the crisis is given by Fouad Zacharia in the collection of his articles on the Gulf Crisis. See *Al-Thaqafa al-Arabiya wa Azmat al-Khalij* (London: Al-Sharika al-Kuwaitiyya lil Abhath, 1991), p. 127.

8. "Instinctive hate" is an apt phrase used by Nadia Khour Dagher in "Lettre a mon Directeur de These," *La Presse* (Tunisia), February 1991.

9. Saddam Hussein expressed his attitude on at least two different occasions. Speaking to a group of Libyans close to the Baath Party, he declared that he had realized that "the language of Islam had become the only way capable of moving the Arab masses and that he didn't have the right to deprive his party of this." To a delegation of Islamists on a mission of goodwill, he said that "it was a long time since he had wished to get closer to Islamic references, but only his anxiety to preserve Iraqi national unity had prevented him from doing so." Private interviews.

10. See interviews with Adel Hussein in *Egypte-Monde Arabe,* no. 4, and with Tareq al-Bishri, ibid., no. 7.

Part 4
Arab–Non-Arab Relations

16

Russia, the CIS, and the Arab World After the Gulf Crisis

VITALY NAUMKIN

The end of the Cold War was marked by three serious crises: one in the Gulf, one in Yugoslavia, and one in the Soviet Union. This soon after these events, it is difficult to be precise about almost any future international developments. The Soviet Union has passed into history and been replaced by the Commonwealth of Independent States (CIS)—whose final nature remains an open question; the Arab world has undergone the trauma of the Gulf War, the full implications of which remain to be seen; the entire international system is in a state of flux, and there is little certainty as to when, how, or in what shape it will stabilize. Yet, the flow of history is not apt to proceed on the basis of a total cancellation of the past. It is therefore logical to assume that Russia and other states of the CIS will have some significance in the Arab world's future. In this chapter, defying the obvious murkiness of the issue at present, I try to identify some of the lines along which relations between the Arab world and the successors to the Soviet Union may develop.

The Legacy of the Soviet Union

Even before the momentous events of the 1990s, Soviet-Arab relations were obviously changing—strained by perestroika, which drastically altered both the essence and policies of the Soviet regime. Under Mikhail Gorbachev's leadership, the USSR no longer regarded the Middle East as an arena for competition with the United States. The Soviet Union was also no longer committed to promoting "revolutionary change" in the Third World. Economic ties soon came to be judged by Moscow on the basis of immediate mutual benefit rather than on ideological considerations. All of this contributed to a worsening of relations between Moscow and its traditional partners in the Arab world.

Yet, not all was bleak in Soviet-Arab relations under Gorbachev. As the international system began to feel the impact of perestroika, Moscow found it possible to establish significant preliminary links with conservative Arab regimes. Progress was made in Moscow's relations with the Gulf states. Diplomatic relations were established between the USSR and Oman and between Moscow and the United Arab Emirates in 1985 and with Qatar in 1988. In 1987, a consortium of Kuwaiti banks offered the USSR a $150 million loan, which was followed in 1990 by a second loan of $300 million. At the same time, the Kuwaiti ambassador in Moscow called for enhancing economic ties between the two states by embarking upon joint ventures in third countries.[1]

Soviet trade with the oil-rich Gulf states nonetheless remained relatively modest in the final years of the Gorbachev regime. The bulk of the USSR's commercial ties with the Arab world involved poorer partners— generally acquired much earlier for ideological and political reasons. Thus, Iraq, Egypt, Libya, Syria, and Algeria accounted for 90 percent of commodity turnover and 85 percent of Arab technoeconomic cooperation with the USSR. Indeed, on the eve of the Gulf Crisis, Soviet-Iraqi economic ties were vitally important for Moscow. In 1990, a draft long-term program for Soviet-Iraqi cooperation was elaborated; it envisaged the modernization of previously constructed projects, the implementation of new ones, and the inauguration of joint ventures utilizing Iraqi capital.

Apart from the incipient economic dimension mentioned above, Soviet relations with the Gulf Cooperation Council (GCC) states particularly unfolded in the development of ties among Muslim communities. In 1990, Soviet Muslims set out on their first mass pilgrimage to Mecca. In sharp contrast with former practice, under which only a few dozen individuals were allowed to undertake the Haij, fifteen hundred Soviet citizens flew to Saudi Arabia on specially chartered Aeroflot planes—accompanied by a Soviet consular group. Following this event, visits by Saudi businessmen to the Soviet Union became ordinary.

However, not all Islamic forces in the Arab world were happy about the changing fortunes of their old enemy—communism. Concern over the rise of Zionism in the Soviet Union and Eastern Europe, and the concomitant beginning of an era of U.S. hegemony, was common in some circles. Egyptian writer Fahmi Howeidi assured a gathering of scholars and political leaders from ten Arab countries at a conference organized by the

London-based Center for Studies on the Future of Islam that the "collapse of Communism will weaken, not strengthen, the Muslim World."[2]

The process of democratization in the Soviet Union opened doors for Jewish immigration to Israel, which in turn strongly contributed to the cooling of Soviet-Arab relations. At the same time, however, the ensuing improvement in Soviet-Israeli relations created new opportunities for launching a peace process in the Middle East, giving Moscow access to all parties involved in the seminal Palestine conflict.

The Gulf Crisis and the Future

From the very beginning of the Gulf Crisis, Moscow's stand against Iraq's occupation of Kuwait satisfied Baghdad's Arab opponents. The Soviet Union had made its choice and, in the process, demonstrated beyond all doubt that it now gave priority to cooperation with the United States. Moscow was soon able to establish diplomatic relations with Riyadh and Bahrain. Intensive consultations between the Soviet Union and the GCC states, at both the bilateral level and at the United Nations, were sustained as the crisis unfolded.

At the same time, however, the definitive implications of this foreign policy posture became a major issue in the Soviet Union's ongoing domestic political struggle. With an eye on his conservative domestic opponents, Gorbachev therefore launched moves—independently of the Western powers—to try to prevent the use of force in resolving the Gulf Crisis. Soviet peace initiatives—conducted with the aid of Gorbachev's special envoy, Eugeny Primakov—met with mixed reactions in the Gulf states. Hopes for a quick, pacific end to the crisis were combined with some suspicion about Soviet aims. In the end, however, Primakov's mission contributed to growing cooperation between Moscow and the Gulf capitals. Significantly after the crisis the same envoy was sent to the Gulf to discuss economic cooperation—and he returned having achieved some success.

The climate that developed between the USSR and the Arab Gulf states during the crisis was perhaps most succinctly and comprehensively expressed by Kuwait's ambassador to Moscow. Speaking to a group of journalists, he said:

> We have no doubts about the sincerity of the intentions of the Soviet Union, and we are grateful to her for her support and help in working to preserve the independence and sovereignty of Kuwait. The peace plan which was put forward by Moscow hasn't had positive results because of the position of Saddam Hussein. His sincerity is what we can't believe. But our relations with the USSR can't be complicated because of that—their basis is very solid.[3]

This was a welcome paean to the new direction taken by Soviet policy under Gorbachev. However, the collapse of the Soviet Union led to a new reality: the emergence of new, independent states with different interests, problems, approaches, and policies. The system of new relations between these new states and the countries of the Middle East is being formed.

Arab states began to express interest in developing relations with Russia and the Muslim republics of the CIS for a variety of reasons, not the least of which was the active interest in that goal first manifested by Iran and Turkey. As the Soviet Union tottered toward collapse, an early sign of a new geopolitical situation was a growing interest in the establishment of a Black Sea Community, a concept that surfaced in 1990. The community was officially created in Istanbul in February 1992, and it strengthened Turkey's role in the region. Azerbaijan, although it has no access to the Black Sea, became a member.

Almost simultaneously, a group of Central Asian republics and Azerbaijan also joined the Economic Cooperation Organization (ECO), an inactive organization whose existing membership included Turkey, Iran, and Pakistan. Finally, a group of states formed yet another economic alliance—the Caspian Group (Russia, Iran, Kazakhstan, Azerbaijan, and Turkmenistan).

Iran's active diplomatic role in forming potential elements of a new subregional system raised fears in the West and led to Western encouragement of Turkey, a secular and relatively democratic state, to seek greater influence among the Central Asian and Transcaucasian republics. This encouragement was amply demonstrated during Turkish Prime Minister Suleiman Demirel's visit to the United States in early 1992.

These swirling currents led some Arab states to express concern over the activities of both Turkey and Iran. Calls were made for a greater Arab role in the newly independent erstwhile Soviet regions. The question promptly became a point of debate within the Arab world. In late February 1992, the issue was addressed at a seminar organized by Cairo's *Al-Ahram* Center for Strategic and Political Studies. Retired Egyptian Ambassador Salah Bassiouni regarded the expansion of the ECO as a revival of the old Cold War Central Treaty Organization (CENTO). He insisted that the formation of a new geopolitical space was in the offing and that it would be harmful to the Arab world. He and other participants expressed alarm over all of the new economic alliances. In each case, their attitude reflected misgivings over the possible development of Turkish or Iranian hegemony. The crux of prescriptive suggestions derived from this perspective was that the Arab world, particularly Egypt and the GCC states, should compete with Turkey and Iran for influence in the southern belt of the former USSR.

A different Arab position was represented by Cairo University's Ali Hillal Dessouki and was supported by other conference participants. This position was based on two premises, the first being that Turkey and Iran would naturally play important roles regarding the Central Asian and Transcaucasian states because propinquity forges natural connections and provides grounds for economic, cultural, and political cooperation. The second assumption was that ethnic and religious ties militated toward the same result. The conclusion was obvious: The possible development of a special role in these republics on the part of Turkey and Iran should not be regarded by the Arab world as a challenge. At the same time, proponents of this view argued that the Islamic republics need, above all, money and technology—and these cannot be provided at required levels by either Turkey or Iran. So, the argument went, the decisive partner for these republics is the Western world, for which Turkey is the main conduit. And this, in turn, opens opportunities for pro-Western Arab regimes.

Seemingly mirroring the theoretical principles articulated by Dessouki and his supporters, Saudi Arabia acted quickly to develop official relations with the Islamic states of the CIS. In early 1992, Saudi Foreign Minister Saud al-Faisal visited these states; promises of financial aid were soon forthcoming.

Such signs are encouraging, but they remain only indications of possible directions of future fruitful interaction between states of the CIS and the Arab world. Arab businessmen have not rushed to Central Asia and Transcaucasia. Most, leery of the leading roles still played by erstwhile members of the Communist Party and the general instability in the region, suspect that the Muslim republics are not yet ready to engage in significant economic cooperation. Thus, relations so far have emphasized trade protocols and aid designed to foster religious ties through the construction of mosques and the facilitation of Islamic education. Nonetheless, investment has not been totally rejected by private Arab sources. Even before the collapse of the Soviet Union, a joint Kazakh-Saudi bank was established. At the beginning of 1992, a group of Arab bankers started a project in Azerbaijan. Yet, Arab businessmen seem to see more opportunities in Russia, where Kuwait has led the way in exploring active economic cooperation.

The Gulf Crisis left the Arab world facing a constantly changing geopolitical environment. The collapse of one of the world's two major powers confronted Arab states with a number of questions. Is the United States now likely to establish hegemony over the region? Does the new global context represent a threat to the Arab world? What international configuration will replace the old, bipolar world? What is the significance to the Arab world of the emergence of the republics in Central Asia and Transcaucasia? Does the post-USSR era imply an expanded definition of the Middle East, one that will include the former southern Soviet republics? Answers to these questions can only be formed over time.

Despite the amorphous political landscape created by such a vast array of unknowns, some Arab governments are clearly serious about pursuing possibilities for economic cooperation with Central Asian republics. To date, Saudi Arabia, Egypt, and Kuwait figure most prominently in this regard. Saudi Arabia's government shows signs of favoring Uzbekistan and Kazakhstan as partners, although Tajikistan has not been ignored.

Glimmers of Arab interest have already generated indications of a probable new reality—one that is likely to become a major element in relations between the CIS and the Arab world. The emerging factor is competition in the Middle East among members of the CIS. Ukraine, Belarus, and the Islamic republics of the CIS are clearly already competing with Russia in a subdued contest to divide the Soviet heritage in the Arab world. On one level, this competition is rather prosaic—involving, for example, such questions as the division of diplomatic premises and equipment. On another, however, it promises to become a significant political factor. By the end of 1991, for example, Uzbek authorities stopped sending their republic's cotton to Russia and began negotiating a deal with Saudi Arabia to exchange cotton for wheat.

Russia will probably remain the major CIS actor in the Middle East. Moscow is determined to retain its role as cosponsor of the Arab-Israeli peace process. Although its role obviously cannot equal that of the United States, Russia's political experience in the region, its history of long and close relations with leading Arab states, and its developing ties with Israel can be useful to those interested in peacemaking—both regional protagonists as well as the United States.

Nevertheless, Moscow's hopes of cultivating a strong position in the Arab world must be pursued in the face of clear obstacles. Apart from ongoing Arab dissatisfaction over the immigration of Russian Jews to Israel, one problem is that of debts created by Soviet credits—primarily for military purchases. However, perhaps an even greater problem is that of future arms sales. Some years ago, the Soviet Union abandoned its policy of facilitating arms transfers on ideological grounds. Yet, arms sales still provide a major and attractive source of hard currency for Russia.

Although all parties involved in the Middle East recognize in principle the advisability of arms control measures, the allure of relatively easy financial gain has proved difficult to resist. In the aftermath of the Soviet Union's breakup, this takes on even more intense meaning. The decentralization that has accompanied the establishment of the CIS means Russia must consider the fact that the most sophisticated sorts of Soviet-developed arms may be transferred to the Middle East by actors no longer under Moscow's control. This consideration alone immeasurably complicates Russia's problem in deciding whether to capitalize on arms sales to the Middle East.

In these fluid times, this problem only underscores a broader issue—
that of determining the values and goals that will ultimately decide the policies pursued by the states that have replaced the USSR. A triangular political scenario has already been formed, and it cannot be conjured away—
Russia, the Islamic republics of the former Soviet Union, and the states of
the Middle East as heretofore generally defined. The confluence of policies
settled upon at each of these three poles will do much to shape the Arab
world's future.

Notes

1. *Izvestia,* June 2, 1990.
2. *Arab Times,* May 6, 1990.
3. *Izvestia,* February 25, 1991.

17

The United States and the Arab World After the Gulf Crisis

HOSAM T. EL-TAWIL

In this chapter I examine Arab relations with the United States in the aftermath of the Gulf Crisis and the U.S.-led international coalition's war against Iraq in 1991. In doing so, I concentrate on three crucial areas that affect that relationship: Gulf security, Israel, and Arab nationalism.

Iraq's invasion of Kuwait brought to the forefront the complicated and often conflict-ridden nature of Arab-U.S. relations.[1] Americans were divided as the crisis unfolded. Some saw no point in getting involved in an intra-Arab dispute. Among these were proponents of the view that U.S. interests would not be harmed by Saddam Hussein becoming the "policeman" of the Gulf. However, what ultimately proved to be the stronger current of opinion was the view that Iraq's aggression was a challenge that could not be ignored.

On the Arab side, controversy over Arab-U.S. relations was soon reflected in two central issues: First, should U.S. troops be involved in an inter-Arab–Muslim dispute? Second, should Arabs support U.S. condemnation of Iraq in view of Washington's long-standing support of Israel—a state that had invaded, occupied, and absorbed much more Arab territory than that represented by Kuwait? The first question had a somewhat religious tone and the second a powerful political and ideological tone. Saddam Hussein used both to generate strong anti-U.S. sentiment, particularly in poorer countries of the Arab world.

Gulf Security

Significant U.S. involvement in the Middle East is at best around sixty years old.[2] In the 1930s, oil attracted private U.S. concerns, although it was not until the 1940s that policymakers began to perceive a national interest in the oil connection. In the wake of World War II, the onset of the Cold War and the goal of "containing" the USSR rendered the Middle East strategically important in Washington's eyes. Finally, the establishment of Israel in 1948, and the pivotal U.S. role in that development, gave both official Washington and the U.S. public an added point of deep concern in the Middle East.

Hence, for over four decades, oil, communism, and Israel formed the triangle affecting U.S. foreign policy in the Middle East.[3] However, by the summer of 1990, the ongoing collapse of the Soviet Union and the Eastern bloc removed the Cold War as a factor in U.S. calculations regarding the Middle East. Washington had no clear goal to pursue in defining its response to the invasion of Kuwait.

The U.S. role in the Gulf War has been the subject of considerable controversy, even among members of the international alliance that faced Iraq. France, for example, was a somewhat reluctant member of the alliance; indeed, the French defense minister resigned twice during the crisis. His first resignation, in September 1990, was rejected; his second, in December 1990, was accepted. Except—perhaps—for Britain, EEC countries were somewhat uneasy over the prospect that events were leading to eventual U.S. hegemony in the Middle East. The unstated question was, What were U.S. objectives?

Something of the same concern was visible in the United States itself. The U.S. Senate opened the way for the White House to order the use of force against Iraq by a slim 52–48 margin. Underlying the variety of reservations expressed by those opposed to the measure was uncertainty over the purpose of possible intervention.

Overcoming all obstacles, the Bush administration forged and sustained an impressive international coalition against Iraq—and did so with the approval of the Soviet Union. The ensuing military campaign terminated with almost embarrassing speed. Notwithstanding Baghdad's rhetoric, there was little resistance, and the near-total collapse of the Iraqi military was humiliating.

It has been argued that U.S. actions were governed by morality and a kind of "American ideology" that seeks to spread liberal democracy and protect human rights. This argument finds support in what is termed a New World Order, the pillars of which are morality and peaceful methods of settling disputes. However, both before and after the Gulf War, the United States has provided support for many dictators.

From an economic angle, it was perhaps oil—the "strategic commodity," as it is often referred to—that was the decisive reason for the intervention. The United States imports 37 percent of its oil needs from the Middle East, and projections indicate an average annual increase of roughly 4 percent. Japan relies on the Middle East for over 90 percent of its oil needs, and Europe gets roughly 85 percent of its needs from the Middle East. It is also worth noting that U.S. companies dominate the oil industry and that the former Soviet Union is a net importer of oil.[4] The conclusion appears to be that Washington could not possibly have let Saddam Hussein control Kuwait's massive oil production, exports, and reserves—particularly in light of his potential threat to the other oil-producing countries.

From a political point of view, Saddam Hussein's growing arrogance after the end of the Iraq-Iran War in 1988 and his attempt to become the policeman of the Gulf were unacceptable to Washington. It is worth speculating that the United States might not have reacted strongly had Saudi Arabia invaded Kuwait. In other words, the fact that to Americans Saddam Hussein is identified with radical Arab nationalism spelled danger.

The United States did not seek the breakup of Iraq after Saddam Hussein's defeat, apparently for fear that the country's disintegration would eventually allow Iran to swallow the Gulf—including large chunks of Iraq. Part—nearly a third—of the Iraqi military machine remained intact.[5] However, with no concrete long-term political strategy, Washington encouraged rebellions by Shi'a in southern Iraq and Kurds in the north—and then let down both groups of insurgents. Again, there were fears that the collapse of Saddam Hussein and his regime, under pressures from both the south and the north within his country, might lead to an Islamic government. However, U.S. policymakers seemed to view Iran as a balancing factor against Iraq in the Gulf. In other words, the U.S. hope appeared to be that the two countries would keep each other in permanent check. In this regard, U.S. thinking—different from Egypt's but close to Syria's—seems cautiously supportive of some Iranian participation in Gulf security.

The United States, however, is very pro-Turkey. Although much attention has been paid to the U.S. encouragement of Ankara's efforts to compete with Iran for influence in the Muslim republics of the former Soviet Union, it is also worth noting that Turkey is seen as having an increasingly important potential role in the development of a broader Middle East system. There is talk of Turkey's involvement in the water issue, not only with Syria and Iraq but also with Saudi Arabia and Israel. Any such developments would certainly give Turkey a more direct role in upholding Gulf security.

The U.S. role in the future security of the Gulf is still unfolding—although Washington wisely declined the post–Gulf War call by Gulf sheikhdoms for U.S. ground troops to be based in the area. At present, the following seem to be the main features of U.S. policy toward the sheikhdoms. Concerning the immediate problem of demarcating the border between Kuwait and Iraq, the U.S. position rests on the 1963 agreement between the two countries and to the 1932 letters exchanged with the British government. Apart from this immediate issue, the United States will be heavily involved in joint defense planning and in improving military facilities in Saudi Arabia and Bahrain, as well as those in Muscat and Oman. However, no ground troops will be stationed in the area, although the U.S. military's capacity to project itself rapidly to the region will be enhanced. More weapons packages destined for Gulf countries have already been announced—nothwithstanding U.S. expressions of concern about arms control in the Middle East. In both Washington and the Gulf, there seems to be a general feeling that the spectacular U.S. military performance in the war, coupled with U.S. air superiority, is enough to deter a future aggressor. However, the exclusion of Iraq from Gulf security arrangements could trigger instability in the long run.

Israel

Periodically, much discussion erupts over what is usually referred to as the "severest rupture" or the "lowest ebb" in U.S.-Israeli relations. This theme has surfaced increasingly since the Iraqi invasion of Kuwait and the subsequent Arab-Israeli peace talks. One of the underlying bases of this argument is that the United States no longer sees Israel as a necessary strategic ally. The demise of the Soviet threat, along with the decline of international communism and the weakening of Arab radicalism, make Israel an unnecessary and a rather costly ally. Indeed, the latest Gulf War showed that Israel's military strength could be potentially detrimental to U.S. interests. Israeli retaliation against Saddam Hussein's Scud missile attacks could have triggered an Egyptian and a Syrian withdrawal from the international coalition.

Such interpretations must be questioned. Over the years, sharp criticisms of Israeli practices and policies have been made periodically by prominent U.S. politicians.[6] Clashes between Israeli and US leaders at the highest levels have also occurred, as have verbal pyrotechnics between spokesmen for both sides. Yet, the basic—and special—tie between Israel and the United States has remained essentially sound. There is no immediately visible reason to believe that this will change because of the mutual recognition of Israel and the PLO and the initiation of direct talks between them in 1993.

Discord, ruptures, and low ebbs that appear periodically between Israel and the United States have been at most tactical and temporary and, most commonly, merely illusory.

Other important factors not only helped establish but also continue to help sustain the special U.S.-Israeli bond. Among these is the Judeo-Christian tradition, which is particularly evident in the pro-Israeli inclinations of U.S. Christian fundamentalists, "estimated at between 30–50 million people."[7] Then too, Americans and Israelis perceive each other as members of "frontier nations." Sharing histories of conquest, expansion, and nation-building, their societies prize aggressiveness and competitiveness. Both countries were established in reaction to European persecution. Americans and Israelis see each other as belonging to the same cultural value system: one of liberal democracy and capitalism.

The most striking and tangible manifestation of U.S. support for Israel is the fact that the latter is possibly the largest recipient in history of economic and military aid from a single country. Between 1949 and 1983, Israel received around $25 billion in such aid; since 1984, Israel has benefited from about $3 billion annually. In general, the bulk of this aid has been in the form of grants. U.S. aid has had an impact on virtually every sphere of Israeli society.[8]

We should recall that strains and occasional tension between Israel and the United States were not uncommon during the years in which this impressive record was compiled. Friction between the two countries had various sources: differences over the quantity, quality, and delivery schedules of U.S. arms supplies; personality clashes between leading figures on each side; Washington's periodic annoyance over what it considered heavy-handed Israeli use of force—such as the 1981 raid on Iraq's Osiris nuclear reactor and raids on Palestine Liberation Organization (PLO) facilities and personnel in Tunis; U.S. arms sales to Arab states; and Israeli espionage within the United States.[9]

More than the history of past squabbles between Israel and the United States engenders skepticism toward claims that post–Gulf Crisis tensions imply a fundamental alteration of their relationship. Washington (as well as the Arabs) accepted almost all Israeli demands in the "peace process" that was launched by the February 1992 Madrid Conference. These demands included no representatives from outside the West Bank and Gaza (that is, no PLO representatives); no freezing of settlements; one Jordanian-Palestinian delegation; no representatives from East Jerusalem; and, finally, a nominal presence of the United Nations, Russia, and the EEC—limited to mere observer status. More important, Washington unequivocally agreed that no U.S. pressure would be exerted on Israel and no U.S. acceptance of a Palestinian state would be forthcoming. Finally, no U.S. proposals or initiatives would be presented without prior consultation with Israel.

Not surprisingly, procedural disagreements arose in regard to the peace process. In general, the United States took positions that either supported Israeli views or came close to doing so. In some cases, even what appeared to be a middle-of-the-road U.S. position proved to be only a slight modification of an Israeli stand. For example, the Arabs had strongly urged that progress in the planned bilateral talks, which were to deal mainly with the return of Arab territories in exchange for Israeli security, be a prerequisite for the multilateral talks that would deal primarily with aspects of cooperation between the Arabs and Israel. However, Israel maintained that the two types of talks should go hand in hand, with more effort devoted to the multilateral forum. After some wrangling, the United States arranged a "compromise": a gap of merely two weeks between the start of the two kinds of talks.

The United States and Israel currently agree that no sovereign Palestinian state should exist in the West Bank and Gaza. Israel's Likud Party calls for local elections, whereas the Labor Party wants some form of local autonomy. Washington's position is perhaps closer to labor's. Regarding the future of the occupied lands, the clearest U.S. stand is a sustained, if low-key, pressure on Arab governments to drop demands for a Palestinian state and for self-determination for the Palestinians. At present, one senses that the idea of a Palestinian sovereign state may not even be a serious Arab demand. The PLO and its various local supporters seem simply to want the maximum possible rights under "autonomy," whatever that is. Indeed, the much-discussed link between returned territories and Jordan would apparently nullify the idea of a Palestinian state.

The substantial issues of peace seem to generate the most severe disagreements between the United States and Israel. The first point of disagreement revolves around the basic frame for the entire peace process: the 1967 UN Resolution 242. The United States—and apparently the Arabs as well—are ready to accept the partial return and demilitarization of the 1967 territories. On the surface, Israel at this point is opposed. Officially, Israel declares Judea and Samaria to be part of Eretz Israel, with annexed Jerusalem as the eternal capital of the Jewish state. Furthermore, Israel seems to consider the Golan Heights as strategically vital and hence not subject to compromise.

However, Israel, particularly under a Labor government, would likely agree to some devolution of Arab territories. Nevertheless, even under a Labor government, this seems to imply Israeli retention of large amounts of Arab territory.

Moreover, Israeli political discourse indicates that any flexibility would be conditioned upon an arrangement under which Jewish settlers retain the right to live anywhere in the currently Occupied Territories. The entire issue of settlements raises the most salient questions concerning the future of the peace process. It is often argued that this issue is a major point of tension between the United States and Israel.[10] This, above all, remains to be seen.

Throughout 1991, Israel conducted a massive and well-orchestrated campaign to obtain U.S. loan guarantees of $10 billion, the declared purpose being to finance the immigration of Soviet Jews at favorable rates. It was publicly stated that the immigrants would be targeted to the West Bank. In September 1991, President Bush called upon the U.S. Congress to delay considering the Israeli request. His purpose was to pressure Israel into participating in the peace process. Congress complied, but only for a limited period of four months. Moreover, Bush had to agree to seek no further delay. The administration linked Israel's request for loan guarantees to a freeze—not a cessation—of settlements in occupied lands. The four-month deadline was reached, Israel continued its refusal to freeze the settlements. Several attempts were made to get a resisting president and a pro-Israeli Congress to compromise. No arrangement was reached, and the issue stood unresolved as Israel drifted into national elections in the summer of 1992. Labor's victory heralded favorable U.S. action on the loan guarantee. All in all, despite its tensions with Israel, the U.S. posture should cause concern to Arabs.

Washington seems to accept the principle that some existing settlements would remain under Israeli control after a final peace agreement is signed. This calls into question what the United States currently understands by the "land for peace" formula in the peacemaking process. Moreover, the United States accepts the idea that large sums of money will ultimately be given to Israel in return for the Occupied Territories. The United States would probably foot the bill; thus, there is clearly an incentive to reduce the extent of territorial return. Finally, limited U.S. interest in the return of the Occupied Territories to Arab control clearly exists only in the context of a variety of restrictions on Arab sovereignty, including demilitarization.

Jerusalem's status is another apparent point of fundamental difference, or at least lack of agreement, between Washington and Israel. Yet, the real degree of difference between Israel's insistence that an undivided Jerusalem must be its capital and Washington's position is open to question. Former Secretary of State James Baker apparently succeeded in getting all parties to the peace process to agree that Jerusalem would be the last item to be addressed in the negotiations. Because negotiations are expected to last for years, and with Israel pressing for the consolidation of its presence in and around Arab (East) Jerusalem, it is daunting to even consider what this implies. The bottom line is that on territorial issues, including Jerusalem, no great gap exists between the United States and Israel that offers Arabs in general, or Palestinians in particular, much hope of attaining their objectives.

The relationship between the United States and Israel does not refute the theoretical generalization that patrons (the United States) have influence on clients (Israel). The United States is capable of pressuring Israel. The actual nature of the relationship between the two countries is determined by a lack of U.S. desire to exert pressure rather than by U.S. inability to do so.

Thus, in the U.S.-Israeli relationship, power differentials have not resulted in the exercise of influence. Actually, the United States sees the Middle East through an Israeli lens. Indeed, Washington consistently pledges that it will not pressure any of the parties to the peace process; in practice, this means the United States will not pressure Israel.

There is no formal alliance between the United States and Israel, and none seems necessary. Persistent and continual statements and declarations leave no room to doubt the U.S. commitment to Israel.

U.S. officials have often argued that a confident and militarily powerful Israel would be more flexible in giving concessions to the Arabs. Former Secretary of State Henry Kissinger, however, made the following assessment: "I ask Rabin to make concessions, and he says he can't because Israel is weak. So I give him more arms, and he says he doesn't need to make concessions because Israel is strong."[11]

It is often assumed that foreign policy decisionmakers are rational actors. In other words, events, issues, and relationships pertaining to two or more nations are supposed to be analyzed by decisionmakers according to cost-benefit criteria. Rational outcomes are supposedly reached. However, this is not necessarily the case. Perhaps a more intuitive approach based largely on past experience, rather than deductive process, determines decisions. In approaching the peace process, Arabs should keep this possibility in mind.

In a nutshell, if any settlement is reached between the Arab world and Israel, it will probably have little to do with U.S. pressure on Israel. The settlement will be a comprehensive normalization of relations in exchange for a return of demilitarized and substantially reduced Arab territories. Arms control means disarming the Arabs and leaving Israel's nuclear, chemical, biological, and conventional weapons essentially intact. Israeli military superiority will be guaranteed by U.S. assistance. Self-determination will remain something to be attained by other people, but not by Palestinians.

The United States and Arab Nationalism

U.S. policymakers have never been pleased with Arab nationalism. In the 1950s and 1960s, the rocky nature of U.S. relations with Gamal Abd al-Nasser's Egypt made this very clear. In more recent times, U.S. policies toward Iraq, Libya, and Syria—the remaining centers of Arab nationalism—further establish the point.

Indeed, as the post–World War II international system evaporated, the U.S. attitude toward Arab nationalism hardened. It can, for example, be argued that the Iraqi invasion of Kuwait led to the last crisis of the old order, whereas the tensions reached by the U.S.-Libyan controversy over the bombing of a Pan American passenger airplane over Scotland constituted one of the first serious challenges to the emerging new international system.

The 1991 Gulf Crisis and the semicritical stage reached by Western-Libyan relations in the spring of 1992 highlight the North-South problem. Both Iraq and Libya have extensive oil reserves, and both propound radical Arab nationalist ideologies. In both cases, the United States led the permanent members of the UN Security Council into adopting a hard-line stand. In both cases, the Arabs faced international pressure orchestrated by former colonial powers—Britain and France—and the dominant neocolonial power, the United States.

U.S., British, and French charges of Libyan responsibility for the sabotage of two passenger aircraft came around three years after the events—and after the destruction and humiliation of Iraq. We cannot avoid the suspicion that in leading the campaign against Libya, Washington was interested less in extraditing individuals allegedly responsible for the Pan American tragedy than in undermining the regime of Muammar Qaddafi. In the wake of the Gulf War and the demise of the Soviet Union, Washington seems gripped by a kind of arrogance based upon superior military power. The United States now seems tempted to settle accounts with former adversaries in the Arab world.

Several international agreements relating to the hijacking or sabotage of civilian aircraft exist. The most important of these are the 1971 Montreal Convention and the 1988 Tokyo Protocol. Under the terms of these instruments, the option of handing over the alleged saboteurs to other parties is exercised at Libya's discretion. Although it has not yet agreed to Western demands for extradition, Libya has shown enormous flexibility in searching for a legal mechanism to resolve the issue. Its initiatives have been soundly rejected. The United States pushed the UN Security Council into Resolution 748's imposition of sanctions even before the International Court of Justice had an opportunity to examine the matter.

The Arab world, including Washington's allies in the war against Iraq, has not been favorably impressed with U.S. actions. A seven-member committee of the League of Arab States criticized the Western "conspiracy" against Libya. Washington is widely seen as intent upon using the United Nations as a cloak of international legitimacy for the pursuit of its own vendetta against the Libyan regime.

There is also widespread suspicion that the third remaining bastion of Arab nationalism—Syria—will yet appear on Washington's list of targets. Syria's participation in the coalition against Iraq, its role in effecting the release of Western hostages in Lebanon, and Damascus's decision to permit Syrian Jews to travel abroad may have helped stay Washington's hand so far.

Yet, many in the Arab world note with misgivings that all is not smooth in Syrian-U.S. relations. For example, Syria's request to be removed from the U.S. State Department's annual list of countries supporting terrorism has not been honored. The United States also seems disturbed by the reopening of two points on the Syrian-Iraqi border and the renewal of postal service between the two countries for the first time in thirteen years. Syria's rejection of any further military attacks on Iraq is further evidence of possible tensions in the relationship. Perhaps most important, the United States is uncomfortable about Syria's visible irritation over the launching of the multilateral peace talks without progress in the bilateral peace talks. The clearest sign of the limits of confidence in U.S.-Syrian relations came when both the United States and Israel threatened to attack a German ship allegedly transferring North Korean weapons to Syria and Iran.

It has been said that history teaches us one important lesson: that no one learns from history. This perhaps applies to the U.S. approach to Arab nationalism. If the United States continues to pursue a trend that seems designed to undermine regimes clinging to Arab nationalist values, it may ultimately only help unleash an outbreak of strife and chaos throughout the area.

Conclusion

Crisis is typically defined as involving rapidly unfolding events that sharply raise the impact of destabilizing forces at the global and regional levels. This implies that crisis involves surprise, high degrees of threat, and little time for remedial action. The Arab world has had its share of this kind of crisis. However, there are other kinds of crisis that might be termed chronic. This condition can involve low levels of threat, little surprise, and a very long time for resolution. This is the sort of crisis now gripping the Arab world.

The United States is the only military superpower in the world, and notwithstanding its relative economic decline vis-à-vis Japan and Germany, it has a formidable scientific, technological, and economic base. Whatever the arguments surrounding a New World Order, the United States is, and will continue to be, the major external power in the Middle East.

This reality has not been lost on Arab governments, most of which now accept—to a far greater degree than in the past—a much larger U.S. role in the region. However, there is significantly less acceptance of this fact among large segments of the Arab masses, particularly those with Islamic and left-wing tendencies, which is why Washington is cool toward genuine democracy in the Arab world.

On the U.S. side, there seems to be a lack of long-term vision. Instead, the United States appears to be engaged in a confused and belligerent search for enemies. This is best expressed in the confused and often contradictory reports about the future U.S. role in world affairs emanating from the Pentagon and other places over the past two years.[12] A new kind of colonialism is perhaps emerging, one covered by the trappings of international legitimacy. It is led by an explosively dominant United States and confronts powerless Arab governments that sometimes appear to want to be dominated, as evident from their 1992 request to the United States not to strike at Libya during Ramadan.

Notes

1. T. G. Fraser, *The USA and the Middle East Since World War II* (New York: St. Martin's Press, 1989).
2. See, for example, Haim Shaked and Itamar Rabinovich (eds.), *The Middle East and the United States: Perceptions and Policies* (New Brunswick: Transaction Books, 1980); Seth Tillman, *The United States in the Middle East: Interests and Obstacles* (Bloomington: University of Indiana Press, 1982); Alan R. Taylor, *The Superpowers and the Middle East* (Syracuse: Syracuse University Press, 1992); Dan Tschirgi, *The Politics of Indecision: Origins and Implications of American Involvement with the Palestine Problem* (New York: Praeger, 1983).
3. Fraser, *The U.S.A. and the Middle East*; Shaked and Rabinovich, *The Middle East and the United States*.
4. Mahmoud G. Warfully, *Imagery and Ideology in U.S. Policy Toward Libya, 1869–1982* (Pittsburgh: University of Pittsburgh Press, 1988).
5. "With Friends Like This," *Newsweek*, May 6, 1991, p. 42.
6. Expressions of concern within the United States that the one-sidedness of U.S. policy toward the Middle East is too costly have not been totally absent. George McGovern, in an article entitled "The United States Should Halt Aid Unless Israel Talks to PLO," noted that he had met Yasser Arafat on four occasions and found him to be "highly intelligent, tough minded, pragmatic, and serious . . . the kind of man we can do business with." *American-Arab Affairs*, no. 33 (Summer 1990), pp. 6–9.
   Perhaps reflecting growing concerns of U.S. taxpayers over heavy U.S. subsidies to Israel, Senator Robert Dole spoke as follows on the Senate floor:

> We all know how it works around here . . . we carry our resolution, or our letter, into the cloakroom. We buttonhole every senator who walks in, and push them for an immediate signature. Half the time, the signer doesn't even read the text . . . so we are all wrong. The process is wrong and the result can be damaging. . . . Now, we have home-

less in America, we have homeless veterans in America, and they're wondering, "Why don't we get the same treatment?"
Cited in *Middle East International,* April 27, 1990, pp. 3–5.

7. Ruth W. Mouly, "Israel: Darling of the Religious Right," *Humanist,* no. 42 (May-June 1982), p. 6.

8. Bernard Reich, *The United States and Israel: Influence in the Special Relationship* (New York: Praeger, 1984), pp. 165–171.

9. U.S. reaction to Israeli activities affecting U.S. national security is, to say the least, bewildering. At various times during the past two decades, Washington has known of (1) Israeli political, military, and industrial espionage activities in the United States; (2) Israeli intelligence services' recruitment of official U.S. personnel; (3) illegal Israeli sales of U.S.-supplied weaponry to third parties; and (4) Israel's supplying U.S. secrets to the Soviet Union in return for facilitation of the emigration of Soviet Jews to Israel. See, for example, Noam Chomsky, *The Fateful Triangle: The United States, Israel and the Palestinians* (Boston: South End Press, 1983).

10. "Declaration of Independence," *Newsweek,* April 6, 1992, p. 32.

11. Cited in Edward Sheehan, *The Arabs, Israelis, and Kissinger: A Secret History of American Diplomacy in the Middle East* (New York: Reader's Digest Press, 1976), p. 199.

12. Mohammed Abd El-Salam, "The Limits of Military Power in the New World Order," *Al-Ahram,* July 10, 1992, p. 7.

18

The Gulf War and the Political Situation in the Middle East

W ALID K AZZIHA

During the Gulf Crisis, major political and social problems that had long haunted the peoples and countries of the Middle East were brought into sharp focus. Perhaps most vivid was the Palestinian question. However, there were other issues underscored by the Gulf Crisis. Among them were:

• The widening gap between rich and poor in the Arab world unfolded as a dominant subtheme of the overall crisis that attended Iraq's invasion of Kuwait.

• The Gulf War revealed a deep-seated crisis in the political nature of the Arab regimes, especially in the area of political participation. In the absence of institutionalized constraints, the Iraqi people—and indeed the Arab nation as a whole—were plunged by the arbitrary action of the Iraqi regime into a conflict that literally became a matter of life and death. Similarly, after the war the Kuwaiti leadership resumed its earlier posture as if nothing had happened, retaining its old monopoly on the reigns of power without inhibition.

• The war in the Gulf focused Arab attention on the double standard the West adopted in dealing with Iraq. Israel was permitted to occupy Arab land and to develop a nuclear arsenal, but Arab countries were to be denied—if need be, by force—the development of a chemical deterrent to Israel's military threat. For many Arabs and Muslims, the Gulf War confirmed their worst suspicions. The West seemed bent on continuing its crusades against Islam, aiming at its final destruction. During the crisis, Saddam Hussein was a source of inspiration for many Muslims in a variety of countries, who regarded him as leading an Islamic stand against the onslaught of the Christian West.

• The war impressed upon the world the threat of allowing the arms race in the Middle East to reach a point at which the use of weapons of mass destruction would become a distinct possibility. Since 1948, military conflicts in the Middle East have tended to involve the use of progressively more sophisticated weapons, which has led to progressively higher body counts in each successive round of fighting. In its four wars with Israel, Egypt lost around 100,000 men total. In the recent war in the Gulf, Iraq probably lost between 150,000 and 250,000 men.

• The Gulf War revealed the lack of any viable security arrangement in the region. The Middle East has proved to be one of the most unstable regions in the world. Plans broached after the Gulf War to cope with the problems of insecurity and instability have not satisfied the security needs of the countries involved. In the Gulf region, the continued exclusion of Iraq and Iran from any security arrangement remains a crucial potentially destabilizing factor.

• To many Arabs, the Gulf War clearly demonstrated the absence of an Arab political order. The events that unfolded during the crisis proved beyond any doubt that the vested political and economic interests of Arab ruling elites were more effective than were pan-Arab values. The assumption that an Arab political order exists is both misleading and inaccurate. The reality of the Arab political situation is that each country forms its own perceived national interest without regard for its neighbors. This fact, however, does not deny the existence of an Arab people who have similar political aspirations and share a wide range of pan-Arab interests.

Arab and Non-Arab Interaction

These major issues became the subject of political discourse among Arabs and between Arabs and non-Arabs. Throughout the crisis, debates and discussions raged among those who were directly and indirectly involved in the conflict. Various historical, moral, politico-strategic, religious, and economic arguments were articulated to buttress all sides. The total impact of these controversies ultimately produced a climate of opinion—regionally, internationally, and at the level of rulers, as well as popular opinion—that emphasized the need to meet the challenges facing the Middle East once the war was over. During the crisis, the powers concerned—most notably the United States—recognized that drastic political and economic changes must occur in the Middle East in order to achieve stability, security, and peace. The burden of responsibility fell largely on the United States.

The Gulf War seemed to test the U.S. political and military will in the new age of international politics. The decline of Soviet power left a power vacuum in many parts of the Third World, and the Middle East was the first area of challenge. In a sense the Gulf War opened the door for the United States to fill the power vacuum and readjust its position to fit the new global situation. With the Soviet Union unable to stem its precipitate decline, Washington became the world's sole superpower.

In this context, it is important to understand that the reality of the U.S. role in the Gulf Crisis is far from Washington's rhetoric about the so-called New World Order and the supremacy of the United Nations and international law. In fact, we can argue that the newly established global order has made the UN little more than a fig leaf for U.S. foreign policy.

However, being at the top, despite the position's advantages, entails serious responsibilities. A power that does not act wisely may ultimately undermine its own position.

The political future of the Middle East will depend largely upon how the United States chooses to deal with the region's major problems. It is too early to form definitive conclusions about the U.S. approach, but we can point to some likely elements that will be central in future U.S. policy in the region.

Shortly after the Gulf War, then Secretary of State James Baker outlined major U.S. concerns. He recognized the importance of searching for a solution to the Arab-Israeli conflict and the Palestinian question. Furthermore, he emphasized the need for a security arrangement in the Gulf based on the participation of the countries involved.

He also alluded to the need for devising feasible plans for regional economic development. On the whole, Washington seemed to be aware of the dilemmas the Gulf War had revealed. Following in Baker's wake, President George Bush also spoke of the need to solve the Arab-Israeli conflict and to guarantee the security of Israel, as well as the "legitimate political rights of the Palestinians." The stage was set for a fresh initiative on the Palestinian issue. However, on other fronts, U.S. policy seemed far less determined.

Today, a major initiative is under way to bring about peace between Israel and the Arab world. By the fall of 1993, it led the PLO and Israel into mutual recognition, a handshake between Israeli Prime Minister Yitzhak Rabin and PLO leader Yasser Arafat, and direct talks between Israeli and PLO representatives. It is important to examine the prospects for this initiative's success or failure based on the underlying U.S. motivation that helped produce it. Past experience shows that the United States has consistently lacked sufficient political determination to pursue even its own initiatives for a peaceful settlement between Israel and the Arab world. What is so different about the new U.S. initiative? Is a strong U.S. determination behind it?

Perhaps one factor that prompted Washington to drive toward current peace efforts was the growing realization that the Middle East has fallen under absolute U.S. dominance, with no significant challenge from any other quarter. The Gulf War increased Arab countries' dependence on the United States. Many Arab regimes today, especially those of the Gulf countries, have become dependent for their security and existence on the physical presence of the United States in the region. However, the Arab-Israeli conflict continues to potentially threaten a solid U.S. sphere of influence. The United States, therefore, is faced with one of two choices: either to tolerate a controlled level of instability or to put its newly acquired Middle East house in order. The Bush administration seemed to prefer the latter alternative. By the fall of 1993, the Clinton administration's support of the PLO-Israel agreement seemed to indicate that Washington remained committed to the same end.

Second, in the absence of a Soviet challenge, the United States may realize that its dependence on Israel as a strategic ally in the Middle East is no longer relevant. Therefore, the United States could pursue a slightly less favorable policy toward Israel without jeopardizing either its own interests or Israel's security. The Gulf War, as well as the Iran-Iraq War before it, highlighted Israel's insignificance within the context of regional conflicts.

However, the most important factor in Washington's reorientation may have been President Bush himself. It seems that during the war, President Bush promised Arab leaders—members of the coalition against Iraq—that after the war he would use his influence to settle the Palestinian question. He subsequently found himself under a strong moral obligation to do so, especially because others could still exploit the Palestinian issue—as the Iraqi leadership did during the war—to incite Arab sentiments against the United States. Convening the Middle East peace conference was one way of clearing the president's conscience. Thus, the most important force behind the rekindling of U.S. interest in the peace process after the Gulf War was probably that it was simply a moral obligation.

We cannot deny that political and strategic considerations also figured in Washington's post–Gulf War approach. However, in the past such considerations had been insufficient to lead to sustained U.S. efforts to promote a general peace agreement. In short, Washington had always proved willing to risk a certain level of periodic turbulence in the region rather than seriously seek a comprehensive peaceful settlement. Over the past few decades, many U.S. and non-U.S. initiatives were buried because the United States did not fear repercussions from its own inaction.[1] Today, the United States has even less reason to fear challenges to its supremacy in the region.

Similarly, since Camp David, Israel has had no incentive to settle the Palestinian question or outstanding border disputes with its Arab neighbors. The regional balance of military power has always been in its favor. The

Gulf War not only reduced the military capability of the most powerful Arab country but also enhanced Israel's military standing vis-à-vis what remained of Arab military power.[2] Presently, Israel has no reason to fear its Arab neighbors and can hope to enjoy military superiority for a very long time without seeking settlements. The intifada was a nuisance, but it was a tolerable nuisance; it is one of the facts of life to which Israel adjusted. The Arab states failed to escalate the intifada, and the Gulf War further strained relations between Palestinians and the oil-rich Arab regimes. It set the Gulf countries on a course that is antagonistic to the Palestinians and created a basically isolationist Palestinian mood, even toward those Arab countries that supported them during the crisis.

It must still be seen whether the handshake between Yasser Arafat and Yitzhak Rabin signals the onset of a fundamental and enduring rearrangement of attitudes and relations in the Middle East. The question, therefore, remains: Who is interested in a settlement in the Middle East? Who genuinely seeks a Middle East peace?

Undoubtedly, the Palestine Liberation Organization (PLO) and the Palestinian people, especially those living in the Occupied Territories and suffering under Israeli military occupation, are keenly interested in an end to Israeli rule. Moreover, given that the growing influx of Russian Jews into the Occupied Territories threatens to overwhelm the last part of Palestine that remains heavily inhabited by Palestinians, the PLO worries that time is not on its side.

Israel, however, feels the pressure of time barely, if at all. On the contrary it sees time as working in its favor. Perhaps, Israel is thus losing its historical perspective. After all, if Israel were to ultimately swallow the Occupied Territories, it would almost surely precipitate an open-ended conflict with the Arab world, including, of course, the Palestinians.

The Occupied Territories remain in the hands of Israel as hostage, a hostage with which the Jewish state can still negotiate a reasonable settlement with the Arabs. However, if Israel decides to gradually settle the Occupied Territories with Jewish immigrants, the Arabs will have no incentive to negotiate any kind of settlement. It would be extremely shortsighted on the part of Israel, the world community, and, most of all, the United States, to allow the situation to deteriorate to such a point.

The Middle East can still be spared the agony and misery of perpetual conflict between Jews and Arabs if those concerned, especially in Israel, perceive the ultimate danger of being blinded by the arrogance of military power. The PLO has done everything within its power to pave the way for a peaceful settlement. Israel and its leadership must now recognize that in the long run, time is not necessarily an advantage and that an end to the occupation of the West Bank and Gaza may open the way for Israel's integration into the region.

If Israelis deny Palestinians their due place, they will never find acceptance among the Arabs, even though their state might gain official recognition. A case in point is the Camp David Agreement, through which Egypt officially recognized the Jewish state. Despite that agreement, few Egyptians have cared to normalize relationships with Israelis so long as the Palestinians were not accommodated.

Syria is another participant in the current peace process that has a keen interest in achieving a settlement. The return of the Golan Heights is of great importance to the Syrian regime, affecting its prestige both domestically and internationally. However, it is a mistake to think that Damascus can afford to ignore the Palestinians for the sake of regaining the Golan Heights. The historical links between the two peoples, the long-standing commitment of all Syrian regimes to the Palestinian cause, Syria's involvement in Lebanon, and the nature of the regime built under Hafez al-Asad are some of the factors that make it difficult for Syria to ignore the Palestinian question.

During the past two decades, the Syrian regime has been trying to gain strategic parity with Israel.[3] Its initial efforts were directed at achieving a deterrent capability, and this was reached by the mid-1980s. However, Damascus's hopes of further enhancing its military position were frustrated by the decline of Soviet arms transfers.

The Gulf War dramatically tipped the military balance of power between Israel and Syria even more in favor of the former. During the war, the United States and the Netherlands provided Israel with Patriot missile batteries, which by definition gave Israel an enormous military advantage over Syria. The United States also pledged to provide Israel with 80 percent of the cost of developing the more accurate Arrow missile system. The total effect of these steps has rendered Syria's deterrent capability obsolete. The lack of a reliable superpower ally willing to serve as a source of more advanced weapons makes it increasingly difficult for Syria to regain its earlier position of strength. At present, Syria is very weak, both militarily and economically, and, therefore, is more willing than ever before to negotiate a settlement with Israel. It remains to be seen whether Israel and the United States will use this opportunity to seek a permanent solution to the Middle East problem.

Jordan emerged from the Gulf War exhausted economically, isolated politically, and eager to renew efforts toward peace. Together with the PLO, Jordan realizes that its future depends on the achievement of a reasonable solution to the Palestinian question. King Hussein has always been a minimalist in his approach to the goal of Middle East peace, and the Gulf War undoubtedly confirmed in his mind the need to remain so. Jordan's strategic depth—that is, Iraq—has been tamed, and the oil-rich Arab Gulf states have turned against Amman because of its support for Iraq during the war. Jordan is thus trying to save what it can by being very accommodating to the demands of the United States and Israel—short of accepting the idea of the country itself becoming the Palestinian national home.

Egypt no longer has any vital quarrel with Israel and, therefore, has no direct incentive to pursue the peace process should Israeli obstructionism prove too burdensome. Yet, Cairo is interested in contributing to the achievement of peace, because such a contribution would bolster its position as champion of the Palestinian cause. It is also in Egypt's interest to draw more Arab countries closer to agreement with Israel, thereby proving to the Arab world that the philosophy of the Camp David Agreement was correct.

On the whole, the Arab world today is more willing than at any time in the past to make peace with Israel. Saudi Arabia suffers from a shortage of funds; it pledged $50 billion for the war effort but has paid only half that amount. Kuwait is also weakened and still owes around $22 billion in war-related debts.

The Arab world is militarily weak and ever more dependent on the United States for its security. The Gulf War left the Arab world fragmented and polarized. In a word, the Arab world has very little leverage in the process of making peace.

Everything is stacked heavily in favor of Israel, but the Jewish state is revealing little flexibility. It enjoys a position of virtually absolute military strength and does not seem inclined to make a historic bargain with the Arabs. The United States is the only power in the world that can make a difference. However, although U.S. policymakers seem to be aware of this fact, there is no guarantee that a sense of moral obligation, such as that apparently felt by George Bush during the Gulf War, will become the principal determinant of U.S. peacemaking efforts. The vicissitudes and pressures of world leadership, as well as Bill Clinton's now being president, underscore the danger of basing hopes for an effective U.S. peacemaking policy on the inclinations of a single individual.

Although the Arab-Israeli conflict has won priority on the U.S. agenda for the Middle East, other issues, including the question of political participation, have not escaped Washington's attention. The Gulf War and its aftermath focused the attention of the United States and the world at large on violations of human rights and the lack of democratic institutions in the Middle East. Not only Kuwaitis and Iraqis were victimized by the war. Palestinians were practically kept under house arrest by Israeli authorities for the war's duration. Almost a million Yemenis were evicted from their homes and jobs by the government of Saudi Arabia. Jordanians, Palestinians, and Sudanese were harassed and expelled en masse from Arab

Gulf countries. When the war ended, Kuwaiti authorities acted vindictively against the Palestinian community as a whole. In some Arab countries that joined the anti-Iraq coalition, demonstrators protesting Iraq's destruction were killed by security forces.

Despite the importance of this issue in the Middle East, the United States has been reluctant to take serious steps to encourage greater respect for human rights. Most of its efforts have been limited to mild appeals.

Neither respect for human rights nor greater political participation can be introduced in the Middle East through the same governments and ruling elites that exercise repression. If the United States seriously hopes to further the development of democratic values and practices in the region, the process will have to be mediated through local forces that are sincerely committed to such ends.

Another potential threat to Middle East stability was illustrated during the Gulf War by the growing rift between the rich and the poor in the Arab world. It was not accidental that many of the area's poorer states sympathized with Iraq. During the crisis, U.S. spokesmen, including Secretary of State Baker, seemed to understand the pernicious role of poverty and underdevelopment in fostering bitter dissatisfaction with the regional status quo; yet, this did not translate into substantial U.S. steps after the war. On the contrary, Washington tended to punish countries such as Yemen, Jordan, and Sudan by reducing or eliminating U.S. economic assistance.

The U.S. approach to the issue of Gulf security has also reflected a gap between American rhetoric and practice. Although Washington has seemed to favor the idea that local actors should assume responsibility for regional security arrangements, the United States has not actively encouraged Arab states to meet this challenge. With Washington now having entered into defense agreements with Kuwait and Bahrain, the United States seems to actually prefer to forge bilateral security relations with the Gulf countries. Although this approach may hold the promise of giving the United States a dominant position in the Gulf, it also carries the danger of permanently casting the major regional powers—Iraq and Iran—in the role of "outsiders." This, in turn, would almost certainly lead to the area's ultimate destabilization.

Regarding the issue of arms control, the United States seems totally oblivious to the Arabs' growing concerns. As Washington enthusiastically pursues a policy of disarming Baghdad, Israel continues to develop its military might—including its nuclear capability—without constraint. The United States has paid lip service to arms control by announcing that an effort should be made to eliminate chemical weapons in the region. Such a step would only benefit Israel, because it would dramatically reduce the Arab deterrent capability while leaving Israel's nuclear arsenal untouched.

Conclusion

The Gulf war had a major impact on the political situation in the Middle East. The war confirmed Washington's political and military dominance in the region and highlighted the crucial role the United States will have in determining the region's political future. Above all, it emphasized the indispensable need for active U.S. participation in the search for a peaceful resolution of the Arab-Israeli conflict. The 1993 PLO-Israel agreement, dramatically formalized at the White House, highlights this fact.

By calling for a Middle East peace conference, the United States took an essential initial step. However, at the basis of the new departure was a sense of moral obligation the U.S. president developed during the Gulf Crisis. It remains to be seen whether the direction taken by George Bush will last long enough under other U.S. leadership to bring the Palestine conflict to a happy conclusion. We can expect that if left totally to its own inclinations, Israel—being swayed more by immediate military arrogance than by long-term vision—will not move toward peace. Despite the fact that the Arab regimes are desperate for a settlement, they lack the political or military leverage to influence the process. Ultimately, the Middle East must resign itself to the fact that the United States is the only power that can shape its future.

Peace, if it is ever reached between the Arabs and Israel, may reduce considerably the tension that has engulfed the Middle East in the last half century. It will help reduce the arms race and may contribute to the region's economic development as military expenditures decline. Furthermore, peace may pave the way for more democratic political systems to emerge, especially in those Arab countries in which ruling elites often limit political participation by imposing emergency measures on the pretext of requirements of national defense. Finally, a peaceful settlement in the Middle East will bring about a greater measure of security and stability to the states of the region. It will enhance the cause of human rights in parts of Palestine where the Arab population has been suffering for almost a quarter of a century under the heavy hand of Israel's occupation.

However, peace will not necessarily eliminate other threats to the political and economic fabric of Middle Eastern societies. Questions of economic disparity, foreign intervention, and Western double standards will continue to cause instability and friction in the region. Until the United States begins to handle these problems effectively and more seriously, the political situation in the Middle East will remain exposed to sudden turbulence and unexpected upheavals.

Notes

1. The Camp David Agreement was the exception simply because there was sufficient Israeli interest in achieving peace with Egypt. The obvious advantage to Israel of this historic agreement was that it neutralized almost 70 percent of the Arabs' military capability by removing Egypt from the ranks of belligerents.

2. See Walid Kazziha, "The Gulf War: A New Cause of Instability in the Middle East," *JIME Review,* no. 13 (Summer 1991), pp. 7–16.

3. Walid Kazziha, "Syria's New Role in the Arab-Israeli Conflict," *Vierter Jahres Breichte,* no. 99 (March 1985), pp. 49–53.

19

The Arab World and the Rest of the World

DAN TSCHIRGI

Perhaps the most disturbing implication of the Gulf Crisis is that it is all too apt to be replayed someday—if, that is, awareness of this danger fails to elicit conscious and deliberate preventive steps. That the Gulf Crisis culminated in tragedy is indisputable. Any thinking person, regardless of how the rights and wrongs involved in the crisis may be perceived, can find little satisfaction in the outcome of the war to liberate Kuwait. The exact number of Iraqi troops, presumably mostly conscripts, who perished under the enormous firepower of the U.S.-led international coalition remains unknown, although it appears to have been well over 100,000. Civilian deaths—including those generated by the war, as well as casualties that occurred during the immediate domestic upheavals the war triggered in northern and southern Iraq—probably numbered several tens of thousands.

The bloody mayhem of war cast slashing ripples in widening circles, placing long-term and heavy burdens on women, children, and other noncombatants far from the scenes of battle. The dead and injured—those physically affected by the hostilities—were only the tip of the iceberg of those harmed.

The pain, the agony visited upon the Arab world had an additional dimension that enveloped individuals throughout the region who were often well removed from either direct or indirect unsavory consequences of the struggle. These were the *intellectuals,* broadly defined as those who thought seriously about the darkening political situation and in some way tried openly to make sense of the Gulf Crisis by placing it in the context of the Arab world's historical trajectory. In this sense, intellectuals included not only academics, journalists, and pundits but also statesmen and articulate men-on-the street. With one Arab state—notorious for having the cruelest and most arbitrary regime in the region—moving against a smaller, rich, and not particularly popular neighbor only to confront international forces led by non-Arab powers, it was often exceedingly difficult for those upholding "Arabness" to offer a coherent perspective.

This applied less to intellectuals who clung to a given ideology, whether pan-Arabist, liberal democratic, Islamic, or any other. For these, the unfolding Gulf Crisis was a relatively black-and-white affair. Their opinions, analyses, and conclusions all followed the dictates of ideological inclination.

It was different, however, for those who struggled mentally against the patent contradictions that immediately assaulted any facile interpretation of the Gulf Crisis. The fact that they frequently lapsed into apparent contradictions—liberal democrats supporting Saddam Hussein, religiously inclined thinkers supporting the quintessentially secular Baath regime in Baghad, determined secularists also supporting the Baath regime—while Saddam Hussein sought to cast his cause as a jihad—was the most telling manifestation of the fundamental confusion assailing Arabs trying to define positions that had to be held in support of "Arabism."

The importance of this monumental intellectual chaos is twofold. First, it graphically reflected the essential lack of clear societal identity that pervades the Arab world at all levels. This, in turn, simply underscores the fragility of links between Arab societies and Arab states, the low level of cohesion between widely held values and values embodied by political regimes. In a word, the Arab world's political underdevelopment was highlighted.

Second, the high visibility of Arab intellectual chaos was significant as a specific example of the more generalized impact of the Gulf Crisis: its magnification of basic realities of the Middle East's political environment. The Arab world's political underdevelopment was only one such fundamental element thrust to the fore. Among others, three stand out—each possibly dire in its implications for the future. Each of these—social class divisions in the Arab world, the rising levels of military capability characterizing the area, and the impact of non-Arab actors on the region—is a constituent feature of today's Arab *problematique*. Because in combination they create a problem that goes far beyond the limited frontiers of the Arab world, one that indeed takes on potentially global dimensions, it is worthwhile to consider each in more depth.

The Arab World's Political Underdevelopment

In attempting to organize themselves in the mold of nation-states, the societies of the Arab world have had limited success. The essential root of the

issue revolves around the problem of sociopolitical identity, which underlies most of the difficulties besetting the contemporary Arab state. The
point is only driven home by the fact that these difficulties are essentially
derived, on the one hand, from fissiparous internal challenges linked to
infrastate identities—whether regional, ethnic, religious, or tribal—and, on
the other, from various suprastate pan-Arabist movements. But the lack of
consensus within Arab societies over the nature and requirements of societal identity is not limited to preferences regarding how Arabs should relate
to Arabs. The inevitable other side of the coin is the issue of how Arabs
should relate to non-Arabs.

Both aspects of the enduring uncertainty that permeates Arabs' sense
of communal identity have long been noted. Different labels sometimes
attached to the phenomenon—identity crisis, moral crisis, cultural crisis,
psychological crisis, spiritual crisis—at bottom refer to the same condition.[1]

This Arab crisis confronts the Arab world—that is, its people and its
leaders—with disquieting concrete questions, the answers to which can
only be formulated in political terms. Regarding the nature of Arab society,
these include various fundamental questions: What is, or should be, the
relationship between Arabism and religion, between individual freedom
and communal responsibility, between rich and poor sectors of the Arab
world, between society and state, between government and citizenry, and
among the existing Arab polities?

The other half of the Arab crisis similarly incorporates a broad range of
unresolved issues pertaining to political, economic, and cultural ties with
the non-Arab world: To what extent, and in what specific ways—if any—
should Arab culture be modified in accordance with non-Arab cultural patterns, values, and norms? How should the Arab world relate to the world
economy, and how should it work to bring about the desired relationship?
How should the Arab world relate to the global political system, and how
should it work to bring about that relationship?

Although this broadly existential crisis has roots extending back at
least to the nineteenth century, its politically unsettling impact increased
following the full measure of independence gained by most of the Arab
world after World War II. The cause of this is found largely in that very
independence, a condition that not only soon undermined dominant elites in
key Arab countries but also saw competing sociopolitical preferences grow
and struggle. Much of the Arab world's history since World War II constitutes the chronicle of this competition. Yet, as Malcolm Kerr noted years
ago, events moved not toward reconciliation but toward greater tension;
toward greater reliance on violence, on extremist stands, on zero-sum pos-
turing.[2]

Leading Arab thinkers recognized the challenge facing their region in the first rush of emerging full independence, as well as the diverse menu of options preferred by those who would meet that challenge. Over four decades ago, Habib Amin Kurani argued that "the key to the future of the Arab World" lay in the nature of Arab response to Western civilization and reviewed the alternatives as he saw them:

> Arabs may be placed on a scale varying between two extremes. On the one end of the scale, there are those who advocate . . . turning westward, and breaking away completely from Arab traditions and beliefs. . . .
> On the opposite end of the scale, there are those who have not reconciled themselves to the superiority of Western culture, who chafe at the greater power of the West and in self-defense reject the West and all it stands for. . . .
> Most educated Arab youth, however, fall midway between the two groups. They believe that Western civilization has possibilities for making significant contributions to the Arabs, but that there are virtues and elements of strength in Arab civilization which are worth preserving. But precisely what elements of Western civilization should be borrowed, or what are the elements of strength in Arab civilization which should be preserved? Is this process of conscious and deliberate cultural selection practical or possible? These are questions which educated Arab nationalists have been able to answer only partially.[3]

Writing at the same time, Constantine Zurayk upheld pan-Arabism as a political goal and attempted to identify both the requisites for attaining Arab unity and possible obstacles to that objective. Zurayk cited industrialization, secularism, scientific training, and the assimilation "of what is best in Western civilization" as four steps necessary for the Arab nation's development. None of this, he noted, would be easy, and success would very much depend upon whether Arab nationalism became "broad or narrow, tolerant or exclusive, progressive or reactionary—whether, in other words, it becomes the outward expression of an inner civilization or contracts upon itself and dies of suffocation."[4] Zurayk offered the following as a necessary (although insufficient) basis for Arab development:

> In facing the difficulties that now stand in the way of their national progress, and to be able to tackle the serious problems that are confronting them, the Arabs are in need of two things: enlightened and capable leadership and a radical change in their attitude toward life. From them the new attitude requires searching self-examination; merciless rejection of all weakening and reactionary factors in their national life; objective appreciation and cultivation of universal values in their culture; readiness to assimilate Western technique; and, above all, the positive intellectual and spiritual tradition of the West. . . . Furthermore, the leaders of the revived Arab nation must be capable and progressive. They must have a real understanding of the political and social conditions of the modern world, and must be able to adjust to the requirements of those conditions.[5]

Kurani and Zurayk wrote as the curtain fell on the first era of modern Arab nationalism. Almost before the ink dried on their tracts, the Nasserist Revolution heralded the demise of first-generation "liberal nationalism" and the eclipse of its aristocratic, Western-educated elite in Egypt and the Fertile Crescent. Kurani's reference to the "superiority" of Western culture would henceforth find little resonance in the Arab world. Zurayk's plea for an Arab nationalism that would be broad rather than narrow, tolerant rather than exclusive, and outward-oriented rather than inwardly focused, as well as his demand for nationalist leaders having "a real understanding of the political and social conditions of the modern world," stood as a description of precisely what was not to happen.

Liberal nationalism was followed by revolutionary nationalism and the bombastic, empty rhetoric of pan-Arabism. Part and parcel of it all was the popularization of political participation through controlled massive mobilization. The age of the one-party state, of the state that hoped to be—but never quite became—all-inclusive, had arrived in the main centers of Arabism—Egypt, Syria, and Iraq—and would rapidly be taken up in other areas of the Arab world, from North Africa to the Arabian Peninsula.

By 1967 the failure of revolutionary nationalism was patent on three fronts. First, rather than promote pan-Arab integration, it had helped divide the Arab world. Bitter cleavages not only separated revolutionary regimes from the remaining conservative monarchies and sheikhdoms of the Arab world but also marked relations among the revolutionaries themselves. Second, instead of understanding and coping successfully with the international global context, revolutionary nationalism led the Arab world into the disastrous 1967 war against Israel. Finally, none of the revolutionary nationalist states had managed to generate a high level of articulation between societal and regime values. The gap between society and state remained disturbingly large, and mediating organizations—controlled by the state—failed to attain high degrees of "institutionalization"; that is, they largely failed to induce widespread internalization of the communal values upon which they ostensibly rested.

In short, as an ideology for nation-building, for political development, revolutionary nationalism had largely run its course by the early 1970s. Only in Egypt was this somewhat forthrightly confronted, as Anwar al-Sadat effectively jettisoned Nasserist principles and inaugurated the age of *infitah*. This reorientation included Cairo's reversal of foreign policy, its move to liberalize Egypt's economy, and its tentative steps toward reorganizing the country's political life along controlled pluralist lines. Other centers of revolutionary nationalism clung to the old rhetoric and strictly maintained single-party regimes. However, as Rashid Khalidi has noted, the principal revolutionary standard-bearers—Syria, Iraq, Algeria—soon launched their own versions of economic and foreign policy *infitah*,

even while retaining their established frameworks of political organization.[6]

These phenomena, plus the fact that the erstwhile struggle between tra-
ditional-conservative and revolutionary Arab regimes was replaced by
more complex interactions as the former agreed to bankroll the latter in
return for a cessation of radical agitation, formed the context of the post-
1967 Arab world. On all sides—although more visibly so for ostensibly
"revolutionary" regimes—the gap between ideological rhetoric and political practice steadily widened into a chasm. Under such circumstances, the
development of meaningful institutionalized mediating bonds between
society and state was at best difficult and at worst impossible.

Yet, in the decades after 1967, Arab regimes generally increased their
control over the societies they governed. The explanation for this lies
essentially in the simple proverbial effectiveness of the "carrot and stick."
On the one hand, good use was made of the state's resources—resources
that expanded considerably as the oil boom exploded and sent financial
tidal waves across much of the Arab world in the 1970s—to co-opt opposi-
tional forces and create regime-supporting dependencies through such
instruments as employment, government contracts, and the like. On the
other hand, heavy reliance was placed on mechanisms of state coercion, the
military, and internal security structures. Post-1967 Arab regimes enjoyed
effective power but faltered in gaining effective legitimacy. The masses of
the Arab world were shorn of realistic alternatives to existing regimes but
were not necessarily brought into consonance with governing political values.

Under the magnifying effect of the Gulf Crisis, the fate of the tens
upon tens of thousands of Iraqi troops who surrendered without struggle to
the advancing forces of Desert Storm eloquently symbolized a more general situation: The regime to which they responded had indeed organized and
used them but had largely failed to establish a link based on fundamental
communal values.[7] The state remained in control of, but essentially distinct
from, society.

Although the example of Saddam Hussein's Iraq highlights such phenomena, no particular "type" of Arab regime enjoys a monopoly on the
strategy and instruments that now entrench authoritarianism in the Arab
world. To one degree or another, all Arab regimes follow the same format.
Whether we look at the remaining revolutionary nationalist regimes, the
constitutional or liberalizing monarchies—such as Morocco and Jordan—
the emerging bourgeoisie-based liberal systems—such as Egypt—or the
traditional states of the Gulf, in each case we find authoritarian regimes.

Admittedly, there are differences—and important ones—in terms of
the manifestations of government control. In some cases (Iraq stands as the

standard stark example), authoritarianism rests largely on the blunt application of force and the conscious instillment of terror. In others, more subtle approaches prevail. In all, the state relies on its own momentary power to establish the limits of acceptable political discourse and activity, thus essentially overriding law and institutionalization at its whim.

It does little good to cavil at this situation. It is simply there—and what remains is to understand and, one hopes, deal with it in ways that may restrict its potentially harmful implications. And indeed, "understanding" the Arab susceptibility to authoritarian rule must inevitably heighten awareness of its potentially harmful implications—not only for those immediately caught up in dynamics of Arab politics but also for those far beyond the borders of the Arab world.

Can the ubiquity of authoritarianism characterizing Arab states organized along different lines and proclaiming adherence to different principles be attributed to coincidence? Probably not. Instead, we look at Arab societies as the common denominator with which regimes must deal. In this light, society—not the state, not the regime, not the leader—is the determinant factor. In other words, forced by historical exigencies to govern societies molded by their pasts into disparate communities, the contemporary Arab state, whether under revolutionary nationalist, liberal bourgeoisie, constitutional monarchical, or traditional regimes, has been forced to override divisive tendencies—and the obvious instrument for doing so has perforce been either the crude mailed fist or its velvet-covered counterpart.

The matrix of it all, in short, is Arab society—different as it is in each region and nonetheless in each region influencing regime strategies for "nation-building," which is the real name of the game. Arab societies on the one hand and Arab regimes on the other have become locked in an unresolved struggle to shape the outlines and dynamics of Arab nation-states.

In the leading sectors of the Arab world, the collapse of liberal nationalism, its replacement by revolutionary nationalism, and the latter's replacement, in turn, by *infitah* signal a trajectory that has progressively promised the masses, the popular sector, a greater say in political affairs. However, given the lack of a consensual base defining the nation-state, regimes had little option but to try to impose their definitions of acceptable political process by force or co-optation.

Having not directly experienced the impact of liberal or revolutionary nationalism, traditional regimes—those of the Gulf particularly—have so far had relatively little difficulty maintaining themselves in power. Yet, here too, the distribution of wealth—through the rentier state mechanism—and heavy reliance upon sophisticated internal security services have been pillars of regime maintenance.[8] In the Gulf, as is largely true elsewhere in the Arab world, societies—or at least their younger generations—are not characterized by widespread commitment to state institutions and internalization of the values underlying them.[9]

The ubiquity of authoritarian systems in the Arab world in itself strongly indicates the determining role of Arab society in the development of Arab political organization. The tragic Hobbesian fate of post-1975 Lebanon—once touted as the "Switzerland of the Middle East"—perhaps best illuminates the dangers of weak central authority in the region. The lesson has been driven home in Iraq, where Baghdad's defeat in the Gulf War led immediately to the Kurdish and Shi'ite rebellions that even today effectively partition the country into three segments.[10]

Much has already been written and said attributing the Gulf Crisis and the ensuing Gulf War to the foibles of authoritarian government. There is much truth in this. Saddam Hussein's decision to invade Kuwait and his subsequent decisions to push the confrontation with the international system to the point of armed conflict were indeed products of dictatorial politics. However, at a deeper level of analysis, the "problem," or "fault," goes beyond dictatorial personalities and requires probing the dynamics of authoritarian systems. What is there in hierarchical political structures—particularly in those whose value systems rest on visions of "absolute truths"—that may promote disastrous decisions?

Nearly thirty years ago, David Apter's classic theoretical work, *The Politics of Modernization,* provided the outlines of an answer: It is the inverse relationship between information flow and the degree of hierarchy in political structures—a relationship that is exacerbated in direct proportion to the extent to which absolute, or "consummatory" (as opposed to "instrumental" or "pragmatic"), values prevail.[11] In short, authoritarian systems based on absolutist ideological visions of reality will brook no interference in decisionmaking from information that runs counter to ideological orthodoxy. This, of course, is a formula for political miscalculation in a fast-changing world.

Having identified Iraq's authoritarian political structure as the villain in the tragic Gulf Crisis, many observers leapt to the conclusion that the "democratization" of Arab political systems is the solution to the region's woes. This is theoretically logical, perhaps, but realistically deficient.

There is little in Arab societies to indicate that democratization offers any clear solution. In Chapter 13, Mustapha El Sayyid stresses that existing elites are unlikely to dilute their own power by undertaking significant democratic reforms. To this we can add several considerations pertaining to the characteristics of Arab societies, among which three appear to be fundamental. First, there is the prevalent and widespread fragmentation of primordial communal identification within existing Arab states, a phenomenon directly related to relatively low levels of identification with national institutions.[12] Second is the predominance—to utilize Apter's terminology again—of consummatory over instrumental values in most segments of Arab societies. In other words, the Arab world on the whole lacks the degree of secular, pragmatic value orientations that seem to be required for the functioning of democratic political systems along Western lines. Finally, the relatively low value Arab culture gives to self-orientation, as opposed to communal conformity, may militate against the early or easy emergence of democratic political systems.[13]

In short, in the foreseeable future, a radical change in prevailing patterns of Arab domestic politics is unlikely. Hierarchical, authoritarian structures will in all probability continue to predominate. As is currently the case, these will not all be alike. Some Arab states—Egypt and Morocco appear to be prime candidates in this respect—may successfully follow liberalizing paths leading to the progressive institutionalization of relatively participatory processes. In others, regime maintenance will continue to depend far more heavily, and perhaps increasingly so, on the sheer application of the state's coercive power. In all, regimes will continue to face the challenge of promoting the state and its institutions as the basis of primordial communal identity.

Social Class Divisions

The most marked characteristic of the relationship between social stratification and political power in much of the Arab world in the years since World War II is the eclipse of narrowly based aristocratic, or "notable," classes and their replacement by ruling elites from lower socioeconomic classes. Although—with the notable exception of Iraq—this has not been the case in most of the oil-producing Gulf states, it has generally held true for the Levant and much of North Africa.

Beginning in Egypt, revolutionary Arab nationalism effectively ended the political dominance of Western-oriented aristocrats in favor of the banner of "popular" control of the state. This met with limited success, because the regime waved the banner but eventually failed to incorporate real popular representation—in the process becoming at once more alienated from the society it governed and more reliant upon rhetorical myth and coercion. Much the same process was repeated in other centers of revolutionary nationalism, the culminating point perhaps coming in Iraq.

In North Africa—Algeria and Libya particularly—the demise of World War II–era elites, although it did not occur until the 1960s, followed the same pattern. Promises of generalized political participation crystallized in the establishment of ruling regimes that sought to mobilize without being responsive, to rule without being responsible. Difficulties in both states in recent years reinforce the point.

After 1967, with Egypt once more in the lead, the composition of erstwhile revolutionary nationalist regimes began to alter somewhat under the impact of policies associated with *infitah*. By the 1980s, Egypt, Syria, Iraq, and Algeria had all been affected. Rashid Khalidi notes:

> In fact, what was taking place was the establishment of a hybrid new elite. This included ex–military officers of varying backgrounds, frequently but not always rural, and sometimes poor . . . professionals and senior managers of the state sector and the government apparatus; well-to-do medium landowners; and a new group of businessmen, contractors, speculators and middle-men, some from the old upper classes, some with close links to the state sector, but all entrepreneurs of a kind which had seemingly disappeared in the 1960s.[14]

The emergence of this heterogeneous elite sector has not diminished the need for Arab governments to address their publics in terms shaped by cultural-national myths appealing to the lowest common denominators: the ideals of pan-Arabism and Islamic purity. Indeed, the elite reorientation entailed by *infitah* policies may have increased pressures to cling to increasingly empty radical discourse in the face of counterelite accusations that essential national and cultural values were being betrayed.

Certainly, this tendency on the part of all Arab regimes was dramatically enhanced by the Gulf Crisis. Saddam Hussein broadened his secularism to the point of near evaporation by engaging in demagogic appeals to xenophobia on both Baathist and Islamic grounds. Jordan's King Hussein capped decades of projecting himself as an energetic modernizer by donning a sharifian mantle to placate his country's agitated masses. Egypt, Syria, Kuwait, and Saudi Arabia used pan-Arabist and religious arguments to challenge Baghdad's pretensions, proclaiming Saddam Hussein to be the single greatest threat to Arab unity and brandishing supporting statements by leading religious figures. No party failed to justify its stand in the crisis as truly in keeping with the higher ideal of "Arab brotherhood."

In Chapter 3, Nicholas Hopkins suggests that the Gulf Crisis and its aftermath may reveal a transnational stratification in the Arab world that does much to explain the region's political dynamics. The notion has evident merit. Existing regimes of all sorts face internal tensions rooted largely in class distinctions. The dissatisfaction of rural populations and the urban poor and lower middle classes has been manifested in many ways— not least, for example, in Algeria's aborted Islamist electoral victory in early 1992 and in Egypt's growing problem with militant Islamic movements. Even in traditional, rentier-organized Gulf states—Saudi Arabia,

Kuwait, and Bahrain stand as examples—internal patterns of stratification promise increasing challenges to currently dominant elites.[15] Additionally, the "street politics" that to some degree swept most of the Arab world during the Gulf Crisis graphically demonstrated that the regionalization of class-based antagonisms is a potentially important political factor.

Rising Levels of Military Technology

It would be superfluous in this context to discuss the military dimensions of Middle East politics at any length. The story is too well-known and can be summed up in what has become a cliché: The Middle East is perhaps the most highly militarized region of the world.

However, it is worth recalling that clichés generally exist because they are true. Budget figures consistently verify high levels of Middle Eastern militarization. In 1990, for example, eleven countries of the Middle East and North Africa—Qatar, Iraq, Israel, Jordan, Saudi Arabia, Syria, Libya, Egypt, Morocco, Kuwait, and Algeria—together spent over $45 billion on defense. This becomes even more meaningful when percentages of gross national product (GNP) devoted to military expenditures are taken into account. Iraq, for example, allocated 32 percent of its GNP to defense, whereas figures for Qatar and Israel during the same period are, respectively, 46.9 percent and 16.6 percent. Saudi Arabia, with a GNP in excess of $95 billion, spent nearly 13 percent of the proceeds on defense. Nearly 12 percent of Syria's GNP was assigned to defense. Egypt, despite more than a decade of peace with Israel, allocated over 9 percent of its GNP to the military. Kuwait spent over 5 percent of its 1990 GNP on defense, and nearly 7 percent of Morocco's GNP was directed to the same end.[16]

The social costs, and even more important, the political determination of the region's regimes to expand and enhance their respective military capabilities, are indicated by considering relevant estimates of per capita income. Egypt, which spent around $3 billion on defense in 1990, had a per capita income of $610; Syria spent over $2 billion on its military, while per capita income was just over $1,700; Israel, with a per capita income of nearly $9,000, spent over $6 billion on defense; and Iraq, whose per capita income stood at about $2,000 in 1990, devoted nearly $13 billion to military expenditures in that year.[17]

These massive outlays should not simply be taken as quantitative indicators. Their real and most ominous import lies in the domain of the qualitative. Clearly, Middle Eastern regimes have steadily sought to enhance their military capacities. But they have increasingly sought to do so not by mere addition to existing forces, not simply by "more," but by "better": through the acquisition of novel, increasingly lethal technologies. Israel's long-standing, thinly veiled status as a regional nuclear power is just one example. Iraq's drive to develop biological, chemical, and nuclear weapons is another. Libya's efforts along the same lines underscore the pattern. Egypt's pre–Gulf Crisis involvement with Argentina and Iraq in an effort to develop an advanced Condor missile is yet another indicator—as was Cairo's foiled attempt some years ago to steal Stealth technology from the United States.

In short, the determination of Middle East regimes to be on or near the cutting edge of military technology is patent, as manifested in their willingness to commit significant resources and efforts to that end. Their relative success is also apparent, if we avoid facile, superficial interpretations of Iraq's defeat in the Gulf War. Self-congratulatory Western enthusiasm over the ease of the international coalition's victory in the Gulf War should be tempered by careful recollection of events. Prewar estimates by U.S. military planners raised the spectre of perhaps twenty thousand or more coalition casualties once hostilities commenced. The most striking feature of postwar comments, particularly those made immediately by U.S. General Norman Schwartzkopf, was their denigration of Iraqi military leadership—implicitly acknowledging that the cost of victory could have been far higher.

A disturbing conclusion is that future military interventions in the Arab world by the non-Arab world may cause even greater suffering and damage to all sides. An even more disturbing point is that the confluence of regional Middle Eastern dynamics and those of the broader global system may produce just such confrontations.

The Global Environment and the Middle East

The international context has always been a major factor shaping the politics of the modern Middle East. To a great degree, today's Arab world has been formed in accordance with, and in reaction to, external influences.

With much justification, Arab as well as non-Arab scholars have generally focused on the pernicious impact of external influences on the Arab world. The history of European colonialism and imperialism provides data for catalogs of ills visited upon the region; this history is replete with multiple examples of oppression, aggression, manipulation, and treachery. The post–World War II involvement of the United States in the Arab world offers a somewhat similar, if less lurid, basis for criticism.

On balance, analyses of relations between the Arab and non-Arab worlds have tended to view the former as threatened—whether politically, militarily, economically, or culturally—by the latter. However, perceptions of threat reversal—that is, of possible threats to the non-Arab world by the

Arab world—have been limited to two realms. The first is formed by periodic, and essentially panicky and uninformed, outcries over the possible use of "oil blackmail" by the Arab world. The second, more enduring and solidly based, is formed by the long-standing recognition that the Middle East in general, and the Arab world in particular, constitute potential threats to world peace. However, on reflection it is apparent that this latter assessment has in the past referred to a *derived* threat rooted in the context of the Cold War. In short, the perceived danger was that Arab or other Middle Eastern actors might serve as catalysts for great-power confrontations having worldwide implications. In and of itself, the region was not usually considered threatening.

A major lesson of the Gulf Crisis is that this perspective is no longer realistic. The Middle East—and, again, particularly the Arab world—must now be seen as potentially threatening to the rest of the world in its own right.

This situation has arisen because of the ongoing interaction of the factors discussed in this chapter: the Arab world's political underdevelopment and consequent tendency toward authoritarian government; the domestic and regional implications of class divisions at the national and transnational levels, which indicate that the utility of demagogic appeals to xenophobic fears and consummatory values will not soon disappear from Arab politics; the high levels of weaponry already available in the Arab world, and the demonstrable determination of Arab regimes to reach ever higher spheres of military capability; and, finally, the impact of the global political environment and non–Middle East actors on the Arab world. This last factor deserves closer consideration, because it was not only significant in the eruption of the Gulf Crisis but will also do much to determine whether the future portends further confrontations between the Arab and non-Arab worlds.

It was hardly coincidental that the Gulf Crisis developed as the Cold War ended. Saddam Hussein's bid to seize Kuwait, and with it the leadership of the Arab world, reflected the breakdown of the post–World War II international order. Whether the Iraqi leader believed Moscow would assert itself on Baghdad's behalf in a desperate effort to shore up its own faltering global position, or whether—as is more likely—he believed the United States would find insufficient reason in the post–Cold War era to oppose the takeover of Kuwait, Saddam's gambit sprang from a miscalculation of international reaction.[18] In a sense, this was understandable. In the transitional political environment that greeted the last decade of the twentieth century, nobody knew what international constraints limited regional actors. This was exemplified by the opposition of influential voices in both the United States and the Soviet Union to the policies both countries pursued during the Gulf Crisis.[19]

To date, the aftermath of the Gulf Crisis, despite much brave talk of a New World Order, has not clarified the nature of the international system that will supposedly emerge from the current transitional period, and this is particularly true of its implications for the Middle East. The one obvious element of the new global political environment is the preponderant role of the United States. The Bush administration's fuzzy indications of its understanding of the New World Order appeared to establish at least some of the notion's supposed conceptual pillars. Principal among these were respect for international law and the will of the United Nations, support for human rights and participatory political processes, and, finally, recourse to collective action when such was deemed necessary by the international community to enforce elements of the New World Order on a recalcitrant member.[20]

Recent U.S. policy in the Middle East has both adhered to and deviated from these guidelines. The most significant result of the new U.S. orientation has been Washington's heavy involvement in the renewed Arab-Israeli peace process—an initiative largely in keeping with the spirit of the New World Order but also clearly a wise political move to remove, or reduce, a festering problem that, as Saddam Hussein proved, is a powerful destabilizing factor in the region. However, the U.S. approach to the peace process has clearly been tempered by pragmatic political concerns rather than simply shaped by abstract principles. Thus, Washington's determination to promote respect for international law and for the will of the United Nations in the Palestine issue pales in comparison to its readiness to exert pressure on Iraq in support of these same values. Further, U.S. encouragement of democratizing steps on the part of its Arab allies—Kuwait and Saudi Arabia—contrasts sharply with barely disguised U.S. approval of the downfall of the democratic process in Algeria when Islamic fundamentalists were about to win power in early 1992.[21]

This is hardly surprising. Considerations of national interest rather than visions of internationalist principle have continued to guide the U.S. approach to the Middle East. Yet, exactly what those considerations imply for the nature and degree of the U.S.-led external impact on the region in the wake of the Gulf Crisis remains undefined. To some, Arabs as well as non-Arabs, the opportunity exists for the imposition of a true Pax Americana in the conflict-ridden Middle East. The force of this conviction among segments of the U.S. populace was highly visible in vocal domestic outcries when the Bush administration refused to become heavily involved on behalf of Iraq's Shi'a and Kurdish rebels in the wake of the Gulf War.[22]

On the other side, the anti-Saddam rentier regimes of the Gulf have not hidden their eagerness to rely on a U.S. security umbrella. By the summer of 1991, virtually all pretense of interest in shoring up the Gulf's security through inter-Arab arrangements had been dropped. In private, the extent of some Gulf elites' wish for U.S. support is often dramatic. Shortly after the Gulf War, a Gulf state ambassador to a major European country enthusiastically regaled me for nearly two hours with his vision of the future U.S. role in the Arab world. He assured me that he spent as much time as possible in Washington trying to advance his views directly:

> The war shows that the United States is the only power in the world . . . and that's that. Power is power, and the United States should dominate the Middle East. U.S. domination is, after all, benign. Americans pay dollars for our oil. The oil itself does us no good. With dollars, not oil, we buy videos, cars, and houses.
>
> We [Arab Gulf states] are rich and the United States is rich. It is natural that the rich should lead the poor. But in the past we were afraid to speak out. And the result is that the radicals—the Nasserists, the pan-Arabists, the PLO—brought disaster to the Arab world. After all, we are the pure Arabs, and we don't need lessons in Arabism from them. The United States must accept the responsibility of dominating so that the Arab world will at last be peaceful and productive and better for all.[23]

The ambassador's words deserve consideration. The Arab world's modern history is such that only the most hard-hearted would scoff at the wish for a new era that would "at last be peaceful and productive and better for all." But the real question is whether any external force—whether the United States alone or the international community under the aegis of a U.S.-led New World Order—can provide such a benefit.

History has shown the fallacy of such hopes.[24] Neither the historical practice of foreign domination in the region nor the current human ability to "engineer" political tranquility offers grounds for believing that the Arab world's troubled and unstable existence can be overcome by outside agents. The problem is simply too rooted in the Arab world itself, and it must therefore be dealt with in historical terms by Arabs themselves.

In the meantime, this conflictive region will continue to pose a potential threat to areas far beyond its boundaries. In relating to the Arab world, therefore, wisdom seems to require understanding the nature of the potential threat and pursuing policies designed to minimize chances of its realization.

Conclusion: Dealing with the Arab World

The essence of the Arab world's potential threat to the non-Arab world lies in the combination of elements inherent in the region itself and in relationships formed between regional and nonregional actors. The contemporary Arab world's characteristics portend instability, conflict, and crisis—and above all, social change. The gloom of this prediction lies most of all in its immediacy. Social change may be desirable and perhaps is inevitable. But the intervening variable between the present and some future marked positively and happily by societies that are more "peaceful and productive and better for all" is all too likely to be violence and suffering for Arabs. Moreover, the great probability seems to be that those Arabs who currently most strongly favor the emergence and development of universal values and the assimilation of—as Constantine Zurayk once hoped—the "best in Western civilization" will be among the first to suffer disillusionment, if not more. These Arabs, who are mostly neither members of the region's current governing elites nor yet driven into the ranks of the region's overtly marginalized, will likely find themselves increasingly caught in the middle and assailed by both extremes.

External powers have little recourse but to continue dealing with the Arab world. Oil and the region's strategic geographical importance will not soon disappear as essential factors in world politics. But if external actors have essentially no choice insofar as involvement, options remain in terms of the nature and degree of that involvement.

The warning that seems to emerge from a consideration of the Gulf Crisis is that external actors, to the extent possible, should refrain from involvement in the tangled dynamics of intra-Arab politics. On the face of it, given the overwhelming Allied victory in the Gulf War, the lesson may seem empty. But on reflection, it bears consideration. Saddam Hussein, in spite of his own gross violation of values associated with Arab brotherhood, was nonetheless able to tap wellsprings of sentiment and link them to what Nicholas Hopkins suggests are regional class divisions. Thus, he managed to plunge the entire Arab world into turmoil, predicated largely on the tension between xenophobic and universal values. Although the war was a "walkover" for Allied forces, we should not forget that early Pentagon estimates raised the specter of around twenty thousand Allied casualties. The fact that this did not occur, and that the war did not metamorphose into a broader conflagration with many more casualties, must be largely attributed to Baghdad's decisions. Iraq refrained from the use of weapons of mass destruction—its chemical weapons capacity—against both the opposing forces and Israel. Given the continuing influx of weapons into the Middle East, the West cannot count on another lucky walkover.

What seems, then, to be in order is a strict appraisal of non-Arab vital interests in the Arab world, one that exposes issues that call for intervention in the region's affairs. Only two such potential issues appear on the political horizon at present. One, for reasons grounded in recent history, is Israel's survival as a sovereign state. The other, stemming from contemporary economic necessity, is the regular, uninterrupted flow of Arab oil. Apart from these, at least rationally, little or nothing calls for non-Arab intervention in Arab affairs.

But so-called rationality is largely the preserve of academics, who tend to favor long-term perspectives. The question is whether non-Arab policy-makers can or will resist the temptation to try to mold the Arab world into patterns they define as "beneficial."

The probability seems to be that they will not. Post–Gulf Crisis U.S. policy provides disturbing evidence for this conclusion. Although the over-all nature of U.S. policy toward the Arab world in the New World Order remains to be established, there are signs—arms sales and, particularly, the 1991 U.S.-Kuwait defense agreement—that shortsighted commitments to existing power structures in the Arab world may come to define the nature of external involvement in the region.

Should this happen, the non-Arab world will almost certainly find itself involved in military confrontation in the Arab world at some future point. One doubts that the outcome will be in anyone's long-term interest.

Notes

1. Dan Tschirgi, "The United States, the Arab World, and the Gulf Crisis," in Dan Tschirgi and Bassam Tibi, *Perspectives on the Gulf Crisis, Cairo Papers in Social Science* 14, no. 1 (Spring 1991) (Cairo: American University in Cairo Press, 1991), p. 6.

For what is arguably the best brief discussion of crises in the Arab world, see Hanna Batatu, "The Arab Countries from Crisis to Crisis: Some Basic Trends and Tentative Interpretations," in *The Liberal Arts and the Future of Higher Education in the Middle East: Papers Presented at the Conference on "The Liberal Arts—A Neglected Dimension of Middle East Development," Sponsored by the Faculty of Arts and Sciences, American University of Beirut, October 23–27, 1977* (Beirut: American University of Beirut, 1979), pp. 3–15. See also Fouad Ajami, *The Arab Predicament* (Cambridge: Cambridge University Press, 1981); Constantine Zurayk, "The National and International Relations of the Arab States," in T. Cuyler Young (ed.), *Near Eastern Culture and Society* (Princeton: Princeton University Press, 1951), pp. 205–224. An extensive discussion of the development of Arab national-ism as a response to, and as a part of, what can be termed *the Arab crisis* is provided by Bassam Tibi, *Arab Nationalism: A Critical Enquiry,* 2d ed. (London: Macmillan, 1990), see particularly pp. 1–26 and 94–141.

2. Malcolm Kerr, *The Arab Cold War: Gamal 'Abd al-Nasir and His Rivals,* 3d ed. (Oxford: Oxford University Press, 1971). In his widely quoted Preface to this edition, Kerr wrote:

> Since June 1967 Arab politics have ceased to be fun. In the good old days most Arabs refused to take themselves very seriously, and this made it easier to take a relaxed view of the few who possessed intimations of some immortal mission. It was like watching Princeton play Columbia in football on a muddy afternoon. The June War was like a disastrous game against Notre Dame which Princeton impulsively added to its sched-ule, leaving several players crippled for life and the others so embittered that they took to fighting viciously among themselves instead of scrimmaging happily as before. This may be instructive for the student of politics, but as one who all his life has had friend-ships and memories among the Arabs to cherish, I have found no relish in describing it.

3. Habib Amin Kurani, "The Interaction of Islamic and Western Thought in the Arab World," in Young, *Near Eastern Culture,* pp. 148, 157–158.

4. Zurayk, "National and International Relations," p. 222.

5. Ibid., p. 223.

6. Rashid Khalidi, "Social Transformation and Political Power in the Radical Arab States," in Adeed Dawisha and I. William Zartman (eds.), *Beyond Coercion: The Durability of the Arab State* (London: Croom Helm, 1988), pp. 210–211.

7. This is not meant in any way to minimize either the effect of the prolonged air bombardment of Iraqi troops prior to Desert Storm's ground offensive or the courage and suffering of Iraqi troops who withstood that assault. Yet, history—much of it recent—shows the difference between troops committed to a cause and those who are not.

8. For a penetrating exposition of the concept of the rentier state and its implications for the politics of the Arab World, see Hazem Beblawi, "The Rentier State in the Arab World," in Giacomo Luciani (ed.), *The Arab State* (Berkeley: University of California Press, 1990), pp. 85–98; see also Dirk Vandewalle, "Political Aspects of State Building in Rentier Economies: Algeria and Libya Compared," in Hazem Beblawi and Giacomo Luciani (eds.), *The Rentier State* (London: Croom Helm, 1987), p. 160.

9. See Faisal A. Al-Salem, "The Issue of Identity in Selected Arab Gulf States," in Tawfik E. Farah and Yasumasa Kuroda (eds.), *Political Socialization in the Arab States* (Boulder: Lynne Rienner Publishers, 1987), pp. 47–63.

10. It makes no difference that the Shi'a and Kurdish rebellions, and the ensuing de facto partition of Iraq, have not yet been crushed by Baghdad because of the active intervention of outside actors, particularly the United States. The point is that both Kurds and Shi'a rejected the institutions and values of the Iraqi regime and capitalized on its moment of weakness to manifest their dissatisfaction by rebellion.

11. David Apter, *The Politics of Modernization* (Chicago: University of Chicago Press, 1965).

12. Al-Salem, "Issue of Identity." See also, for example, Nicholas Hopkins's comparison of an Egyptian and a Tunisian village, which finds that despite significant differences between them, "in both . . . a strong sense remained that the community was an appropriate arena for politics and that it was in various ways opposed to the state or the wider society." Nicholas Hopkins, "Clan and Class in Two Arab Villages," in Farhad Kazemi and John Waterbury (eds.), *Peasants and Politics in the Modern Middle East* (Miami: Florida International University Press, 1991), p. 267.

13. Apter, *Politics of Modernization,* details the link he posits between "instrumental" values and open, or relatively participatory, political systems.

Although social scientists continue to debate the relationship of cultural and individual values to systemic political change, it is generally agreed that some relationship does exist. At the same time, no consensus exists regarding precise identification of dominant cultural values in Arab societies—or of their ultimate political significance.

Nonetheless, I find myself fully in accord with Nazih Ayubi, who in a recent work—whose implications (as the author explicitly understands) go far beyond the "Islamic" focus of its title—makes, inter alia, the following observations:

> The concept that ethics in Islamic society are public and not private, collective and not individual, is partly related to the fact that in the "original" solidarity-based Arab society, shame-related values have usually been more important than guilt-related values. This point should not be exaggerated out of all proportion, but I think that it is fairly

valid, as the Arab is still usually more concerned about apparent, collective norms and behaviour, with the frightening likelihood of a scandal, *fadiha,* than he is with regard to private, discreet matters that nobody can see. . . .

To the ordinary citizen in a Muslim country, deprived for centuries of the means (and the skills) to express himself politically and to defend his own interests via political action, the pains and conflicts that go with . . . modernisation may appear [to be] like a basically "moral" problem. . . . He may then join ranks with others who feel the same way . . . this is not basically because Islam is a political religion—as many maintain—but because it is premised on the *collective* enforcement of *public* morals.

The fact that the modernizing secular [Arab] State has also partly dismantled and partly dominated the economic sector has meant, by way of reaction, that "culture" is turned *par excellence* into the arena in which the civil society may express itself and preserve its cohesiveness.

Although focusing on political Islamist currents, Ayubi repeatedly points out that the same dynamic affects other religious groups in Arab societies: "The process is mutually reinforcing, for the return to sectarian allegiances is bound to strengthen a religionist ideology." See Nazih Ayubi, *Political Islam: Religion and Politics in the Arab World* (London: Routledge, 1991), pp. 43, 44, 222 (emphases in original).

It is instructive to compare Ayubi's analysis of the modernizing Arab world—and the importance he gives to cultural-sectarian support of the concept of ethics and morals as public phenomena—with the emphasis political philosophy as well as behavioralist-oriented political science have typically given to "individualist" ("self-oriented" as opposed to "collectivist-oriented") value systems as requisites for successful democratic political organization. Since the Classical Age, the idea that internalized values must link the individual to his social context has dominated. As democratic thought developed, the dominant opinion inclined progressively toward the premise that individual responsibility must be given priority over social conformity if democracy is to function. A contemporary consideration of the issue and its antecedent philosophical formulations puts it this way:

Liberal-Democratic theory gave rise to a conception of the citizen which made civil disobedience by real citizens conceivable. . . . While liberal-democratic theorists realized that some subordination to authority, some loss of individual autonomy, was required if the collective endeavor were to succeed, a recurrent intent of their thought has been to minimize the individual's subordination to purposes other than his own.

See Elliot M. Zashin, *Civil Disobedience and Democracy* (Free Press: New York, 1972), p. 35.

For excellent discussions of the development of behavioralist approaches linking self-orientation to modern, participatory political systems, see James A. Bill and Robert Hardgrave, Jr., *Comparative Politics: The Quest for Theory* (Lanham: University Press of America, 1981), pp. 50–57; Joel S. Migdal, "Studying the Politics of Development and Change: The State of the Art," in Louis J. Cantori and Andrew H. Ziegler, Jr. (ed.), *Comparative Politics in the Post-Behavioral Era* (Boulder: Lynne Rienner Publishers, 1988), pp. 385–409.

14. Khalidi, "Social Transformation, pp. 210–211.

15. For example, Saudi Arabia witnessed organized protests during the Gulf Crisis by women activists seeking the right to obtain driver's licenses. Demands for more effective and wider participation heightened in Kuwait following the Gulf Crisis. A survey of Bahraini students in the early 1980s found that 63 percent "expressed a wish to see a revolution." Al-Salem, "Issue of Identity," p. 55.

16. Data taken from *PC Globe,* produced by PC Globe, Inc., Tempe, Arizona, 1990.

17. Ibid.

18. Tschirgi, "The United States," pp. 44–45.

19. On the United States, see ibid., pp. 45–46. See also Henry Kissinger, "Bush Has Crossed a Rubicon in the Saudi Sands," *International Herald Tribune,* August 20, 1990; and Zbigniew Brzezinski, "The Goal Is Assuring Oil Supply," *International Herald Tribune,* August 17, 1990.

I am indebted to many Russian professional students of Middle Eastern and world affairs for insights into the Soviet Union's internal and, at least initially, generally quiet debate over Moscow's approach to the Gulf Crisis. I particularly wish to thank Dr. Andrei Shoumikhin, of the U.S. and Canada Institute, and Drs. Irina Shadrina, Victor Nadein-Raevsky, and Aziz Kamilov of the Institute of World Economy and International Relations. Interviews, Moscow, March 1991.

20. Dan Tschirgi, "The United States and the Arab World," *JIME Review* (Summer 1992).

21. Following the establishment of the High Committee of State, which suspended Algeria's electoral process after the resignation of President Chadli Ben Jedid, Washington initially described the event as being in accord with the Algerian constitution. Within twenty-four hours, however, the State Department announced "a definite change of position" and proclaimed strict U.S. neutrality toward developments in Algeria. This did not prevent the U.S. Export-Import Bank from subsequently confirming that its credit support for major Algerian development projects was unaffected by the collapse of the constitutional process. One unidentified State Department official explained the dilemma Washington faced once it became apparent that the Islamist FIS would almost certainly win free elections in Algeria: "Obviously, we believe in the democratic process . . . but obviously we would not be particularly comfortable with an authoritarian regime that did not believe in democracy and human rights."

See *Keesing's Record of World Events,* News Digest for January 1992, p. 38,703; *Middle East Economic Digest,* March 20, 1992; "Islamic Shock," *Newsweek,* January 20, 1992, pp. 36–37.

22. See, for example, Elizabeth Drew, "Letter from Washington," *New Yorker,* May 6, 1991; "Desert Shame," *New Republic,* April 29, 1991; Albert Wohlstetter and Fred Hoffman, "The Bitter End," *New Republic;* Morton Kondracke, "Kurdled," *New Republic;* May 13, 1991.

23. Confidential interview.

24. This point is most persuasively presented in L. Carl Brown, *International Politics and the Middle East: Old Rules, Dangerous Game* (Princeton: Princeton University Press, 1984), pp. 268–277.

The Contributors

IBRAHIM AWAD is based in Geneva and serves as a consultant to the International Labour Organisation. During 1991–1992 he was adjunct assistant professor at the American University in Cairo.

L. CARL BROWN is director of the program in Near Eastern studies at Princeton University.

FRANÇOIS BURGAT is researcher at the National Center for Scientific Research in Paris and at the Center for Economic, Juridical, and Social Studies and Documentation in Cairo.

AHMAD SIDKI AL-DAJANI is a member of the Royal Jordanian Academy and the Royal Moroccan Academy and is the author of over thirty books dealing with political matters in the Middle East. He has been a member of the Palestine National Council since 1964, chairman of that body's Higher Council for Education, Culture, and Science since 1977, and a Central Council member since 1972. From 1977 to 1984, he served on the Executive Council of the Palestine Liberation Organization.

ADEED DAWISHA is professor of government and politics at George Mason University.

NADER FERGANY is director of the Al Miskat Center for Research and Training in Cairo.

NICHOLAS S. HOPKINS is professor of anthropology at the American University in Cairo.

SAAD EDDIN IBRAHIM is professor of sociology at the American University in Cairo and director of the Ibn Khaldoun Center for Developmental Studies, also in Cairo.

WALID KAZZIHA is professor of political science at the American University in Cairo.

RIAD AL KHOURI is director of Middle East Business Associates, Ltd., in Amman, Jordan.

BAHGAT KORANY is director of the Arab Studies Center and professor of political science at the University of Montreal. During 1991–1992, when he researched this chapter, he was at St. Antony's College, Oxford.

VITALY NAUMKIN is president of the Russian Center for Strategic and International Studies and assistant director of the Russian Institute of Oriental Studies in Moscow.

CYNTHIA NELSON is professor of anthropology and dean of the School of Social Sciences at the American University in Cairo.

ROGER OWEN is director of the Middle East Centre and professor of economic history at St. Antony's College, Oxford University.

ALAN RICHARDS is professor of economics at the University of California in Santa Cruz.

MUSTAPHA K. EL SAYYID is professor of political science at Cairo University.

HOSAM T. EL-TAWIL is assistant professor of political science at the American University in Cairo.

BASSAM TIBI is director of the Center for International Relations and professor of political science at Georg-August University in Gottingen, Germany, and research fellow at the Center for International Relations Studies, Harvard University.

DAN TSCHIRGI is associate professor of political science at the American University in Cairo.

Index

267

About the Book

The full significance of the 1990–1991 Gulf crisis remains unclear—though clearly of deep concern to all those interested in the Arab world and its place in today's fast-changing global environment.

This book brings together the work of nineteen eminent Arab, European, and North American scholars who focus on the political, economic, social, and theoretical implications of the Gulf War. The key questions they address revolve essentially around two major issues: the meaning of the Gulf War for inter-Arab relations, and for future relations between Arabs and non-Arabs.

Designed to appeal to a range of readers, this book will be especially valuable to students. The areas of disagreement highlighted by the contributors, as much as those of consensus, make it an essential tool in efforts to understand today's Arab World.